"Benedictine Father Anscar Chupungco writes about the liturgy with the authority of a world-renowned scholar and the familiarity of a dear old friend. He treats both worship and Christian faith with an admirable and attractive sense of wonder. No one who cherishes the liturgical reform of the past fifty years can afford to overlook this delightful book. It's an inspiring read."

—John F. Baldovin, SJ
Professor of Historical & Liturgical Theology
Boston College School of Theology and Ministry

"The genuine voice of Anscar Chupungco sounds in these pages—with the characteristic notes of deep fidelity to Catholic tradition, utter clarity, gracious wisdom, Benedictine humility, and gentle hints of humor. That voice is a treasure. Chupungco articulates a vital memory of the very heart of the liturgical movement and many of its formative leaders, and one slowly comes to see that he himself has been one such leader. He speaks a clear and authoritative criticism of the recently too frequent cases of liturgical reaction on the part of some Roman Catholic leaders, yet he loses neither hope nor dignity in the process. Reading this book, you will discover again the basic principles of Catholic liturgical reform and its ecumenical resonances. You will also be encouraged to *sentire esse ecclesiam*, to recover the empowered sense of being the church: yourself with others as you gather around the presence of Christ now in word and sacrament."

—Gordon W. Lathrop
Professor of Liturgy Emeritus
Lutheran Theological Seminary at Philadelphia

Anscar J. Chupungco, OSB

What, Then, Is Liturgy?

Musings and Memoir

Foreword by
Mark R. Francis, CSV,
and Keith Pecklers, SJ

A PUEBLO BOOK

Liturgical Press   Collegeville, Minnesota
www.litpress.org

A Pueblo Book published by Liturgical Press

Cover design by David Manahan, OSB. Illustration by Frank Kacmarcik, OblSB. Photo of the Cathedral of Manila, courtesy of Noli Yamsuan.

Photo on page v is of Gaudencio B. Cardinal Rosales and Anscar Chupungco, OSB. Courtesy of Ferdinand Bautista.

Library of Congress Cataloging-in-Publication Data

Chupungco, Anscar J.
    What, then, is liturgy? : musings and memoir / Anscar J. Chupungco ; foreword by Mark R. Francis and Keith Pecklers.
        p.   cm.
    "A Pueblo book."
    Includes index.
    ISBN 978-0-8146-6239-7 — ISBN 978-0-8146-6022-5 (e-book)
    1. Catholic Church—Liturgy.   2. Liturgics.   I. Title.

BX1970 .C573
264'.02—dc22   2010004671

For His Eminence
Gaudencio B. Cardinal Rosales
Archbishop of Manila

Contents

Foreword

For more than thirty-five years thousands of students from countries around the world have had the great fortune to study liturgy with Fr. Anscar Chupungco, OSB. In the best of the Benedictine tradition, he not only imparts his knowledge of the sacred liturgy but also his deep love for the Church as the Mystical Body of Christ. The following pages offer a good idea of what classes and informal conversations with Fr. Anscar are like. He describes this book as a liturgical memoir, sharing with the reader his "memory of people and events" that shaped his profession as a liturgist.

Rather than giving a dry academic presentation, Fr. Anscar invites the reader to engage with him as a fellow believer in an account of the liturgical renewal, defined by a deep and profound sensitivity to the liturgy's potential for strengthening a life-giving relationship with Jesus Christ. Drawing on what he learned from his own mentors, Fr. Anscar compares the study of liturgy to entering a forest. He warns us that it is not necessary to stop and admire every tree but to have a picture of the entire forest firmly in place. In other words, he has imparted to his students that to fully appreciate the liturgy and be transformed by it, much more is needed than a mere understanding of rubrics or issues surrounding the text, because the whole of the liturgy is greater than the sum of its parts. In his own words: "We should beware of ranking the rubrics ahead of good theology, historical consciousness, and pastoral care. Rubrics are meant to lead the faithful to an ever-deepening experience of the paschal mystery."

This book, then, essentially proposes a vision of the Church's liturgical life that comes from the Second Vatican Council. Fr. Anscar's mentors who were influential in both the drafting of the Constitution on the Sacred Liturgy and the crafting of the renewed liturgical rites of the Church exercised a profound influence on his approach to liturgical studies. Having studied at Sant'Anselmo in the 1970s, he had the good fortune of living and studying with some of the greatest liturgical scholars of the twentieth century and founders of the Pontifical Liturgical Institute: his doctoral mentor Fr. Burkhard Neunheuser, expert in liturgical history; Fr. Salvatore Marsili and Fr. Cipriano

Vagaggini, renowned liturgical theologians; Fr. Adrien Nocent, specialist in the areas of the liturgical year and Christian initiation; Fr. Herman Schmidt, SJ, who held a dual appointment at the Pontifical Gregorian University and the Pontifical Liturgical Institute.

From these masters he learned that there is an intrinsic relationship between liturgy and life to which we should be attentive. The liturgical assembly itself is called to live out this relationship. In the words of Fr. Anscar:

> The liturgical assembly invites human society to make a collective effort to affirm human equality, eliminate social injustice, and promote true fellowship among all. In this sense the liturgical assembly, like a prophetic symbol, will always contain an element of counterculture.

Because of this attention to the assembly, Fr. Anscar naturally emphasizes the importance of both history and culture as keys to helping the liturgy more effectively invite believers in the twenty-first century to enter into the mind and heart of Christ through communal worship. This serves as a helpful antidote to the unbridled individualism characteristic of so much of our postmodern society. Since active participation of the lay faithful in the liturgy is a hallmark of the reforms of the Second Vatican Council, this subject becomes an overarching concern for his convictions regarding worship, as is well demonstrated in this book.

As the Second Vatican Council maintains, "full, conscious, and active participation" of God's people would be impossible without proper adaptation of the rites to their own cultural context. To this end, Fr. Anscar has been at the forefront of exploring what has come to be called "liturgical inculturation." Having served as president of the Pontifical Liturgical Institute, secretary of the Filipino Bishops' Liturgical Commission, and founder of the Paul VI Liturgical Institute at the behest of the Filipino bishops, he has both developed his thought in this area and had the opportunity to implement his vision—a vision that has influenced and inspired many scholars and pastors throughout the world, both in the Roman Catholic Church and beyond.

As a loyal son of the Church and a faithful Benedictine monk, Fr. Anscar has always been respectful of the Church's tradition as expressed in her worship. And as a consultor to the Roman Congregation for Divine Worship and the Discipline of the Sacraments for many years, he has put his erudition and pastoral sensitivity at the service of the Holy See and, therefore, the universal Church. His profound love and appreciation for that tradition puts him in a unique position to offer constructive critique on the current liturgical tradition and offer a way forward.

As former doctoral students who have inherited the teaching of his two major courses at the Pontifical Liturgical Institute—"The Theology and Principles of Liturgical Inculturation" and "Liturgical History Across the Cultural Epochs"—we see the wisdom of our Catholic liturgical tradition, to which Fr. Anscar has given his professional life, reflected in the pages of this book. Today, thirty-five years later, he continues to enrich the Church's liturgy through his scholarship and pastoral sensitivity. We are all very much in his debt.

Mark R. Francis, CSV
Keith F. Pecklers, SJ
Rome, Feast of the Epiphany, 2010

Preface

I began to teach the theology and spirituality of liturgical worship in 1973 at Maryhill School of Theology in the Philippines. Though it is one of my favorite subjects, this is my first book about it. For several years the lion's share of my publications were on the topic of liturgical inculturation.

Unlike some of my previous work, the method of exposition I follow here does not merit to be called scholarly: I dispensed with documented footnotes and technical apparatus. I consider this book the product of my musings on liturgical worship after three decades of studying and teaching it. It is also a book of liturgical memoir. In it I share with my readers my memory of people and events that shaped or influenced my profession as a liturgist. When people compliment me for my liturgical output, I always answer that if I seem tall, it is because I stand on the shoulders of giants.

This work is not meant to be a textbook, but its contents can be useful to people who want to know more about liturgical theology without the usual book references and highly technical vocabulary. For several years I taught this subject according to the rules of the academe, but it dawned on me that the awesome mystery of Christ and the Church should also be the object of prayer and meditation. After explaining such profound topics as Christ's presence or the role of the Holy Spirit in the celebration of Christian worship I would always advise my audience to sit still and ponder.

In the course of this work I quote patristic writers again and again. I might disappoint those who expect me to footnote my quotations using the most recent editions. I take most of my patristic sources from the Liturgy of the Hours, and that is surely not the scholarly way to quote them. But I thank the experts that chose those passages for the Office of Readings, causing them to be objects of prayerful meditation. Reading patristic writers in a little book called Liturgy of the Hours is a treat. I take delight in the literary freshness and extravagance and in the lyrical beauty of several of them. Indeed, how else are we to speak about the awesome mystery of God in us?

I was formed in the liturgy of Vatican II at a time when the council ended and the work of postconciliar reform was in full swing. My professors at the Pontifical Liturgical Institute were all active in the various Vatican commissions or the Consilium for the Implementation of the Liturgy Constitution. Obviously, my work is strongly premised on the principles and criteria of liturgical reform as my professors understood and taught them.

I have always upheld the principle that we do not enjoy the liberty to question the conciliar decisions that the fathers made with the guidance of the Holy Spirit. I believe, however, that there are postconciliar revisions of the liturgical books and cases of implementation of the reform that are open to debate and further consideration in view of pastoral and cultural changes in local churches. This was true in the early Church as well, where after a heated debate on whether or not to impose the Mosaic Law on pagan converts, the apostles wrote a letter announcing: "For it has seemed good to the Holy Spirit and to us to impose on you no further burden than these essentials" (Acts 15:28). It is in this same sense that the interpretation of the conciliar decrees should be subject to healthy and helpful critique.

With a critical but respectful disposition I deal with some current trends that appear to me as a problematic reading of the mind of the Constitution on Liturgy. I am honestly ill at ease with anything approaching criticism of official position with respect to some controversial issues. Navigating on murky water requires skill, prudence, and the fundamental virtue of obedience. I hope that in this book I did fairly well in that regard. We can debate, but at the end of the day what matters are not personal opinions but what truly contributes to making the prayer of the Church an encounter with the person of Christ.

As I was writing this book I often remembered those gratifying hours when I stood before my students who believed that liturgical inculturation was not the only subject I could teach. I thank them—their number is countless—for their trust. In particular I thank Josefina Manabat who urged me to put down in writing what I had been teaching about liturgical theology.

Given the influence of my students, I planned this book like most textbooks of liturgical theology. Chapter 1 deals with the basic premises. It opens with the tensions generated by the liturgical reform of Vatican II. Why is it that fifty years after the reform there is still discontent with the "new" liturgy in some sectors of the Church? Is there a need to reform the reform of Vatican II? The rest of the chapter deals with some of the challenges facing the global Church today: the place of technology, the observance of Sunday, progressive solemnity, the role of women, the shelved issue of inculturation, and the Liturgy of the Hours. The chapter concludes with a treatise on the human body as an essential component of liturgical worship.

Chapter 2 attempts to define what liturgy is. I have always considered liturgical worship something so multifaceted that it defies any satisfactory definition. When something is both human and divine, like the Incarnate Word, we can only stand in awe and be lost in wonderment.

Chapters 3 and 4 follow the typical treatise consisting of the Trinitarian and ecclesiological components of liturgical worship. The third-century *Apostolic Tradition* (chap. 7, 8, 9, and 21) has this doxology: "Through your Son Jesus Christ, through whom be glory and honor to you, Father and Son and Holy Spirit, in your holy Church, both now and through all ages. Amen."

Chapter 5 refers to the outward shape of liturgical worship, namely, symbols, language, rites, music, and vesture. I borrowed the title *Per Ritus et Preces* from the Constitution on Liturgy: "Through a good understanding of the rites and prayers the faithful should take part in the sacred service conscious of what they are doing, with devotion and full involvement" (48).

The concluding chapter completes the treatise by expounding the deeper meaning of liturgical worship, which is spirituality. With Pope Paul VI, we breathe the air of optimism that because of the liturgical legacy of Vatican II, "supernatural faith is reawakening, eschatological hope is guiding ecclesial spirituality, and charity is reassuming its life-giving, active primacy."

Studying the theology of liturgy is like entering a forest of doctrines, symbols, metaphors, and poetry. We may take delight in the loftiness of a doctrine or in the beauty of a symbol, but we should not lose sight of their deeper spiritual meaning. In the liturgy every metaphor hides an aspect of divine reality; every piece of poetry conveys the message of salvation. It is my hope that this volume will aid the reader to discover the face of God in liturgical worship.

Acknowledgments

Excerpts from the English translation of *Rite of Baptism for Children* © 1969, International Committee on English in the Liturgy, Inc. (ICEL); excerpts from the English translation of the non-biblical readings from *The Liturgy of the Hours* © 1974, ICEL; excerpts from the English translation of *The Roman Missal* © 1973, ICEL; excerpts from the English translation of *Rite of Penance* © 1974, ICEL; excerpts from the English translation of *Rite of Confirmation (Second Edition)* © 1975, ICEL; excerpts from the English translation of *The Ordination of Deacons, Priests, and Bishops* © 1975, ICEL; excerpts from the English translation of Dedication of a Church and an Altar © 1978, ICEL; excerpts from the English translation of Pastoral Care of the Sick: Rites of Anointing and Viaticum © 1982, ICEL; excerpts from the English translation of the Constitution on the Liturgy, the writings of Pope Paul VI, and the postconciliar documents until 1979 from *Documents on the Liturgy, 1963–1979: Conciliar, Papal, and Curial Texts* © 1982, ICEL; excerpts from the English translation of Book of Blessings © 1988, ICEL; excerpts from the English translation of *Rites of Ordination of a Bishop, of Priests, and of Deacons* © 2000, 2002, ICEL; excerpts from the English translation of The General Instruction of the Roman Missal © 2002, ICEL; excerpts from the English translation of The Roman Missal © 2010, ICEL. All rights reserved.

Passages from other documents of the Second Vatican Council are from *Vatican Council II: Volume 1, The Conciliar and Post Conciliar Documents*, by Austin Flannery, OP © 1996 (Costello Publishing Company, Inc.). Used with permission.

Excerpts from the following patristic texts are my translation: *Didaché*, Tertullian, Hippolytus of Rome, Saint Ambrose, and Saint Augustine (*Didaché*, ed. W. Rordorf-A. Tuilier [Sources Chrétiennes 248, 1978]); Tertullian's *De Baptismo* (Corpus Christianorum 1/1, 1954); *La Tradition apostolique de Saint Hippolyte*, ed. Bernard Botte, (Münster 1989); *De Sacramentis/De Mysteriis*, ed. Bernard Botte (Sources Chrétiennes, 25bis, 1962).

Excerpts from the English translation of the *Catechism of the Catholic Church* for use in the United States of America copyright © 1994, United States Catholic Conference, Inc.—Libreria Editrice Vaticana. English translation of the *Catechism of the Catholic Church: Modifications from the Editio Typica* copyright © 1997, United States Catholic Conference, Inc.—Libreria Editrice Vaticana. Used with permission.

Chapter One

Both Human and Divine

> For you, the former rite of Mass is a sign of your false ecclesiology and
> a matter on which to assail the Council and its work of reform. You
> take as pretext or as your alleged justification that only in the former
> rite are the authentic sacrifice of the Mass and the authentic ministerial
> priesthood preserved, their meaning unobscured. We reject out-of-
> hand this erroneous judgment and unjust accusation; we cannot per-
> mit the divine Eucharist, sacrament of unity, to be made the source of
> division (see 1 Cor 11:18); we cannot permit you to make use of it as an
> instrument and symbol of your rebellion.

These stern words were addressed by Pope Paul VI to Archbishop
Marcel Lefèbvre on October 11, 1976. The archbishop, who was a council father, had accused the Holy See of embracing neo-Modernism and
neo-Protestantism as clearly proven by the decrees of Vatican II and
the postconciliar reforms. Perhaps there is no better way to describe
Lefèbvre than as a person who could not accept that times and culture
have changed even in the Catholic Church and that the Holy Spirit
has continued to guide the course of Church events after the Council
of Trent. To complete the story, I merely note that in a fatherly effort
to mend division, Pope John Paul II allowed in 1984 and again in 1988
a restricted use of the Tridentine Missal. Finally, on July 7, 2007, Pope
Benedict XVI published *Summorum Pontificum*, permitting the wider use
of the said missal as *forma extraordinaria* of the Roman Mass.

The tenor of *Summorum Pontificum* allows us to believe that the
Holy Father issued it as a final gesture of peace and reconciliation to
those who still adhere to the Tridentine liturgy. His paternal gesture,
however, put the clock back by forty years. Surely he does not mean
to lessen the importance of the Vatican II liturgy, which he wants to
retain as the *forma ordinaria* of Catholic worship. *Summorum Pontificum*
is in the genre of *via media* or compromise to please both sides. This ingenious technique was often employed during the council's debate on
the liturgical reform.

As I mused on the possible effect of the Apostolic Letter on the liturgical reform and the global Church, I confess that I entertained a bad thought, which I hope would not be taken as insolence. In 1957, on the eve of Vatican II, Pope John XXIII issued the letter *Veterum Sapientia*, insisting on the use of Latin in seminaries. When the council met, the first document to be discussed was the Constitution on Liturgy. The fathers spent several days debating the use of the vernacular in the liturgy. Finally, a *via media* was reached, allowing Latin to remain as the official liturgical language but opening the way to the use of the vernacular at the discretion of the local Ordinary. Consequently, local churches shifted to the vernacular liturgy, and Latin was practically abandoned. The shift from Latin to the vernacular in the liturgy had a parallel effect on the use of Latin in seminaries. Because of the Latin debate in the council, *Veterum Sapientia* did not get off the ground. Will *Summorum Pontificum* suffer the same fate in those places where Latin is a dead language and the Tridentine Mass a historical curiosity? Will it not be flying in the face of the irreversible reality of cultural and theological changes?

As expected, there were different reactions to the Liturgy Constitution and the subsequent implementation of its directives. One reaction was gratitude, which was sometimes mixed with reckless euphoria. Another was outright disenchantment with the reform itself. It was a type of disenchantment that failed to make the needed distinction between conciliar principles of reform and postconciliar implementation. I have always held that there may be instances when the postconciliar interpretation and implementation of the Liturgy Constitution are debatable, but we should carefully distinguish them from the principles promulgated by the ecumenical council. My liturgy mentor, Fr. Adrien Nocent, was a zealous advocate of the Liturgy Constitution, yet he was an outspoken critic of the postconciliar rites of confirmation and penance. Asked what could be done to improve them at that late hour of the conciliar reform, he replied with typical repartee, "Nothing is ever late; there is always time to reform the reform."

After several decades of liturgical reform there are still contrasting opinions about what the council had really intended to achieve. I had the occasion to ask Fr. Cipriano Vagaggini, another mentor of mine and one of the framers of the Liturgy Constitution, what "substantial unity of the Roman rite" meant. The phrase is obscure, yet crucial to inculturation. His answer was quite revealing: "I asked the same question when we were drafting the Constitution but no one in the commission had an answer!" Strange indeed are the ways of the Spirit during the council and surely after the council. But if it is any consolation at all, tension can be considered an encouraging sign that people's interest in the liturgy has not abated over the years. When Abbot Primate Benno Gut of the Benedictine Confederation established the Pontifical Liturgical Institute in Rome in 1962, professors of theology, like prophets of doom, alerted him that liturgy was a fad that would not exceed their lifetime.

In his posthumous book *The Reform of the Liturgy, 1948–1975* Annibale Bugnini keeps record of much opposition to the conciliar and postconciliar reform. Among the antagonistic groups that he has identified the following clearly harbor a countercultural mentality. The first is *Una Voce*, an international group, for the defense of Latin, Gregorian chant, and sacred polyphony against the vernacular and modern music. The second are splinter groups that were often hostile to the liturgical changes being advanced by the Holy See. Among them Bugnini names the American Catholic Traditionalist Movement and individuals like the Italian journalist Tito Casini, who in his book *La tunica stracciata* acidly attacked the use of the vernacular; Cardinal Alfredo Ottaviani and Cardinal Antonio Bacci, who staunchly supported opposition to the new Missal because of its alleged "heretical," "psychologically destructive," and "Protestant" elements; and the French Abbé Georges de Nantes, who called for the ousting of Pope Paul VI, whom he accused of heresy, schism, and scandal. Even some of the devout faithful that frequented the Mass were adverse to the use of the vernacular. In the Church of Sant'Anselmo an elderly lady corrected me as I was offering her Holy Communion: *"Non dicitur 'Il corpo di Cristo,' sed 'Corpus Christi'!"* (In perfect Latin she bade me say "The Body of Christ" in Latin, not in Italian.)

Bugnini himself, then secretary to the Congregation of Divine Worship, was not spared. He was a systematic person who programmed the liturgical reform and courageously pushed its implementation against all opposition. I remember that in one of his visits to the Pontifical Liturgical Institute he declared, "I am the liturgical reform!" In more ways than one his self-assessment was correct. The postconciliar reform would not have progressed with giant steps had it not been for his dauntless spirit and tenacity. To crown his liturgical accomplishments the Vatican promoted him to the rank of papal delegate to Iran, where he became famous in the secular world for successfully negotiating the release of American hostages.

The title and content of this preliminary chapter are inspired by the lofty opening lines of the Constitution on Liturgy: "It is of the essence of the Church to be both human and divine, visible yet endowed with invisible resources, eager to act yet intent on contemplation, present in the world yet not at home in it; and the Church is all these things in such wise that in it the human is directed and subordinated to the divine, the visible likewise to the invisible, action to contemplation, and this present world to that city yet to come which we seek" (2).

In his address at the opening of the Second Vatican Council on October 11, 1962, Pope John XXIII reminded the fathers that it was not the principal task of the council to discuss Church doctrines again. "For such type of discussion alone," he said, "there was no need to convoke an ecumenical council." What needed to be done, he explained, was to translate the deposit of faith in word and deed that the people of today could understand and accept. It was a clarion call for the Church to set out with a fresh vision into a world that had changed long ago. The word *aggiornamento*, or updating, with which he laid down the agenda of the Second Vatican Council, became a catchword and the order of the day. In every sector the Church needed to engage in *aggiornamento*, not of course by being conformed to this passing age but "by thrusting itself boldly and without fear in the work demanded by our time."

It was to be expected that *aggiornamento* would be the undercurrent of every conciliar document. This we read like a refrain in the first document, the Constitution on Liturgy, promulgated by Pope Paul VI on December 4, 1963. I should note that the opening line of the document carries the vision-mission statement for the *aggiornamento* not only of the liturgy but also of every aspect of Church life: "This Sacred Council has several aims in view: it desires to impart an ever increasing vigor to the Christian life of the faithful; to adapt more suitably to the needs of our own times those institutions that are subject to change; to foster whatever can promote union among all who believe in Christ; to strengthen whatever can help to call the whole of humankind into the household of the Church." Properly understood and fittingly celebrated, a renewed liturgy can contribute immensely to the realization of this conciliar vision. At the turn of the twentieth century the Benedictine Lambert Beauduin, who fathered the classical liturgical movement that the council later adopted, advanced such a scheme of Church renewal. Consequently, the opening line of the

Constitution announced that "the Council sees particularly cogent reasons for undertaking the reform and promotion of the liturgy."

The drafters of the Constitution were convinced that every liturgical rite, if adapted to the culture and traditions of the people, has a message to convey to the modern world. A renewed liturgy nourishes the spiritual life of the faithful, promotes Christian unity among the Churches, and contributes to the Church's mission of evangelization. In short, the liturgy is a major protagonist of the conciliar *aggiornamento*. In fact, liturgical reform, ecumenical understanding, and evangelization held a prominent place in the agenda of the classical liturgical movement.

Who drafted the Constitution on Liturgy? A couple of them were my mentors and my future colleagues at the Pontifical Liturgical Institute. They were pastors and scholars who supported and actively promoted the cause of the liturgical movement. Burkhard Neunheuser rightly claimed that thanks to them the fifty-year-old liturgical movement entered the council hall and was finally enshrined in its most fitting place: the conciliar document on the liturgy.

After Pope John XXIII had announced that he was convening an ecumenical council, a preparatory commission on the liturgy was established on June 6, 1960. Cardinal Gaetano Cicognani was president (succeeded by Cardinal Arcadio Larraona in 1962) and Annibale Bugnini secretary. The members were Karel Calewaert, Bernard Capelle, Enrico Cattaneo, Romano Guardini, Josef Jungmann, Joseph Malula, Johannes Quasten, Mario Righetti, and Aimon-Marie Roguet. Among the consultors were prominent liturgy scholars: Bernard Botte, Antoine Chavasse, Godfrey Diekmann, Balthasar Fischer, Pierre-Marie Gy, Anton Hänggi, Johannes Hoffinger, Pierre Jounel, Theodor Klauser, Boniface Luykx, Frederick McManus, Aimé-Georges Martimort, Herman Schmidt, Cipriano Vagaggini, and Johannes Wagner.

Although Pope Paul VI applied himself to the work of ecumenism and evangelization, he is best remembered for having courageously and solicitously undertaken the arduous postconciliar reform of the liturgy. In his 1964 letter *Sacram Liturgiam* he writes that it has been "the concern of earlier popes, of our self, and of the bishops of the Church that the sacred liturgy be carefully safeguarded, developed, and, if needed, reformed." He deserves the epithet "architect of the liturgical reform," though he was at the same time the indefatigable engineer who attended hands-on to the progress of the entire project.

On February 2, 1966, I had the singular privilege of offering a candle to Pope Paul VI at a ceremony in the Vatican Basilica. I was struck by his piercing eyes that seemed to probe my innermost thoughts. When I informed him in my nervous Italian that I was from the Philippines, he smiled subtly and said, "I bless the Philippines!" In 1990 some Philippine bishops urged me to return home after twenty-four years in Rome to establish a liturgy institute. I did not have to search for a name. It was going to be the Paul VI Institute of Liturgy. A colleague in Rome wondered why I did not name the Institute after Pope John Paul II. I quipped that had I the chance to ask him what name to give the Institute, he would have surely replied, "Paul VI." The noble simplicity of Paul VI's funeral at Piazza S. Pietro, emceed by my former mentor Archbishop Virgilio Noè, was the epitome of the conciliar liturgical reform's *sobrietas romana* and noble simplicity that his papacy championed with clear vision and firm determination. The coffin was slightly raised above the ground. It was draped in plain white cloth with the Book of the Gospels on top and the paschal candle nearby. The rite was carried out with dignity, gravity, and noble simplicity. The spontaneous applause of the people as the coffin was carried inside the basilica for interment was a moving tribute to the pope who successfully steered the Church through the calm and tempest of Vatican II's *aggiornamento*.

The Constitution on the Liturgy has a monocular view of liturgical reform. Article 14 reads: "In the reform and promotion of the liturgy, full and active participation by all the people is the aim to be considered before all else. For it is the primary and indispensable source from which the faithful are to derive the true Christian spirit." Active participation, which I will address again in connection with contemplative worship, is vital to Vatican II's agenda of liturgical reform. It is the reason why article 21 of the Constitution instructs that "both texts and rites should be so drawn up that they express more clearly the holy things they signify and that the Christian people, as far as possible, are able to understand them with ease and take part in the rites fully, actively, and as befits a community." In the council's thinking, active participation involves not only congregational acclamations, songs, and gestures but also, as article 29 explains, those ministerial functions exercised by servers, readers, commentators, and members of the choir. The faithful take part in the celebration not only by being active members of the assembly but also by ministering to its needs.

Full, intelligent, and active participation urged the Church during and after the council to reform the liturgy of Trent. Active participation was the matrix within and from which the entire reform was to take shape. It was to be the source and expression of Christian spirituality. To promote active participation the council fathers approved the use of the vernacular, the revision of existing rites, the creation of new rites if opportune, greater involvement of the laity in liturgical ministries, and inculturation.

The liturgical reform was expected to be a ferment of change stirring up the entire Church after the council. Like other changes of this magnitude, it drew forth contrasting reactions and caused uneasy tension among Church leaders and the faithful. There were those that wanted the liturgy to retain its aura of timelessness in a world helplessly swept away by change. They regarded any departure from the familiar way of doing things as a breach in the Church's fidelity to its tradition. Tension was fueled by a type of liturgical romanticism. With my classical background I treasure the Latin language and delight in Gregorian chant. Nevertheless, I question the wisdom and pastoral prudence of reviving them as the normal language and song of the liturgy. In my thinking such revival is an indication that there are people who have not followed the historical process and kept up with the changing times.

It is true that articles 36 and 116 of the Constitution, given the peculiar circumstances surrounding the council declared Latin and Gregorian chant to be among the distinctive elements of the Roman liturgy. It is also true that until the fourth century the Roman Church deferred replacing the Greek *koinè* with the vernacular Latin as its liturgical language. But in the end it had to let go of Greek, the language that had been hallowed by the biblical books and its numerous martyrs. But in our time, to restore Latin as the everyday language of the liturgy, regardless of whether or not the assembly can follow the readings and prayers, is to my historical mind a departure from the Roman "sound tradition" and an impediment to what the council fathers had anticipated as "legitimate progress" of liturgical worship.

But there are two sides to a coin. While there are people who want the liturgy to be hermetically sealed from the contemporary world, there are others who hold that the liturgy needs to be in constant dialogue with what goes on in the Church and the world. They rightly claim that if the liturgy is to be an agent of renewal, it should address today's cultural, religious, socioeconomic, and political issues. We must admit, though, that during the early stages of reform exaggerations marred its image, compelling the Congregation for Divine Worship to issue in 1970 the Third Instruction, *Liturgicae instaurationes*. The Instruction lamented that under the pretext of pastoral needs some people "could not wait for the promulgation of the definitive reforms. In consequence, they have resorted to personal innovations, to hasty, often ill-advised measures, to new creations and additions or to the simplification of rites. All of this has frequently conflicted with the most basic liturgical norms and upset the consciences of the faithful. The innovators have thus obstructed the cause of genuine liturgical renewal or made it more difficult."

I belong to the generation of postconciliar liturgists, and I still recall the proliferation of newly composed Eucharistic Prayers, some of which can be censured for mediocre content and literary style, the blaring sound of jazz ensembles, and, alas, the reported proscribed use of wafers and soft drinks for the Eucharist. Wishing to curtail abuses, the Congregation had to set down stringent rules: "Any liturgical experimentation that may seem necessary or advantageous receives authorization from this Congregation alone, in writing, with norms clearly set out, and subject to the responsibility of the competent local authority."

Wanting to make the Eucharist more relevant to our contemporary situation, someone seriously entertained the horrendous idea of "fast-food Eucharist," open twenty-four hours a day so that the faithful could come any time at their convenience. All they had to do was switch on the television for the Liturgy of the Word and afterward approach the altar for Communion. The idea was motivated by a desire to make the liturgy conform to the situation of people on the move and to the declining value of family meals. What I detect is the failure to regard the liturgy as a countercultural statement, as a Christian critique of modern conventions and systems that impair the foundations of human community and family life.

The liturgical reform of Vatican II generated tensions and uncertainties about the proper implementation of the conciliar decrees. There were people who received liturgical changes grudgingly or simply resisted them because they invaded their comfort zones. They courted the preconciliar liturgy with an attitude often deprived of historical and pastoral basis. They behaved like a terrier snapping at the heels of conciliar reform. What dismays me, to push the analogy, is that today the number of such terriers is on the rise. The humility to accept an ecumenical council's decision is surely a more salutary attitude than a romantic adherence to the past, however glorious that past might have been. In the Office of Readings for Wednesday of the Twentieth Week in Ordinary Time St. Augustine has this timely reminder about "the good old days" that we tend to idealize when new ways of doing things disrupt our routine: "You hear people complaining about this present day and age because things were much better in former times. I wonder what would happen if they could be taken back to the days of their ancestors—would we not still hear them complaining? You may think past ages were good, but it is only because you are not living in them." I would not present an honest picture, however, if I did not mention those who, driven by an unquenchable thirst for novelty, chose to ignore the right order of things. They were the recklessly euphoric who, unwittingly, gave others a reason to be wary of the conciliar reform.

CHALLENGES OF THE LITURGICAL REFORM

In his October 29, 1964, address to the members and consultors of the Consilium for the Implementation of the Liturgical Reform, Pope Paul VI compared the liturgy to "a mighty tree, the continual renewal of whose leaves shows its beauty; the great age of whose trunk, with deep roots and firm in the earth, attests to the richness of its life. In matters of liturgy, therefore, no real conflict should arise between present and past." In another address to the same body two years later he reminded them of the necessity to respect liturgical tradition. The criterion, he said, is what is best, not what is new. "Nevertheless," he concludes with this vigorous statement, "the voice of the Church today must not be so constricted that it could not sing a new song, should the inspiration of the Holy Spirit move it to do so." The Consilium must move ahead with its projects in order to let the Church sing a new song, while bearing in mind that the Church possesses "a priceless heritage worthy of veneration."

Much has been achieved, yet much still remains to be done, even as the Church, caught between tradition and progress, pursues its pilgrimage amid the changes and chances of this world. What role should liturgical worship play in the Church's mission as advocate of authentic values and progress? The liturgical movement and the council wanted worship to be an agent of human renewal. There are times when, as I step back to view the state of liturgical reform, I become disheartened by what seems to be a misplaced concern for rubrical details that have little consequence on what goes on in the world.

Conflict among ethnic groups resulting in genocide, armed strife resulting in political tyranny, and socioeconomic inequity resulting in poverty and ecological destruction—this is the reality of the world in which the Church moves; it is the reality with which the liturgy should dialogue. Despair casts its shadow also on the community of believers. There are Christians who fall away from the Church or no longer talk to God because the meaning and purpose of life have eluded them. There are Christians who commit suicide or practice euthanasia because there is nothing more to look forward to in a life dominated by pain and suffering. This too is a reality with which the liturgy should dialogue if it is to be an agent of spiritual renewal. Is the postconciliar reform of the liturgy capable of addressing some of the challenges of our time?

What are the challenges? Bugnini identified three basic challenges facing the reform of the liturgy after Vatican II: the translation of liturgical texts into the vernacular, the revision of Tridentine liturgical books, and adaptation, which is better known today as inculturation. Below are some of my musings. I realize that they are limited in scope and number and that they represent only the tip of the iceberg. I am not so naive as to think that a truly meaningful celebration of the liturgy will radically and immediately change the course of world events, but I believe that in time it can become a leaven of renewal. For example, when liturgical worship absorbed the culture and preoccupations of the Greco-Roman world, it gradually and subtly imprinted the Christian mark on Western civilization. In the words of Josef Jungmann (*The Early Liturgy to the Time of Gregory the Great*), "Society, political life, the lives of the people, family life, the position of women, the appreciation of human dignity, whether slave, child, or infant yet unborn—all this was transformed in a slow but sure process of fermentation: out of a pagan society a Christian society was born."

Liturgy and Technology

Culture is in constant evolution. Although many of its traditional components have survived the test of time, new elements are continually being introduced and integrated into it. Societies that have been traditionally agricultural are quickly shifting to industry. The Fourth Instruction on the Liturgy, issued by the Congregation for Divine Worship on January 25, 1994, is keenly aware of this. It calls for a balanced approach to this situation: "Liturgical inculturation should try to satisfy the needs of traditional culture, and at the same time take account of the needs of those affected by an urban or industrial culture." Once upon a time people earned their living by hunting, fishing, and farming. Because liturgy mirrors what transpired in the world and indeed accompanies humans in the different aspects of their life, the Church instituted liturgical feasts in the context of agricultural and pastoral life. Masses were held to ask God to intervene by sending rain in time of drought or to stop excessive rain so as to have fair weather for planting and harvesting. The four seasons of the year became the basis of the liturgical calendar of feasts and festivals.

With the advent of the industrial age should we not expect the Church to incorporate this reality in the liturgy? If we confine our attention to agricultural liturgy, we might leave out the daily affairs and cares of a great number of the faithful in urban communities. Our medieval liturgy still bears, and very rightly so, the marks of agricultural realities. Obviously, our earth must continue to produce enough food, which is a basic requirement of industrial and technological advancement. But should we not perhaps consider a liturgy for people who live in an industrialized setting, where labor unions, strikes and pickets, layoffs, and collective bargaining agreements play as important a role in the life of industrialized world as do the changes in the seasons of the year in agricultural societies? Will the creation of such liturgy contribute in some measure to the realization of the council's agenda "to gather the dispersed children of God" divided by industrial systems?

But even before the liturgy turned its attention to the industrial world, another reality made its presence felt. I refer to technology and, particularly, to what is known as information technology. When asked what I thought about the use of laptop computers to replace the Sacramentary on the altar and the Lectionary at the ambo, I thought the question was meant to be included in the book of liturgical humor. But it was asked in earnest because a priest had already mastered the use of a "liturgical laptop." As I said, my instinctive reaction was hilarity. How did the assembly react to the carrying of the computer in procession and to incensing it? What part of the computer did the priest kiss after reading the gospel from it?

When I was taking the intricate course on liturgical books, Prof. Adrien Nocent warned that if we did not learn them we would be handicapped the rest of our lives. Studying the liturgy without being familiar with its sources, he declared, is like studying Scripture without knowing the biblical books. His warning was one compelling reason why I held printed sacramentaries, lectionaries, and the Book of the Gospels in great honor.

This background held me back from giving outright justification for the use of computers in the liturgy. On the surface it looks too banal for liturgical use. But if we regard modern technology as one of God's greatest gifts to humankind, can we simply ignore or dismiss its entry into the domain of liturgical worship? In short, can we allow computers to replace our printed liturgical books? When libraries are now being built to store the collection of computer disks rather than books, should the liturgy of the new millennium stick to printed books? I still have to make up my mind whether information technology is so helplessly secular that it cannot have a place in a sacred action. I am reminded of the controversy between Rome and the Church of Milan about the rite of washing the feet of neophytes as they came out of the baptismal pool (*De Sacramentis* III, 4–7). Rome had sharply criticized St. Ambrose for the practice on claims that it was a secular symbol of hospitality and as such had no place in the sacred rite of baptism. The *Rule of Benedict* (chap. 53) directs the abbot and the entire community to wash the feet of guests as a gesture of hospitality. The answer of St. Ambrose was a retort: "Rome used to wash the feet of neophytes, but it stopped the practice when their number considerably increased. If Rome has its reason to stop the practice, we in Milan have our reason to continue it."

Sunday Observance

My musings lead me to another challenge that touches the heart of the Church, namely, the observance of Sunday. Article 106 of the Constitution on Liturgy urges the faithful to gather together on Sunday so that through the word of God and the Eucharist, "they may call to mind the passion, the resurrection, and the glorification of the Lord Jesus." It exhorts that Sunday, which is the first among all the holy days, should "become in fact a day of joy and of freedom from work." I remember those preconciliar times when people confessed the sin of servile work on Sunday. There were people who could not afford not to work for pay on Sunday. These people had to confess again and again the same sin, which they could not avoid because of poverty. The conciliar decree on "rest and freedom from work" on Sunday puzzled me the first time I read it. For a council that declared to be pastoral, this particular decree seemed to be out of character.

I did a little research on the conciliar proceedings and was relieved to find out that it had not been the council's intention to make Sunday rest an absolute norm. The council in fact regarded it as a matter of secondary importance, compared with the Sunday celebration of the Eucharist that defines Sunday as the Lord's Day. Emperor Constantine introduced the Christian observance of Sunday rest in order to encourage the faithful to participate in the solemn celebration of the Eucharist. Up until then Saturday was kept as a holiday in the Roman Empire, and Christians, like all others, worked on Sunday, though they set aside the early morning hours of the day for the Eucharistic celebration. We know that the Jews, who had been accidentally privileged by the Roman civil holiday on Saturday, were annoyed by the change that favored the Christians.

Today, in developed countries and among the middle class Sunday has become part of the modern phenomenon called weekend. Weekend, which grew in some way from the observance of the Sunday rest, is characterized by tourism and recreation. This has caused the problem of absence on Sunday from one's parish and in some instances also of diminished participation in the Sunday Mass. But in the situation of poverty where it becomes necessary to earn a living even on Sunday, freedom from work is like an unreachable dream. The reminder of the *Catechism of the Catholic Church* is timely: "Those Christians who have leisure should be mindful of their sisters and brothers who have the same needs and the same rights, yet cannot rest from work because of poverty and misery" (2186). In *Sacramentum caritatis* Pope Benedict XVI counsels that while people rightly uphold the dignity of human work, they "should not allow themselves to be enslaved by work or to idolize it, claiming to find in it the ultimate and definitive meaning of life" (74).

For the parish community, Sunday rest should not mean rest from works of love and social concern. The professional service of doctors, lawyers, and teachers offered freely to the poor of the community should become a distinguishing mark of the parish Sunday observance. The Sunday assembly does not end in church but continues on in parish clinics and classrooms. Lay leaders visit the sick and the homebound in order to bring them Eucharistic Communion and the community's spiritual comfort. Sunday Eucharist is incomplete if it does not overflow into community service. Apropos I quote the Decree of the Second Plenary Council of the Philippines reminding all that "service should complement worship in sanctifying Sunday as the Lord's Day" (art. 38, no. 2).

Weekday Order of Mass

For many years now I have been toying with the idea of a "ferial Order of Mass." As things stand, the same Order of Mass published in 1970 is observed every day, with minor features—like the Gloria and Creed and a second reading— added for Sundays and solemn feasts. This gives the impression that the ferial, or daily, Mass is a slightly simplified version of Sunday Mass. The fact, of course, is that we do not have a ferial Order of Mass. This reminds me of a somewhat similar case. Until 1969 there had been no rite of baptism specifically prepared for children. The rite of baptism published by Pope Paul V in 1614 was merely a shorter version of the rite of baptism for adults with all those gruesome formulas to expel the demon from the child.

Pope Gregory the Great mentions *Missae cotidianae*, or daily Masses, in one of his letters (*Letter* 9). He contrasts these with Sunday Masses. The litanies, he informs us, are not said in daily Masses, and "we recite only the *Kyrie eleison* and *Christe eleison*." Gathering bits and pieces of information from medieval sources, we can only guess the format of the daily Mass in the time of Pope Gregory, but guesswork at this point is both futile and unproductive. We wrestle with difficult historical data. What I wish to propose instead is that we apply the principle of progressive solemnity to justify the ferial Order of Mass. Without progressive solemnity the system of ranking the liturgical feasts cannot be fully appreciated.

The concept of the liturgical year is premised on the distinction between feasts and ordinary days, and the degree of solemnity proper to the feast is reflected in the way Mass is celebrated. The ferial Order of Mass will furthermore free the theology of the liturgical year from the exaggerated notion that one day is as good as the other. I keep reminding people with a penchant for festivity that if daily Masses are celebrated with the full complement of a Sunday Mass, they will have to stretch and strain imagination to satisfy progressive solemnity. Although the daily Mass is rightly regarded as the center of the daily rhythm of worship, it should be neatly distinguished from Sunday Mass. I should point out that the presence of a large congregation at a weekday Mass is not a valid reason to elevate it to the rank of a Sunday Mass. On the other hand, a small assembly should not be an excuse to strip the Sunday Mass of those distinctive elements that belong to its celebration.

Prominent liturgists have written about possible revision of the present Order of Mass. Many of them appeal to the *sobrietas romana* as criterion. I refer to Adrien Nocent, Robert Cabié, and Mark Searle, who favor a simple entrance rite consisting only of a greeting, silent pause, and the opening prayer. Thomas Krosnicki, a classmate of mine in Rome, shows partiality to the greeting *Dominus vobiscum*. I agree with him. The other biblical greetings are surely rich in doctrine, but I find them long-winded. Frederick McManus, the eminent canon lawyer and liturgical scholar I profoundly respect, thinks that the offertory *berakah* ("Blessed are you, Lord God of all creation") should be suppressed and the rite of the offertory streamlined. It seems to me that the application of the traditional *sobrietas romana* to the Order of Mass is a challenge that the postconciliar reform should address.

Although the ferial Order of Mass will be somewhat shorter than the *forma typica* of the Roman Missal, progressive solemnity, not brevity, is the overriding criterion. It can happen, however, that the ferial order will exceed the typical form, especially in those instances when the assembly comprised of religious and seminarians takes its time reflecting silently after the readings.

What shape do I envisage for the ferial Order of Mass? To avoid arbitrariness it is useful to recall a rule set down in the *Directory for Masses with Children*: "Apart from adaptations that are necessary because of the children's age, the result should not be entirely special rites, markedly different from the Order of Mass celebrated with a congregation" (21). Sharp contrast between the typical form and the ferial order will not be pastorally productive. Bi-ritualism can be very demanding upon any assembly. Hence, I believe that new rites, acclamations, and responses should not be introduced. Novelty of such sort can produce a jarring effect on the flow of the celebration. Ancient *Ordines Romani* (57) do not dispense with the responsorial psalm. However, elements not considered integral parts of the Mass, like the penitential rite that on occasion is replaced by another rite and the sign of peace that is optional, need not be regular features of the ferial order. The penitential rite is more meaningful in Lent. Likewise, it is quite meaningless to retain songs of accompaniment when the action is not fully performed. I do not see much sense in singing an entrance song while the priest walks from the adjacent sacristy to the sanctuary or chanting the *Agnus Dei* when only one host is broken. The invitation "Behold the Lamb of God" before Communion can take care of the biblical symbol of the lamb. Regarding the washing of hands, McManus remarks that "possibly the symbolic washing before the Eucharist begins—or even before the preface of the anaphora—might have saved it from recent neglect and even disrepute" ("The Roman Order of Mass," *Shaping English Liturgy*).

Below is how I would shape a ferial Order of Mass.

Introductory Rites

After the people have assembled, the priest goes to the altar, making the customary signs of reverence before he goes to the chair. After the sign of the cross, he greets the assembly: "The Lord be with you." During Lent the penitential rite may follow the greeting, otherwise the priest recites the opening prayer after the invitation "Let us pray."

Liturgy of the Word

After the first reading the responsorial psalm is sung or recited. If the Alleluia is not sung, it may be omitted. If there is no homily, a period of silent reflection follows the reading of the gospel, after which the general intercessions are made.

Liturgy of the Eucharist

The priest prepares the Eucharistic offerings in silence. The berakah is not said and the rite of the washing of hands is not performed. Then the priest says: "Pray, brothers and sisters," and recites the prayer over the gifts.

The daily singing of the Sanctus is recommended. If the memorial acclamation is not sung, it may be omitted, so that the priest continues the Eucharistic Prayer without interruption.

After the Lord's Prayer the embolism is omitted. The doxology "For the kingdom" concludes the Lord's Prayer. The sign of peace is omitted, but the preceding prayer "Lord Jesus Christ" is said. Thereafter, the priest invites the assembly to Holy Communion. After a period of silence the priest recites the prayer after communion.

Concluding Rite

The celebration ends with the usual greeting, simple form of blessing, and dismissal.

If there are liturgical days that call for greater solemnity because they are feasts, there are others that do not because they are not feasts. In tradition these days came to be known as ferial days. They do not recall any particular aspect of Christ's mystery or celebrate a saint. The foregoing ferial Order of Mass is my idea, call it reverie, of providing the ferial days with a corresponding *ordo*.

Role of Women

As I turn my attention to another challenge, I should preface my musings with a word to the reader that I will be treading on uneven ground. No one ignores the giant strides the Church has made allowing women to take active ministerial roles in the liturgy. Women may read the word of God in the sanctuary, where in the past they had to read it outside the sanctuary. Women are neither ordained deacons nor instituted as lectors or acolytes, but they can hold the functions of extraordinary ministers of communion, altar servers, and readers. They can preside at Sunday assemblies in the absence of a priest. In some parts of the world bishops deputize women catechists to administer solemn baptism. They also delegate women to assist as official witnesses at Church weddings when no priest or deacon is present (Code of Canon Law 861 and 1112). These are some encouraging gains that we can regard as significant stirrings of progress in today's Church. They reassure us that legitimate progress in the liturgy can be achieved without prejudice to sound tradition.

The reinstitution of the permanent diaconate and the lay ministries of lector and acolyte are a gift of Pope Paul VI to the Church. Even if, by some superior option, these ministries are reserved to male persons, they implement in a limited way the council's principle of full, active participation by God's people through active ministry. But I wish to recall that our liturgical tradition, which does not know of women presbyters, knows of women deacons who received from the bishop the sacramental hand-laying or *cheirotonía*. Church documents as early as the third century speak of the ordination of women to the diaconate. History attests to the ministry they exercised in the Churches of Eastern and Western Syria, Chaldea and Persia, Egypt, Armenia, Constantinople, Gaul, Italy, and Rome until the end of the tenth century, despite the earlier prohibition by Pope Gelasius. Things changed around the year 1000 when adult baptisms gave way to infant baptisms. This new development caused the gradual disappearance of women deacons, whose principal role had been to anoint adult women catechumens during baptism. Now that adult initiation is restored, should the Church consider reopening the question of the ordination of women to the diaconate? Or does it remain a closed book?

There was a lively debate between two eminent liturgists on the ordination of women to the diaconate. One was Fr. Cipriano Vagaggini, who presented ancient documents to prove that the deaconesses in the early centuries were sacramentally ordained. The other was Msgr. George-Aimé Martimort, who countered that women were not sacramentally ordained, although they were designated with the title of deaconesses. The present official thinking of the Holy See favors the second opinion. I suspect that there is a lurking fear that the ordination of women to the diaconate might lead to their ordination to the priesthood, and God knows, eventually to the episcopate.

I am not in a position to address the question of the ordination of women to the priesthood. I leave that to systematic theologians and canon lawyers. A statement from the Congregation for the Doctrine of Faith affirmed that the practice of not ordaining women to the priesthood is part of the deposit of faith. The statement is puzzling. I cannot comprehend that the apostles deposited nonexistent practices as an item of our belief. I always thought that the deposit of faith is an existing doctrine or practice, not the absence of it. All I know is that the ordination of women to the priesthood does not exist in liturgical tradition, and I will not make the blunder of arguing against the current doctrine and discipline of the Church. I want to believe that there is pastoral prudence and centuries-old wisdom in its decisions and declarations. What interests me is, so to speak, not the entire loaf of bread but the crumbs that fall from the table: the ordination of women to the diaconate. Several years ago the International Theological Commission discussed this issue. The conclusion was that if ever the practice would be reintroduced in the Church, it should not be regarded as a sacramental ordination, even if these lucky women will be called deaconesses.

The institution of women lectors and acolytes is, it seems to me, a slightly easier question to settle. When Pope Paul VI issued *Ministeria quaedam* in 1972, he cited the "ancient tradition of the Church," which reserved these instituted ministries to men. We know that because of their close connection to the liturgy, the lectorate and acolytate had been called minor orders. In the late fourth century Pope Siricius started the movement to clericalize liturgical ministries. As a result, lectorate and acolytate were reserved to male persons. Though *Ministeria quaedam* has extricated them from the clerical state, it continues to require them as stages of the clerical *cursus*. Apparently this is the reason for not instituting women to these ministries. Circumventing the *Motu proprio*, the Church gradually allowed women, without the benefit of institution, to be readers, extraordinary ministers of Communion, and altar servers, in keeping with their duty and right to share, where possible, in the Church's ministry. Given these progressive changes, I like to picture Pope Paul VI, the pope of liturgical *aggiornamento*, smiling complacently at the prospect of women being instituted as lectors and acolytes.

Inculturation

The topic of inculturation received a good deal of attention from the Liturgy Constitution. It was Burkhard Neunheuser who established the course on liturgical inculturation in the Pontifical Liturgical Institute. Because of my dissertation, which advocated the adaptation of the Easter symbols in places where it is summer or autumn at Easter time, I was invited to teach the course in 1973. I literally groped in the dark about the shape of such a novel course, but in time I managed to create a decent outline and publish a couple of articles. My first two books on the topic (*Towards a Filipino Liturgy* and *Liturgical Renewal in the Philippines*) were published in Manila in 1976 and 1980. My third book (*Cultural Adaptation of the Liturgy*) was published by Paulist Press in New York in 1982.

At a time when some people in the Church began to be cynical about the present state of liturgical reform—think of the indult restoring the Tridentine Mass and the official preference for the literal translation of liturgical texts—the Instruction "Roman Liturgy and Inculturation" was a timely affirmation of the Holy See's continued commitment to the conciliar decrees. For some time I chaired the Vatican committee that drafted the document, and I take pride in having successfully pressed for the adoption of my definition of inculturation. I had always insisted that inculturation is a dynamic translation of the typical edition of the liturgical books. Inculturation does not create alternative rites. What it does is translate the Roman rite into the language of the local Church by integrating suitable cultural elements. By translation I mean dynamic equivalence, not formal correspondence that is highly favored today in some Church circles. With due respect to authority, I feel that *Summorum Pontificum* has cast a menacing shadow on the future of inculturation. But I have a word to the wise: take note of a door the Apostolic Letter has opened. It established two forms of the Roman Rite, one ordinary and another extraordinary. I would like to consider this a basis for the Holy See to declare inculturated forms of liturgy as "other extraordinary" forms of the Roman Mass along with the Tridentine rite.

What are some of the challenges of inculturation? Let us form a mental picture of a Sunday assembly composed of people from various races, languages, and socioeconomic circumstances. A Hispanic sits next to an Asian. The underprivileged mingle with the wealthy, the children with the adults, the employees with their employers, and no one feels like a stranger: they all belong to the *domus ecclesiae*. Different ethnic groups are allowed, even encouraged, to express the faith of the Church in the language, rites, and symbols of their traditional culture. Every member of the assembly is grateful for the experience of singing to the tune and rhythm of another's native music, delighted to listen to the children's choir, and attentive to the announcement by an employee of a forthcoming strike. Yet no ethnic group is hurt when told that a certain rite indigenous to one's country of origin or a type of musical rhythm is not liturgically appropriate or suitable. Everyone accepts the fact that there are liturgical rules as well as cultural premises that need to be respected. This is, of course, an idealized image of a liturgical assembly, but I should like to think that it aptly describes what inculturation means for multicultural and multiethnic communities that are now a sociological reality in many parts of the world.

The challenge concerns our readiness for liturgical pluralism rooted in cultural or ethnic diversity. Will the community be comfortable with the Sunday Mass in which the different languages spoken in the parish are used: prayers in English, readings in Spanish, song lyrics in Filipino? Actually, the idea is not the product of my fantasy. We know that until the seventh century the liturgy of Rome was bilingual because of the migrants from Eastern Europe. Liturgy highly values hospitality. Greek *koinè* and Latin were used for the readings on special occasions like Easter and Christmas and for some rites of adult catechumenate. The tradition lives on in the solemn papal Masses that are celebrated in a variety of tongues in consideration of the faithful who come from every part of the world.

Another question is whether the community will allow the architecture and furnishings of the church to be influenced by native architectural and artistic designs. Viewed from one angle, the *domus ecclesiae* will look African, and from another, Hispanic or European. It will not look like the traditional gothic or baroque church; it might not even pass for a postmodern building. What it will represent is not the fixed canon of church architecture but the image of a multicultural community gathered in worship, a sign of unity in our divided world. I can make the same observation on the style of the Eucharistic table, lectern, vessels, and vestments.

There is, of course, a principle involved here, namely, the need to produce a sense of harmony among the different cultural symbols, a kind of unity among various elements, an eloquent symbol of the multicultural and multiethnic community that is gathered as a liturgical assembly. This form of inculturation affirms that in the sight of God and the Church all races and ethnic groups are equal. It means that all languages are suitable for the worship of God; that all musical forms, provided they enhance the liturgy, are welcome; and that all cultural rites and symbols, provided they harmonize with the true and authentic spirit of the liturgy, can be raised to the status and dignity of ritual language and symbols. To paraphrase a well-known line in George Orwell's *Animal Farm*, in the Church no culture should claim to be more equal than others.

The success of genuine inculturation is in the hands of the local bishops and the Vatican Curia. The two agencies need to work together in mutual respect and understanding. Bishops, who are the liturgists of their dioceses, are expected to master not only canon law but also liturgy. On the other hand, Vatican officials will do well to immerse themselves in the culture and traditions of local churches. The apostolic visits of Pope John Paul II to the different continents of the globe bore good fruit. In his speeches he gave his support to the progress of liturgical inculturation. He formulated its definition, laid down its theological foundation in the mystery of the incarnation, and adopted the neologism "inculturation" to make certain that changes in the liturgy would not remain on the surface of ceremonies.

I cannot forget the time I was called by Cardinal Josef Ratzinger to a meeting with the Congregation for the Doctrine of Faith. The subject for discussion was the type of flour to be used for the Eucharistic bread. In my excitement I prepared a short paper about the question of using non-wheat flour. It soon dawned on me that my paper was nothing more than youthful impertinence, because it turned out that the meeting was called to deal exclusively with the query whether honey could be added to the flour to sweeten the host. We were informed that some groups were doing it under the inspiration of the psalm: "Taste and see that the Lord is sweet"!

On another occasion the good cardinal asked what I thought about this invocation of ancestors in the entrance rite of the Zairean Mass:

"Oh you, our ancestors of righteous heart, stay with us." The obvious problem is that the ancestors who had not been baptized are now invoked together with the Christian saints. In my answer I recalled the disastrous decision of Rome banning the Chinese ancestral rites. The hundred-year controversy between the Jesuits and the Franciscans with their Dominican ally fuelled the antagonism of the Chinese people toward the "Western" religion. History might be telling us that it would not be prudent to delete the Zairean invocation, since the veneration of ancestors, as in China and other parts of the world, is the bedrock of African civilization. The invocation stayed, but as the cardinal wisely noted, no explanation should be made about it.

Liturgy of the Hours

My final consideration deals with the Liturgy of the Hours, which I shall discuss below in connection with the official character of the liturgy. The breviary is sometimes called the priest's wife. It should be his companion day and night and he is expected to remain faithful to it, finding strength, consolation, and joy when he prays it. But I am not sure this matches reality. A good number of priests confided to me that they do not find their "wife" attractive enough. Although the Liturgy Constitution stresses the two chief hours of Lauds and Vespers as the hinges of the prayer life of the Church, we are aware that these hours do not necessarily figure in every priest's daily routine.

The crusade to bring the Liturgy of the Hours back in reach of the faithful resulted in a form that is more suited to public or communal, rather than private, recitation. Every liturgical action is, of course, an action of the entire Church, even if it is held in the privacy of one's bedroom. But I am afraid that this has disadvantaged the principal users. In 1535 Cardinal Quiñones published a type of breviary for the use of the clergy. Marked by brevity and simplicity, it gained popularity among the priests. However, it neglected the communal aspect of its celebration. It was withdrawn from use in 1568.

The message is clear. The Liturgy of the Hours is liturgy and should, at least theoretically, be shaped for public prayer. Vatican II's reform did not envisage a form of the Liturgy of the Hours for private recitation. Instead, it adopted a form that includes antiphons, a great majority of psalms that even the Jewish faithful did not recite every month, and a format that is not user friendly. A simpler format with a limited selection of prayerful psalms might have been more attractive to priests who are engaged in pastoral ministry day and night and who, in all probability, will not be able to form a stable community of laypeople with whom they could pray at least the chief hours of Lauds and Vespers.

My musings on the Liturgy of the Hours bring me to the question of the Office of Readings. Once upon a time it was a nocturnal vigil observed by communities of monks and nuns. Now it is meant to offer priests daily spiritual reading. If this is the intention, there is perhaps a need to reexamine its form. Let me think aloud at this juncture. Should not the Office of Readings be connected with the priest's ministry of Sunday homily? If so, should not the readings be grafted, so to speak, on the Lectionary for Mass, with special attention to the gospel of the day, and with corresponding commentaries both patristic and contemporary so that the priest will be provided with useful material to prepare his Sunday and daily homilies?

Daytime prayer does not enjoy the prominence that Lauds and Vespers have in the estimation of the Church, but in the daily grind of pastoral life its significance should not be passed over. It is the propitious time of the day for priests to pause from work, sit back, and converse briefly with the Lord. In antiquity prayers were said at nine o'clock, twelve, and three. Because of their brevity they were called little or minor hours. Tertullian (*De oratione* 25) explains that these hours "stand out in daily life, because they divide the day, establish the rhythm of business, and are signaled by public bells." The minor hours are thus a momentary pause from daily business or routine, "compelling us to snatch a moment from business" in order to pray. All too often our day can appear like an endless movement from one meeting to another, with a lunch break hurriedly taken, and a short nap to prepare for whatever surprises the afternoon might bring. I propose that the daytime prayer is an interlude that breaks the routine, allowing us to recollect, recover a lost good humor, and secure us from the dreaded disease of being "burnt out" in the service of the Lord.

However, to require active priests to recite three psalms or three segments of a long psalm at midday can be quite unrealistic and even inconsiderate. I believe that daytime prayer can be reformatted in consideration of the reality of pastoral ministry. Why not merge it with the prayer before the midday meal, in much the same way that we recite the Angelus before lunch? Salvatore Marsili had pointed out that the Angelus is a popular Marian version of the Liturgy of the Hours, consisting of three antiphons followed by a Hail Mary, a verse, and the concluding prayer. Several years ago I was appalled when I heard that

Pope John Paul II was toying with the idea of declaring the Angelus a substitute of the daytime prayer. Today I am no longer appalled, but I propose that an abbreviated daytime prayer be integrated with prayer before the midday meal.

Visions, tensions, and challenges: to my mind these are the essential components of liturgical *aggiornamento*. Visions breed tensions, but tensions generate challenges. Vatican II seems like many ages ago, but I like to believe that it still echoes down the corridor of our time. My musings rest upon liturgical tradition and pastoral sense. But I admit that imagination and fantasy are also at work in them. Perhaps certain issues I address—none of them merits the adjective "ebullient"—create uneasiness among those who do not wish to rock the boat or stir the waters. Although I made sure that I have some historical and theological basis for my musings, some of them might seem groundless affirmations that are best ignored. To some others they might cause a feeling of disaffection. However, fantasy is the mother of science. We know that when we lose the gift of fantasy, we lose vision as well. When the Paul VI Institute of Liturgy opened in 1990, a bishop exhorted me: "Just teach your students the basic liturgy found in approved books. Forget all about creative liturgy; it is all fantasy."

THE CHURCH INTENT ON CONTEMPLATION

Active participation in the liturgy is one of the many gifts of Vatican II to the Church in modern times. It amazes me that shortly after the council active participation became a conventional phrase among Catholic faithful. We do not, of course, overlook the fact that in 1909 Dom Lambert Beauduin advocated active participation in the liturgy as an effective remedy for the socioreligious apathy among many Catholics. But are not a hundred years rather long to achieve active participation? I would say no, if we consider that at the close of the patristic era active participation had begun to wane and that it was only in the twentieth century that the Church gave serious thought to active participation.

I have often heard the claim that Rome is eternal. Should we be surprised if its liturgy takes an eternity to be recast? Patience is a virtue I have acquired when dealing with Rome's lengthy process of liturgical renewal. I beg not to be charged with impertinence. I believe that the proverbial prudence of Rome should be matched by the patience of the faithful. After all, prudence and patience are twin virtues. Perhaps there is a less intimidating way to put my thoughts across. I should say that the Roman Church periodically adapts its form of worship to the changing times. My study of history tells me that the liturgy has time and again been assessed, revised, and edited to suit contemporary needs. But the Roman Church with its proverbial wisdom of the ages takes its time.

Before Vatican II, the last major revision of the liturgy took place after the Council of Trent. It contested Protestant innovations that were then considered harmful to the Catholic faith. To crush the danger of gratuitous innovations, Pope Pius V decreed in 1570, under pain of apostolic wrath, that no one was henceforth allowed to introduce changes in the Tridentine Missal. Although active participation was not envisioned, I think the decree was an enlightened move. For one thing, it definitely warded off any unwarranted innovation for the next four hundred years. For another—and this is also praiseworthy—the mystic and arcane way in which the Mass was celebrated encouraged contemplation of heavenly realities. To those who wish to abandon the Tridentine Mass, its protagonists make the timely reminder that countless number of saints drew spiritual nourishment from it. Who would doubt historical facts?

But times changed. At the dawn of the twentieth century the Church faced fresh challenges brought about by new scientific findings, modern philosophy, secularization, industrialization, labor disputes, socialization, civil uprisings, and the weakening of the Christian faith. The council fathers of Vatican II were deeply aware of this. They responded with the insightful and inspiring Constitution entitled "The Church in the Modern World."

The advent of modern times had a profound effect on Catholic worship. The Tridentine liturgy lost much of its relevance for a good number of Catholics living in a secularized society. There was a compelling need to introduce new ways of drawing spiritual nourishment from the liturgy. I suspect that the nineteenth-century Age of Enlightenment had subtly influenced the way the Church formulated its answer to challenges: the liturgy should not merely serve as an occasion or backdrop to contemplate divine realities; it should above all be understood, so that the assembly can pray it and actively participate in it. If its texts, symbols, and gestures are understood, the liturgy can enlighten, exhort, and persuade the assembly. I have always maintained that active participation requires from churchgoers some measure of liturgical comprehension. If they do not understand Latin, can they claim that they take active part in the Latin liturgy merely because they are able to recite the Latin formularies? If the rites and symbols of the liturgy are alien beings in their world of symbols, can they participate actively? In order to pray the liturgy, should they not understand the words they say or hear?

Intelligent and active participation became a byword in the liturgical renewal of Vatican II. Probably the word "canon" would be a more accurate word than "byword." I have read again and again the conciliar provision on active participation, and I admit that sometimes it strikes me as a kind of obsession. Article 14 of the Liturgy Constitution is purposeful: "In the reform and promotion of the liturgy, full and active participation by all the people is the aim to be considered before all else. For it is the primary and indispensable source from which the faithful are to derive the true Christian spirit." There is determination and precision in these words: reform and promotion, full and active participation, all the peoples, aim before all else, primary and indispensable source, true Christian spirit. These were the same words my mentors in the Pontifical Liturgical Institute zealously iterated as I sat in awe at their feet. They were the architects of the conciliar liturgy constitution and the postconciliar reform. They were the giants that roamed the world of Christian worship.

How can I forget my mentors in Sant'Anselmo on the Aventine Hill? Cipriano Vagaggini, Salvatore Marsili, Adrien Nocent, Burkhard Neunheuser, Jordi Pinell, Emmanuel Lanne, Herman Schmidt, Augustinus Mayer, and Virgilio Noè are masters I have always admired and emulated. After their morning sessions in the Vatican, they would come to the classroom with contagious enthusiasm to share with their fascinated students the progress of the reform. Every so often other giants visited us to add to the excitement of acquiring more information that frequently included funny and juicy trivia. That was the time I had the privilege to listen to Georges-A. Martimort, Pierre-Marie Gy, Balthasar Fischer, and Annibale Bugnini. What springtime in my liturgical formation that was! I cannot thank my mentors enough. Words fail me. I should add that even later when I had the honor to be counted among them as a young colleague, their solid scholarship, deep humility, and unsullied loyalty to the Church never failed to awe me. I remember with gratitude the Jesuit Herman Schmidt, who prevailed upon the authorities of the Gregorian University to give way to the Benedictines of Sant'Anselmo to open the liturgical institute. Liturgy, he argued, belonged to the sons of St. Benedict. He took particular interest in furthering my liturgical career by having my articles published in the periodical *Concilium* and inviting me to join him in some of the meetings he attended. I enjoyed especially the meeting with Jewish scholars about the proposal to observe a common Easter date. Yet he bragged that he had given me a barely passing mark for his course on Introduction to the Western Liturgy.

Earlier, I remarked that when the Tridentine liturgy lost its appeal to secularized Christians, Vatican II had to devise a new strategy in order to offer them the spiritual nourishment the liturgy had been able to provide in earlier times. The strategy was to re-propose to the people the doctrinal resources contained in the liturgy. In a sense it was a question of repackaging the contents of the liturgy. The council was convinced that, if understood correctly, the liturgy could nourish the spiritual life of the faithful. If understood correctly—in my opinion this is the basic requirement for the strategy to work. Hence the task assigned to the postconciliar reform was to recover the original noble simplicity of the Roman liturgy that had disappeared in the tenth century due to external influences from the Franco-Germanic Churches.

As a matter of fact, those young Churches in Northern Europe had been tampering with the noble simplicity and sobriety of Rome's liturgy since the eighth century. In earnest they introduced into the Roman rite their local traditions, thereby producing a hybrid type of liturgy that can be named Franco-Germanic Roman liturgy. Among their local traditions were prayers and symbols that appealed to the senses, human emotions, and down-to-earth concerns that we find especially in their book of blessings. I should not neglect to point out that there was beauty and refinement in their church architecture, liturgical furnishings, miniatures, graphic arts, music, and poetry. These were veritable contributions to the cultural treasury of Christian worship. However, in the process of inculturation—that was what they were doing—the simplicity, sobriety, and practical sense of the Roman liturgy gave way to useless repetitions, allegorical interpretation of rites, and the mystery-laden symbols that were typical of the northern people at that time. The loss of the *sobrietas romana* was the price paid for inculturation. The German popes of the tenth century (Clement II, Damasus II, Leo IX, Victor II, and Stephen IX) adopted this hybrid type of liturgy for the city of Rome. The Tridentine Mass was a by-product of this hybrid liturgy.

Why did Vatican II's agenda include the restoration of the original seventh-century Roman rite? Would it not brand the conciliar reform as an archaeological exercise in the twentieth century? The council's reasoning is crystal clear: the simpler the rites and symbols are, the easier they will be understood; and the better the people understand, the more fully they can participate. Since the liturgy is "the primary and indispensable source from which the faithful are to derive the true Christian spirit," every effort should be made to lead the people to fully and actively participate in it. The council's adoption of the vernacular has a historical precedent. To make sure that the people really understood the liturgical texts, the Roman Church officially allowed in the fourth century the use of the vernacular Latin to replace the elitist and foreign Greek *koinè*.

Active participation is Vatican II's prized gift to the Church. As I ruminate on this, my thoughts turn to the vibrant participation I often witness in some parts of Asia, Africa, and Latin America, especially in some of their remote villages. People do not just sing: they sway and cheerfully clap their hands. The atmosphere of festive and active participation is electrifying. Having been brought up in the tradition of *sobrietas romana* and reverential awe of the sacred, I admit that I am not always comfortable with such mirthful manifestations. As a liturgist whose main hobby is inculturation, I always encourage and enjoy the celebration of inculturated liturgies where local rites and symbols are sometimes displayed like ostentatious and frolicsome rococo art. But at the end of the day I confess that my personal preference is still in favor of the sober, short, and unencumbered Roman rite that I studied at the feet of my masters and have learned to love.

But the majority of my experiences of active participation point to a composed and collected assembly that recites the Lord's Prayer without having to hold each other's hands, that sing without the deafening electric instruments to accompany them, that observe the prescribed postures and gestures without the clapping of hands, and that dutifully laugh or smile only when the presider decides to amuse them with a joke. Knowing where my mentors, who were architects of the postconciliar reform, were coming from, I might be correct in my conjecture that the above scenario of active participation was what they had in mind. I am quite certain that most of them would frown upon swaying or dancing, clapping, kissing, and roaming the length of the church to offer the sign of peace. On the other hand, I can imagine how they would have reacted to restrained, somber, and expressionless participation.

I consider our Sunday liturgy in Sant'Anselmo on the Aventine Hill when I was student and professor a classic example of hieratic liturgy.

All the rites were performed with gravity and demureness typical of monastic restraint. The liturgy looked very much like a still-life painting. Adrien Nocent had a classic name for it. He called it the "liturgy of the death of God." In fairness, I should admit that owing to Sant'Anselmo's liturgy, especially of the Easter Triduum that sharply contrasted with my Philippine experience, I came to understand and appreciate the meaning of *sobrietas romana*.

A frequent lament about active participation is that, unlike the Tridentine liturgy, it does not foster prayerful and contemplative celebration. It is averred that while the Tridentine liturgy encourages contemplation, the Vatican II liturgy, which requires active participation, does not leave room for contemplation. The lament is probably born from the erroneous conception that action and contemplation are mutually exclusive, or that the liturgy of Vatican II does not support dignity, prayerfulness, and awe in the celebration of Christ's mystery. To argue thus is, I believe, to stand logic on its head. I believe that the framers of the Liturgy Constitution were preempting such debate when right at the beginning of the document they wrote: "It is of the essence of the Church to be both human and divine, visible yet endowed with invisible resources, eager to act yet intent on contemplation, present in this world yet not at home in it" (2). In the Church "the human is directed and subordinated to the divine, the invisible likewise to the invisible, action to contemplation." The contrasting binomials are consistent with the traditional description of the Church: human and divine, visible yet invisible, eager to act yet intent on contemplation. What I find significant is the unqualified subordination of action to contemplation.

Active participation should lead the worshipers to the contemplation of the sacred realities they celebrate. Frankly, as a presider I have always found this challenging, and I suspect that worshipers struggle with the same problem. Not that I have ever committed the mistake of equating contemplation with ecstasy, rapture, or transport to the seventh heaven. A presider simply cannot afford to experience such heavenly bliss while standing at the Eucharistic table. Would it not be odd if the assembly went into ecstasy at the elevation of the sacred host? Such disruption of the rite is surely "un-liturgical"!

What is contemplation? It is a state of awareness of God's presence in the assembly, in the proclamation of the word, in the breaking of bread, and in the shared fellowship. Contemplation is awareness of divine presence. When I mean the words I say, words as routine as the greeting "The Lord be with you," I become conscious of God's presence in the assembly. When I utter the awesome words "This is my body," I perceive in faith that Christ is truly present in the lowly element of bread. When I recite the words of absolution, my thoughts return to the parable of the merciful Father and I vicariously experience the compassion of God. When I accompany the dead to their resting place, the liturgy persuades me to feel at least in my heart the pain of the mourners. These are surpassing moments of encountering God and recognizing the face of Christ in his people, in his words, and in his sacraments. Contemplation is awareness of God's presence, and the liturgy provides the assembly with the words, symbols, and fellowship so they will experience that presence.

Sometimes, in an honest effort to make the liturgy spirited and vivacious, we end up producing a celebration that has the features and qualities of showbiz. In the process we overlook the liturgy's awesome and hieratic character. The cross always casts its long shadow on our celebration. Amid the festivity of song and dance there always appears the image of him who "offered up prayers and supplications with loud cries and tears" (Heb 5:7). Enthralled by this *mysterium tremendum*, worshipers turn spontaneously to prayerful silence. In this type of contemplation actions and words can become quite superfluous. Silence supersedes the rituality of the liturgy. I am a believer in the value of silence, the kind of silence that offers occasion to relish in the depth of the heart God's presence in the celebration. Not surprisingly, the Liturgy Constitution regards silence as one of the constituents of active participation: "To promote active participation, the people should be encouraged to take part by means of acclamations, responses, psalmody, antiphons, and songs, as well as by actions, gestures, and bearing. And at proper times all should observe a reverent silence" (30).

Silence is not a momentary pause from activity; it is a form of liturgical activity when the mind and heart ponder the *mysterium tremendum*. Silence is the language of contemplative prayer. It is the attitude of a worshiper who gazes with awe on Christ the *Pantokrator* in the apse of a Romanesque church or with tenderness on the Child resting in the arms of his mother. Silence is the only valid response to Christ's mysterious words "This is my body which will be given up for you." Awe elicits silence. "Let all mortal flesh keep silence" as the liturgy transports us into the sacred realm of the Last Supper, the cross of Calvary, and the empty tomb of Easter. The Liturgy Constitution assures us that in the earthly liturgy we already have a foretaste of that heavenly liturgy where we shall behold Christ the Lord sitting at the right hand of God (8).

"In the reform and promotion of the liturgy, full and active participation by all the people is the aim to be considered before all else. For it is the primary and indispensable source from which the faithful are to derive the true Christian spirit." This conciliar declaration should not be read in isolation from the other conciliar declaration that orients and subordinates action to contemplation. Action and contemplation are not mutually exclusive words, but there is a hierarchy of relationship between them. While active participation should not distract from contemplation, contemplation should not disengage itself from active participation. The liturgy is the action of Christ and the Church: it should not be regarded merely as background for personal contemplation. One without the other would not be representative of the council's vision of liturgical reform. This is obviously easier said than done. To strike the correct balance between the two will always be a challenge. Perhaps a good way to conclude this rumination is to quote article 12 of the Liturgy Constitution: "The spiritual life is not limited solely to participation in the liturgy. Christians are indeed called to pray in union with each other, but they must also enter into their chamber to pray to the Father in secret."

LITURGY AND THE UNIVERSE

It was Salvatore Marsili who introduced me, as a young student of liturgy, to the function of the natural world in the liturgy. His spiritual insights, steeped in patristic thinking, on springtime, spring equinox, and full moon relative to the theology of Easter left a deep impression on me. Born and raised in a country where the only appreciable changes in the climate are the wet and dry seasons, I took delight in the northern hemisphere's seasonal shifts. Autumn, with its riotous colors and temperate climate, appealed to my sense of drama, especially when I realized that it foreboded the death of nature. I was quite disappointed to discover that the liturgy has little use for my favorite season.

Under the guidance of Burkhard Neunheuser and Balthasar Fischer I set about to research the roles of spring, equinox, and full moon in the history, theology, and calendar date of Easter. I entitled the work "The Cosmic Elements of Christian Passover," an esoteric title I have since regretted. My avowed aim was to propose that in their own right the other seasons of the year were as suitable as spring to express the Easter symbol of new life in Christ. In the equator Easter falls during the summer months of March and April when nature is scorched by the sun. On the other hand, the month of May is marked by rainfall and an abundance of fruits and flowers. In my thinking at that time, May would be the perfect time to celebrate Easter in the tropics. Neunheuser was obviously alarmed. He pressed me to think again and think in favor of not messing up with the date of Easter. We reached a happy compromise. My work would propose new symbols for Easter drawn from the season (or month) of the year like summer (in the equator) or fall (in the southern hemisphere) but stick to the traditional date. A youthful enterprise is how I would describe my first serious liturgical work.

The liturgy engages the entire person: mind, heart, soul, spirit, and body. Worship in spirit and truth is a performative act that involves the participation of the mind that understands, the heart that ponders, the soul that is nourished, the spirit that soars, and the body that performs the action. The liturgy is thus an activity that is spiritual and physical, intellectual and emotional, heavenly and earthly. It is in light of this that I see the universe as an integral element of the liturgy. The heavens, the seasons of the year, the cycle of day and night, the elements of fire, water, and earth, the fruits of the land, and the products of human labor constitute an essential unit of the liturgical action. Baptism uses water, the Eucharist uses bread and wine, and confirmation and anointing of the sick use oil. Feasts orbit around the seasons of the year, the months, and the weeks, while the Liturgy of the Hours tracks the daily rhythm of day and night. The participation of the universe in divine worship is encompassing.

I perceive a theological thesis in it. In the Middle Ages it was believed that the unconsecrated hosts were consecrated by contact with the consecrated hosts in the same ciborium. The theory was called *virtute contactus*. The belief is just short of being theologically ingenuous and should not be entertained, but I would not consider it entirely idle and unprofitable. Does not fire transmit heat by mere proximity? Do not intimacy and fellowship induce character change in people? Does not a dominant culture alter or subject itself to the culture it gets in contact with? I would like to consider the medieval case of consecrated and unconsecrated hosts an example of what happens to the universe when the liturgy absorbs its properties and qualities.

A ceremony at the start of the Easter Vigil illustrates the relationship between the liturgy and the universe. I am always fascinated by the liturgical text used for preparing the paschal candle before it is lit and brought inside the church. The text is crisp and concise, solemn and powerful. It reverberates in the silence of the night as it claims that by his resurrection Jesus Christ has gained dominion over the entire universe: "Christ yesterday and today / the beginning and the end / Alpha / and Omega, all time belongs to him / and all the ages." These sublime words, which are biblical in origin, project on the wide screen of the universe the powerful image of Christ the *Pantokrator*.

This particular text has been a constant object of my rumination. I say "rumination" because I have not gotten close to doing scientific research on it. I am afraid I have not cudgeled my brains enough. Yet I have dared time and again to share my thinking with anyone willing to listen. It embarrasses me to admit that I tinker with a venerable liturgical text. But I justify my action purely from a sense of theological satisfaction that I derive from it. Somehow the product of my unscientific meditation has enriched my understanding of the Easter Vigil. That perhaps is justification enough, even if my liturgy mentors did not tolerate undocumented affirmations. Adrien Nocent inherited the intransigence of his master Bernard Botte, who in typically dismissive words wrote in his review of a liturgy book: "If we accept what this author claims as the origin of the Gregorian Sacramentary, we have every reason to believe that Christ was born in Yugoslavia."

"Christ yesterday and today / the beginning and the end / Alpha / and Omega / all time belongs to him / and all the ages." These words are a profession of the Church's faith that by his resurrection Christ gained dominion over the entire universe and all ages. He is the key to the Christian understanding of the universe, the human world, and us. The current year is written on the paschal candle to signify that this year, like all the preceding and coming years, is also the year of the Lord, that is to say, it belongs to him.

"Christ yesterday and today." This segment is a shortened version of the original biblical text from Hebrews 13:8 that proclaims, "Jesus Christ is the same yesterday and today and for ever." The biblical context is a warning about being swept off our course by all sorts of strange teachings. The risen Christ is the one and same person begotten by the Father before all ages and born of a woman in the fullness of time. His life and teachings are not subject to periodic revision. There is something here about history being irreversible. We cannot reinvent Christ, though we can delve deeper into his person and the meaning of his words. To know the Jesus of history I avidly studied theology. Brought up in the Thomistic school, I was initially perplexed, yes even scandalized, by the way non-scholastic theologians described his person, conjectured about his human relationships, and interpreted his doctrine. But as time went on I realized that there are so many loose ends in my historical knowledge of Jesus. As I read the gospels, I found myself asking all sorts of strange questions: Did he really say that? Was it how he said it? What did he mean by it? Was it really a miracle or was it an interpretation, perhaps, a perception of faith?

Who is Jesus Christ, the one who is "the same yesterday and today and forever"? My theological training had led me to search for the answer in the Church's enchiridion of conciliar and dogmatic definitions. What other document could offer a more secure guarantee of truth about Christ? However, that phase of my quest for the person of Christ suddenly came to a standstill when I studied liturgy. What and how does the liturgy speak about Jesus Christ?

We are familiar with the axiom *lex orandi, lex credendi*, which is somewhat difficult to interpret. The rule of prayer is the rule of belief, provided of course that orthodox belief has previously quickened the liturgical rite. In this sense it is also correct to say that the rule of belief is the rule of prayer. The corpus of the Church's official worship, consisting of texts, rites, symbols, and feasts, is a compendium of what the Church preaches about Christ, "from his incarnation and birth until his ascension, the day of Pentecost, and the expectation of the blessed hope and of the Lord's return" (SC 102). The Church unfolds the whole mystery of Christ as it celebrates the Eucharist, the sacraments, the Liturgy of the Hours, the sacramentals and blessings, and the liturgical year.

What differentiates the liturgy from systematic theology is what I would describe as "the experience of the mystery." By mystery I mean the person of Christ, his life, and his saving work. Systematic theology feeds the mind with doctrinal statements about Christ. Liturgy, on the other hand, furnishes us with the surpassing experience of Christ's presence *per ritus et preces* in the assembly's celebration of worship. In the liturgy believing is the same as experiencing. Understanding the doctrine of the faith entails the formation of personal relationship. Intellectual assent leads to the persuasion of the heart. What the worshiper encounters in the liturgy is not the compendium of the Church's beliefs about Christ but the amazing person of Christ himself.

When we experience the presence, the power, and the compassion of Christ in the liturgy, questions about the historical Christ and the historicity of the gospel passages are silenced by the heart. They become peripheral. "Jesus Christ is the same yesterday and today and for ever." The liturgy offers the security of faith that the love he manifested during his earthly ministry has not waned. He still speaks with power against God's enemies and whispers words of comfort and hope to the oppressed. He comes to the wedding feast and drinks from the couple's cup of joy. He has not ceased to hold the children in his arms and shield them from harm. He still calms the anxiety of the sick and the family. He continues to bring peace and reconciliation to sinners. He joins those who mourn for their dead, as once he shed tears for his friend Lazarus. Jesus Christ yesterday and today is still here with us in the preaching of the word, the breaking of the bread, and the fellowship of the assembled worshipers.

The second segment of this Easter Vigil text, from Revelation 21:6 and 22:13, declares that Christ is the "beginning and the end." The opening line of the Book of Genesis reads: "In the beginning God created the heavens and the earth. . . . God said . . ." The opening line of the Gospel of St. John is a lyrical echo of this creation theme: "In the beginning was the Word, and the Word was with God, and the Word was God. He was in the beginning with God. All things came into being through him, and without him not one thing came into being." The Genesis account of creation prefaced every act of God with the celestial words reverberating in the firmament: "God said." God created the universe by his mighty word. The Fourth Gospel identifies this word as the Word of God through whom all things were made and declares that the Word was God, took human flesh, and lived among us.

The Greek word for "beginning" (*arché*) carries the meaning of dominion or sovereignty. This meaning is faithfully kept by Colossians 1:16 and 18: "For in him all things in heaven and on earth were created . . . he is the beginning, the firstborn from the dead, so that he might come to have first place in everything." On Easter night the Church solemnly proclaims that by his resurrection Jesus Christ gained universal sovereignty. The whole of creation belongs to him and is subject to his authority and power because it was created through him and for him. My thoughts carry me away to that moment beyond time when God appointed the Word as the architect through whom he would create the universe. God saw the result and declared that it was good. The Letter to the Colossians says that it was for the sake of Christ that God created the universe. Christ is the reason why the universe exists. Rightly then, God handed it over to Christ after his resurrection as his possession. Would it not be great to see the name of Christ written all over the universe as its architect and possessor? "All things have been created through him and for him" (Col 15).

The Greek word for "end," on the other hand, connotes completion and fulfillment. Christ as the end does not merely represent the consummation of the world. When I meditate about Christ as the culmination of God's creating power, what springs up in my mind is the thought of finality. Christ is the finishing touch of God's creation. But I can appreciate fully the beauty and endowments of creation when I acknowledge Christ as the person that imparts meaning to creation and brings it to completion. As I gaze on the Milky Way that spans the immense heavenly space or listen to the myriad of stars that noisily chatter on a clear night, I ask myself the question that the ancient humanists have posed but have not answered conclusively: is humankind the ultimate reason why the firmament exists? It is a humbling thought to consider humankind the center of the universe, yet the biblical account of creation supports this bold statement. God entrusted creation to humans, and humankind has been continually conquering the space, unraveling its secrets, and claiming ownership of creation. When Christians affirm that Christ is the beginning and the end of all created things, they perfect the thinking of the ancient humanists. For Christians it is not humankind as such but the person of Jesus Christ that bestows meaning and purpose to the universe of created things.

Christ is the beginning and the end: his name is written across the universe and etched in every part of it. Believers should be able to read Christ's name in the heavenly bodies and in all the things that make up planet Earth. "At the name of Jesus every knee should bend, in heaven and on earth and under the earth, and every tongue should confess that Jesus Christ is Lord, to the glory of God the Father" (Phil 2:10-11). Indeed, the universe is a sacrament: it reveals Christ, it speaks about Christ, and it leads to Christ. Sometimes I receive amused grins from students of liturgy when I invite them to delight in the delicate beauty of a flower, rave about the dazzling sunburst, or experience nostalgia at sunset. To value the sacramental character of the universe, we need to fill our senses with the smell of burning leaves, the texture of stones and wood, the coolness of spring water, the heat of the scorching sun, and the doleful howl of night animals. We need to possess a keen sensitivity to the properties and workings of nature if we are to recognize it as a sacrament of Christ and ultimately as a venue for encountering him in the liturgy.

When the liturgy avails itself of the vast resources of nature and employs them as mediums to communicate the divine, nature rises to a higher level of existence. From being merely cosmos it acquires a "sacramental" character, a Christian attribute. What I have in mind is that the wonders, beauty, and order of the universe exhibit the presence not only of the Creator but also of Christ, the Incarnate Word. I cannot gaze at the immensity of the heavens and not direct my thoughts to Christ, who came to this planet Earth to make it his home. The tiny spring flowers on the grass as much as the raging winds from which I shield myself reveal to me Christ's tenderness and mighty power. Spring or the burgeoning of new life tells me what happens to the world when Christ is close at hand. Winter, on the other hand, conjures the image of a world that has distanced itself from God.

We relive this sacramental being of the universe in the liturgy as we celebrate the mystery of Christ in it. When we cleanse ourselves with water, eat bread, drink wine, and apply oil on our bodies, we remind ourselves that in the liturgy these same elements function as sacraments of Christ's presence. Bread and wine are the fruits of the earth and the work of human hands, but in the Eucharist they are the sacraments of Christ's body and blood. When we chant with the psalmist, "The heavens are telling the glory of God; and the firmament proclaims his handiwork" (Ps 19), we behold in creation the image of Christ who is the glory of God and the perfect work of his hands. As every page of Scripture speaks about Christ, so every part of the universe mirrors the face of him through whom all things were made. In the liturgy the world crosses the boundary that divides the sacred from the profane. Nothing in this world is purely profane. The Latin *profanus* originally meant people and things excluded from the temple. The presence of Christ's saving mystery in creation has torn down the barrier of the world's alienation from God. No one and nothing, except sin, is any longer profane or excluded from Christ's temple and realm of influence.

The third segment of the liturgical text at the beginning of the Easter vigil is from Revelation 1:8, 21:6, and 22:13. Jesus Christ is the Alpha and the Omega. These are the first and last letters of the Greek alphabet. Earlier I thought it curious that the Book of Revelation should give such titles to Christ, who is more familiarly known as Son of God, Son of Mary, Savior, and Lord. In fact, even though the Easter liturgy chants year after year that he is the Alpha and the Omega, I have not heard anyone addressing him with these letters of the alphabet.

Perhaps this is due to the rather impersonal and non-relational character of these letters. We relate more easily to Christ as our Lord and Savior than as our Alpha and Omega!

And yet the Greek alphabet is an active unit of the scientific lexicon. Astronomy, mathematics, and medicine identify their discoveries, inventions, and products using letters of the Greek alphabet. Alpha is the chief or brightest star of the constellation, while beta stands second. Gamma is used in conjunction with radioactivity. Science rightly employs the Greek alphabet, considering the rich legacy bequeathed to Western civilization by the Greek philosophers Socrates, Plato, and Aristotle, and the Hellenistic schools of Athens and Alexandria. Greek Alexandria was the center of mathematics, science, biology, and medicine. Hellenism, which the Arab scholars inherited and perfected, is synonymous with science and philosophy. The language of Hellenistic culture was Greek, and it was in this language that human progress and scientific discoveries were transmitted.

Hence it seems to me that it is not far-fetched to call Christ by the first and last letters of the Greek alphabet. These two letters encompass the whole range of the Greek alphabet. Christ is the Alpha, and the Beta, and the Gamma of all human knowledge, which we express through literature, mathematical formulas, scientific findings, and advancements in technology. For believers, Christ is at hand in every form of human knowledge and can ultimately be found in it. If every page of Scripture speaks about Christ, so does every work of culture and every form of human progress.

St. Augustine is credited for having Christianized the philosophy of Plato, and St. Thomas Aquinas, that of Aristotle. Thanks to the works of these two philosopher-theologians, medieval Christianity was able to make use of the two pillars of Western thought to construct its philosophy and theology. Modern technology, from the invention of the printing press up to the advent of space travels and informational technology, is a tribute to him who is the Alpha of human civilization. We are grateful to the medieval Benedictine monks, who with foresight and wisdom spent years, sometimes a lifetime, copying ancient manuscripts for posterity. They collected, preserved, and disseminated literary works of antiquity, both sacred and profane. If not for their scriptoria, we would probably not have known Plato, Aristotle, Caesar, and Cicero. The monks saved even the erotic works of Ovid and Sappho, because by some process of rationalization they were able to predicate Christian sentiments to them.

Christ is the Alpha and Omega of human progress. While it is not taxing for the mind to relate culture and arts to Christ, it takes some effort to see the connection between him and technology. Telephones, mobile phones, computers, and internet are some of the greatest and most fascinating inventions of humankind; they defy time and space. Connections with people in any part of the world through information technology and space travel have reached an unprecedented stage of progress. Our power to traverse in a few seconds the immense oceans and continents through a tiny mobile phone simply stuns and amazes me.

The myth of the god-messenger Hermes wearing winged sandals and the fable of the flying Daedalus and Icarus are deep-seated aspirations for fast communication among humans across the expanse of time and space. Modern means of communication have succeeded to make such aspirations a reality. The possibilities for further technological progress are limitless. Some would push for the sky as the limit. However, human achievement should not degenerate into the ill-fated Tower of Babel. For Christian believers, modern inventions would indeed be another Tower of Babel if the name of Christ, the Alpha and Omega of human progress, is not etched in them. Colossians 1:16 reminds us: "All things have been created through him and for him"— and all should ultimately find their meaning and purpose in him.

The Constitution on the Church in the Modern World explains that the "autonomy of earthly affairs" from the faith should not be taken as if the world did not depend on God and that we could use it as if it had no relation to its Creator. In fact, "the humble and persevering investigator of the secrets of nature is being led, as it were, by the hand of God, for it is God, the conserver of all things, who made them what they are" (36). The popular song written by Eleanor Farjeon, "Morning Has Broken," is an idyll of Christ's presence in creation: "Praise for the sweetness / Of the wet garden, / Sprung in completeness / Where his feet pass."

Time and again I have raised the question of why our liturgy has not outgrown its agricultural past. It can be argued, of course, that in this age of ecology and fear of global warming an agriculturally pervaded liturgy is exactly what the world needs. Yet the liturgy should not be defined extensively in the context of the natural phenomena with little attention given to technological advances. To be fair, though, the Book of Blessings lists some modern inventions. But to my knowledge, people do not ask that their mobile phones and computers be blessed.

In our technological age I do anticipate liturgical songs that will extol the ascendancy of Christ over the instruments of technology. Christ, after all, is not Lord only of the awesome cosmos but also of the formidable conquests of human genius.

The fourth segment of the Easter Vigil text reads: "All time belongs to him and all the ages." I find resonance in 1 Thessalonians 5:1-2, which alerts Christians regarding the second coming of the Lord: "Now concerning the times and the seasons, brothers and sisters, you do not need to have anything written to you. For you yourselves know very well that the day of the Lord will come like a thief in the night." "Times and seasons" is a cliché that affirms that God is outside time and yet exercises control over it. The statement "All time belongs to him and all the ages" broadcasts that Christ is the Lord of the ages and of human history. I do not know how well it will sit with some people, even believers, but I have this intuition that the text is telling us that Christ the Lord of all times has authority and influence on the course of events in the cosmos and the world. For believers, things happened, happen, and will happen with reference to Christ's entry into the world. I know that what I say sounds rather arbitrary, but how else can I explain the meaning of "when the fullness of time had come, God sent his Son, born of a woman, born under the law" (Gal 4:4)? "Fullness of time" is the time God has appointed. It is the messianic age that fulfills the yearning for salvation that every age in human history knowingly or unknowingly has expressed in hundreds of ways. All seasons belong to Christ and all times; they all converge in him and he binds them together.

The study of history is always a pleasant and rewarding occupation. What often arrests my attention in my study of history is the connectedness of events. The mind boggles at a seemingly insignificant incident that had a ripple effect on succeeding generations, or a decision of a leader that shook a nation or sometimes the world. More importantly, as a believer, how do I make the connection between historical events and Christ? Or for that matter, where do I position Christ in the scheme of what happens in my personal world?

Christ is the key that opens the door of our mind to the events both great and small that make up the history of the world and the story of every person. We interpret world events in the light of his person, mission, and teaching. This is not an easy thing to do. One instinctive reaction is skepticism. What has Christ to do with war, natural calamities, scientific progress, and human development? How has his gospel changed the course of human history? How is it that after two thousand years the majority of the world population has not yet accepted, and seemingly will not accept, him as Son of God and Lord of history? I guess that only a profound faith in the mystery of the incarnation can satisfy such queries. In a word, one has to be a Christian to write the name of Christ across the borders of time and history.

If Christ binds together all times and seasons, he cannot be far away from them. He has risen and ascended into the heavenly realm, into the timelessness of eternity. But he has not dissociated himself from the affairs of the world; he has not distanced himself from human concerns. Christ is the bridge that connects time and eternity, the new *Pontifex* who not only builds the bridge but takes it upon his person to be the bridge. It is through him that we commune with the other world. Through him we can converse with those who inhabit that mysterious, silent world beyond us. We find no difficulty praying to God who is present everywhere in creation, but how do we speak with a relative or friend who has departed from this life? The answer is always Christ. They live with Christ and we can reach them through Christ. We can traverse the dark and unexplored gap between earth and the heavenly domain through him who had visited the earth and returned to where he came from.

The invention of telecommunication has beguiled the tenses of time. In some delusive but not illusory way the present, past, and future are compressed in one when two persons talk to each other from two different time zones. They are present to each other, though they are separated not only by immense distances but also by time differences. One speaks to the other who is still in yesterday's or already in tomorrow's time zone. Modern technology has effaced the distance that separates the three tenses of time. It has provided us with a basis to believe that we on earth are able to commune with the other beings outside the boundaries of time. When Christ by his incarnation broke into our time, he did not leave his Father's side. He pitched his tent among us but he continued to dwell in the bosom of God. He is the bridge that connects eternity and time.

"Christ yesterday and today / the beginning and the end / Alpha / and Omega / all time belongs to him / and all the ages." I conclude this meditation with a passage from the homily that Pope Paul VI delivered in Manila in November 1970: "Once again I repeat his name to you Christians and I proclaim to all: Jesus Christ is the beginning and the end, the alpha and the omega, Lord of the new universe, the great hidden key to human history and the part we play in it. . . . Remember: it is Jesus Christ I preach day in and day out. His name I would see echo and reecho for all time to the ends of the earth."

THE HUMAN BODY AND LITURGY

Mel Gibson's film *The Passion of the Christ* is a gruesome depiction of Christ's suffering and crucifixion. It is violent, nauseating, horrifying, and savage. It deviates from the sober crucifixion scenes and jeweled crucifixes we are used to. It is said that after watching the film Pope John Paul II muttered, "It is as it had been." Christ suffered in his body. I have so often read and preached about the gospel passion narratives and listened prayerfully to Bach's *St. Matthew Passion*, but somehow I failed to connect the narration with brutality. In her travelogue notices about the Good Friday celebration in fourth-century Jerusalem, Egeria reports that the bishop read the story of the passion in the Church of Golgotha amid the loud wailing and weeping of the assembly. The location must have contributed to such emotional outburst, which I would like to regard as a component of active participation in the liturgy. I am serious about it. Smiles, laughter, weeping, and moaning are human expressions that should naturally accompany liturgical celebrations. Why should the assembly not smile at a presider's jokes or antics? Why should the bereaved not shed tears during the funeral rite? Liturgy engages the whole person.

The entire mystery of Christ happened in his human body. The Prologue to the Gospel of John tells the story: "The Word became flesh and lived among us." His human body unfolded the rest of the story. In that body the Word grew and matured as a human person. In that body he preached, healed, and defended the rights of people. Before he delivered his body to the torment of the cross he bequeathed to the Church, which is his mystical body, the august legacy of his incarnation, the sacrament of his Eucharistic body.

Pope Pius XII called the Church the mystical body of Christ. Vatican II's *Lumen Gentium* echoes it: "By communicating his Spirit, Christ mystically constitutes as his body those sisters and brothers of his who are called together from every nation" (7). The word "mystical" has invariably puzzled me when used for the body of the Church. I guess it is because the word connotes something that is neither apparent to the senses nor obvious to the intellect. My understanding of the mystical body of Christ is sensory: it is composed of people existing in physical, material bodies. The liturgy deals with humans in their bodily reality from the time of baptism to the rites of funeral. The sacraments require the bodily presence of those who receive them.

The obligation to respect the human body explains why the Constitution on the Church in the Modern World makes this important reminder: "People may not despise their bodily life. Rather they are obliged to regard their bodies as good and hold them in honor since God has created them and will raise them up on the last day. . . . The dignity of human beings requires that they should glorify God in their bodies, and not allow them to serve the evil inclinations of their heart" (14). Not only should people not despise their bodily life, they should also hold their bodies in honor because they are sacraments that reveal the Creator; they have been raised to extraordinary dignity by Christ's incarnation; and they are integral members of Christ's mystical body. Similarly, the *Catechism of the Catholic Church* teaches that "the human body shares in the dignity of the image of God; it is a human body precisely because it is animated by a spiritual soul, and it is the whole human person that is intended to become, in the body of Christ, a temple of the Spirit" (364; cf. 1 Cor 6:19-20; 15:44-45).

"The human body shares in the dignity of the image of God." I am not disturbed when God the Father and the Holy Spirit are depicted in human bodies, although only the Word assumed human flesh. Religious representations of the Blessed Trinity in human form reflect the stunning words of Genesis: "Let us make humankind in our image, according to our likeness" (1:26). It is naive to think that God, the pure spirit, resembles us who are corporeal. I think it goes the other way around: we resemble God. Richard Clifford, in his commentary on Genesis (*The New Jerome Biblical Commentary*), wrote that "the human is a statue of the deity." My liturgical frame of mind is inclined to replace "statue" with "sacrament." If inanimate creation displays the wonders of God and allows us to sketch an image of God, I should think that in the totality of their being, humans provide a more accurate description of God. Bodily human activities involving the soul, mind, and spirit share in God's qualities and portray God as creator, lover, savior, and provider. Human love, the acts of procreation, prayer and work, family life, and works of love and service all happen in the human body, and they splendidly depict the creative power, love, and mercy of God. Humans are sacraments of their Creator and their "human body shares in the dignity of the image of God."

The value and dignity of the human body was rejected by Manicheans who, like the Gnostics, believed in the eternal struggle between good and evil, regarded the body as evil, and hence frowned on marriage and procreation. Pope Leo the Great fought them resolutely through homilies and euchological compositions. The Christmas prayer he composed proclaims the *humanae substantiae dignitas* (dignity of human beings) that God had created wonderfully and still more wonderfully restored through Christ. If the Word assumed the human body, how could it be evil? It might have been misused and abused, but it did not lose the original dignity that God had bestowed on it when he created it.

This brings us back to the Book of Genesis. God made humans in his image, so that as God is creative, they would in their bodies be procreative. By their procreativeness man and woman become sacraments of God's creative power. As spouses delight in their sexual relations, they participate in God's pleasure upon seeing the product of his creation, which he declared good and indeed very good. Even though sin defaced God's creation, it did not blot out humankind's participation in God's creative power. The first nuptial blessing, which predates the other two by several centuries, proclaims that married life is "the one blessing that was not forfeited by original sin or washed away in the flood."

The dignity and beauty of the human body are nowhere exhibited with such spectacle as in renaissance art, particularly in the works of Michelangelo. Who does not wonder at the perfect proportions of Christ's dead body and of the stately body of his grieving mother in the Vatican Basilica's *Pietà*? The statue in the Church of Sopra Minerva of the naked Christ embracing his cross could pass easily as a copy of an image of the Greek god Apollo. David's flawless body depicts the beauty and grace of youth and forecasts the splendor of the resurrection. The original beauty of human bodies created in the image of God was not defaced by sin. In the Sistine Chapel even the damned men and women in torment and agony possess perfectly proportioned bodies. That most of these artworks are in churches where the liturgy is celebrated confirms my insistence that the human body is a major player in the performance of the liturgy.

I must admit that as a young man trained to exercise modesty of the eyes, I was thoroughly scandalized when I first visited the Sistine Chapel with its plethora of naked men and women, and when I saw in a church the statue of Christ like Adam before the Fall. There was a time when I had to close my eyes when I saw a picture of the Blessed Mother breast-feeding her Child! In my young mind the liturgy surely needed the human body, but the body should be wrapped in decent clothes. I simply could not comprehend why the saints or whoever entered the church in the form of art should be without clothes. Neither could I tolerate the opinion that words referring to human sexuality should be inscribed in the liturgical lexicon. But I have outgrown that stage. A religious group, wishing to avoid the mortifying word "womb" in prayer, replaced the Hail Mary's "fruit of your womb" with "fruit of your love," not realizing the flustering implication. I had the occasion to explain to the group the nobility, dignity, and sanctity of the womb: after all, we all came from there. Rightly, the baptismal font, where Christians are born again, is called the womb of the Church. At the end of life's journey it will be the womb of Mother Earth that will enfold us: from the womb to the tomb.

A saying from Tertullian that I find truly lapidary is *caro, salutis cardo*. The phrase says that the human body is the hinge of salvation. In simpler words, it affirms that God achieved his saving deed by using the human body. That is why Christ took the human flesh, worshiped the Father in the body, performed his mission of preaching and healing in the body, submitted it to crucifixion and death, was buried, rose from the dead, and returned to heaven in a glorified body, and will come again on the last day in a heavenly body. Salvation history took place in the human body of the Incarnate Word. Obviously, the liturgy, which extends the presence of salvation history, takes place also in the human body. The human body is an essential component of the liturgy, just as the body of Christ was the instrument of his work of salvation.

Tertullian has a very fine description of what the liturgy does to people through their bodies: "The body is washed so that the soul may be cleansed; the body is anointed so that the soul may be consecrated; the body is signed so that the soul may be strengthened; the body is overshadowed by the laying on of hands so that the soul may be enlightened by the Holy Spirit; the body is fed with the body and blood of Christ so that the soul may be nourished by God" (*De resurrectione mortuorum* 8). Tertullian speaks of body and soul. Although the phrase suggests philosophical dualism, its message bears out the unity between soul and body, between what is visible to the senses and what is invisible to them. Through the human body God touches the soul, in the same way that Christ cured the body in order to heal the whole person. The human body is like a door that opens to the heart, to the soul, to the spirit. Through the body we fathom a person's innermost sentiments and thoughts.

In baptism the human body is washed or immersed in the water of rebirth. This is a necessary condition for the person to receive the Spirit of adoption who is present in the water. Bodily contact with the sacramental water is the means whereby the Spirit claims the baptized person as daughter or son of God. The other sacraments require some kind of bodily presence. The body of the sick is anointed with the oil of healing in faith and hope that both body and soul will receive the comforting power of the Holy Spirit, the Paraclete. In the Middle Ages anointing was performed on the five senses or on that part of the body that hurt most. Although this therapeutic factor of the sacrament eventually gave way to a penitential character of the same—sin and hence illness entered the body through the senses—the overriding concern was always the healing of the human body and ultimately the spirit.

An eloquent liturgical symbol is hand-laying on the body of persons that receive the sacrament. In confirmation, the rite of penance, holy orders, and anointing of the sick the priest lays his hands on the body of the recipient to signify the overshadowing of the Holy Spirit on the whole person. The Holy Spirit consecrates, forgives, and heals through the minister's contact with the human body. Tertullian's axiom is always worth remembering: *caro, salutis cardo.*

In the course of the liturgical year, feasts celebrate the bond between salvation history and the human body. What else does the Solemnity of the Annunciation commemorate but the conception of the Word in the virginal womb of Mary? The Word took flesh from her so that God might appear in human body and in it accomplish the work of salvation. What is Christ's nativity but his coming forth from his mother's womb in the body of an infant? Previous to the calendar reform of Vatican II the Octave of Christmas was called Feast of the Circumcision. Considering that in my country male circumcision has no religious significance and is often connected with the boy's coming of age, it amused me that a liturgical feast should be so named. I made my amusement known. During a homily my mentor Adrien Nocent painstakingly vindicated the meaning of the feast: the Son of God not only took a human body but he also chose to belong to the race of Abraham from which God had required circumcision as a bodily mark of membership. Although the requirement is moot for Christians, his circumcision has bound his members to Father Abraham and enrolled them among those that share the promised inheritance. I found his explanation most satisfying. But sad to say, after I began to appreciate the mystery of the circumcision, the feast was renamed Solemnity of the Mother of God, which is simultaneously Octave of Christmas and World Day of Peace.

The memorial of the Last Supper when Christ instituted the sacrament of his body and blood solemnly ushers in the Easter Triduum. Who is not perplexed by the awesome declaration he made as he dined with this disciples: "This is my body; this is the cup of my blood"? His body would henceforth be symbolized by the broken bread, because it was a body that would be "given up," that is to say, offered in sacrifice. The fraction rite at Mass signifies that his body was "broken" so that it could be shared as sacrament. Breaking is a painful experience: broken home, broken dreams, broken heart. The Eucharist is the sacrament of Christ's body that he willed to be "broken" on the cross in order to be shared with us. For there is no other way to express love than by sharing, and there is no other way we can share than by breaking ourselves for the persons we love. The Eucharistic bread acquires its full meaning when it is broken and shared in Communion. The popular devotion of making vigil before the Blessed Sacrament on Holy Thursday night heightens the sacrificial character of the Eucharistic bread. Mel Gibson's *The Passion of the Christ* is a lesson in Eucharistic catechesis. During the passion it makes several flashbacks on the Last Supper to remind the viewers that the two events are indeed inseparable.

"This is my body; this is the cup of my blood." These mysterious words have since echoed down the corridor of time. With these comforting words Jesus assures us that he is present in what goes on in our world, that he is part of our homes, and that he accompanies us through life. And he stays with us not with words alone but with his body and blood, with his own gracious self. For our faith tells us that when these sacred words are recited over bread and wine, the almighty power of God transforms them into the body and blood of Christ.

But his words refer also to us. When they are spoken at the table, Christ rests his glance upon us; he recognizes and claims each one of us to be his own body and blood. He tells us in effect: "You also are my body." He identifies himself with us. I believe this is what celebration of the Eucharist is all about. Not the bread on the table or tabernacle alone, but the assembly as well. Whatever our station in life, poor or rich, saint or sinner, we are his body; we are the grains of wheat ground and baked to become one bread, Christ's body. This is not the place for homily, but I believe that the topic presents itself as a timely occasion for some soul-searching reflections. Christ identifies himself with us, yet we witness daily the reality of human bodies being subjected to torture and abuse for sheer pleasure and selfish gains. People close their eyes to the squalor of poverty that surrounds them. They plug their ears to the cries of hunger and injustice. "You also are my body." These are the words Jesus speaks to us, and these are the words we should learn to speak to others. Every person we meet is our brother or sister, whose bodies we are enjoined to respect and honor as if they were our own.

Saints are also celebrated in the liturgy, especially on the day of their *transitus*, or passage from this world to the Father. In the beginning only martyrs (except for the Beloved Disciple) were honored in the liturgy. The shedding of blood configures martyrs to Christ, the Martyr of Calvary. To honor the body of the martyrs a chapel called a *martyrium* was built on top or beside the tomb for the celebration of the Eucharist, especially on the anniversary of their martyrdom. We are told that every year the faithful gathered at the tomb of Saint Polycarp to honor his remains and find spiritual strength in the face of persecutions. The practice of interring relics of saints under the altar originated from the *martyrium*.

The veneration of the bodies or relics of saints is a sad chapter in the history of the liturgy. In the Middle Ages dealers made a big business out of the sale of bones purportedly of saints but later discovered, thanks to modern technology, to be of animals. Unsuspecting devotees bought them and built magnificent chapels to house richly adorned reliquaries. When I was a student in Europe it was one of my diversions to look for some of the most amusing kinds of relics: a feather of St. Michael the Archangel, a piece of cloth stained with the milk of the Blessed Virgin, one of the prepuces of the Child Jesus, and, believe it or not, a bottle containing the darkness of Egypt! The great reformer Martin Luther, appalled by aberrations committed on relics, fiercely took issue with the Catholic Church. Indeed, who would not be scandalized by reports that when priests were compelled to celebrate only one Mass a day to stifle the abuses surrounding Mass stipends, some had the temerity to simulate the Mass and raise the relic of a saint at the supposed moment of consecration? I can still hear my mentor Adrien Nocent's dismissive remark when he listened to stories of relics, private apparitions, and saccharine devotions: "It's another religion!"

Gradually, the deaths of non-martyr saints, starting with Martin of Tours, were also marked in the Western Church with annual liturgical feasts. These saints did not shed blood physically, but their daily struggles to grow in the love of God and neighbor was considered another form of martyrdom or witnessing to Christ. As someone from the Congregation for the Causes of Saints pointed out, "sometimes it takes only some hours to die as a martyr, but it takes a lifetime of martyrdom to remain loyal to the faith."

Abstracting from the deviations of the past and from the odd practice of displaying dismembered parts of the bodies of saints for public veneration, it is important to keep in mind that the liturgy gives special honor to the human body, whether it is of a great saint or a departed ordinary Christian. The reason, as told by Tertullian and worth repeating, is that "the body is washed so that the soul may be cleansed; the body is anointed so that the soul may be consecrated; the body is signed so that the soul may be strengthened; the body is overshadowed by the laying on of hands so that the soul may be enlightened by the Holy Spirit; the body is fed with the body and blood of Christ so that the soul may be nourished by God."

With regard to the practice of honoring the bodies of saints, the Catholic Church believes that God granted a singular privilege to the Mother of Jesus: her body did not suffer the corruption of death. The belief is celebrated in the feast of the Assumption. It originated in the fifth century in Jerusalem after the Council of Ephesus (431), which defended the doctrine of the Theotokos, Mother of God. By the sixth century the feast came to be known as the "falling asleep" or "dormition" of the Blessed Virgin Mary and was extended to the whole Byzantine Empire by Emperor Maurice. The feast reached Rome in the seventh century. In the eighth century it came to be known in Rome as the "Assumption of Mary."

For Catholics the dogma of the Assumption of the Blessed Virgin Mary should not cause ecumenical embarrassment. After her death she was raised body and soul to heaven, because it is not possible that the body from which the Son of God took flesh should see the corruption of death. Mary's assumption is a pledge of what awaits the bodies of the other members of Christ. In Mary's assumption we are made to contemplate the image of the Church in its future glory. At the same time, her assumption is a symbol of hope and comfort, especially in our world torn by misery and war. Mary's bodily assumption assures us that life does not end in the death of the human body: there is something glorious that awaits us, and Mary has preceded us in its attainment. Pope Paul VI wrote in *Marialis cultus*: "This is a celebration that offers the Church and all humankind an exemplar and a consoling message, teaching us the fulfillment of our highest hopes: our glorification is happily in store for us whom Christ has made his brothers and sisters" (6).

The Christian notion of death as a falling asleep recalls the words that Jesus declared concerning the dead daughter of Jairus: "She is not dead but sleeping" (Luke 8:52). We find similar words in the case of Lazarus: "Our friend Lazarus has fallen asleep, but I am going there to awaken him" (John 11:11-13). The disciples took his words literally; but Jesus was talking about death, while they thought that he meant ordinary sleep. The idea is beautifully expressed in a song quoted in the letter to the Ephesians: "Sleeper, awake! Rise from the dead, and Christ will shine on you" (5:14). The human body rests in the sleep of death until such time as God awakens it to his embrace. The Greek icon of Mary's dormition shows her on her deathbed, while Christ who stands beside her embraces her as if she were a little child clad in white funeral robes. It is a touching gesture where the roles of Mother and Child are reversed.

To conclude, let us read again the teaching of the *Catechism of the Catholic Church*: "The human body shares in the dignity of the image of God; it is a human body precisely because it is animated by a spiritual soul, and it is the whole human person that is intended to become, in the body of Christ, a temple of the Spirit" (364). Is it any wonder that the liturgy sanctifies, celebrates, and venerates the human body, because it "shares in the dignity of the image of God"?

Chapter Two

"And So, What Is Liturgy?"

The first liturgy class I attended as a student at the Pontifical Liturgical Institute in Rome is still fresh in my memory. The council had just ended, and the initial reform of the liturgy was making giant strides in many places in the Catholic world. We were 120 student-priests from all over the world. Most of us could follow the lectures in Latin and Italian because of our Latin training in the seminary. When Professor Salvatore Marsili entered the lecture hall he was welcomed with a nervous, eerie silence. His fame as a theologian, liturgical iconoclast, and cofounder (with Adrien Nocent, Emmanuel Lane, and Cipriano Vagaggini) of the Pontifical Liturgical Institute preceded him. In a radio interview he described the bishop's ritual of un-vesting at the altar as a kind of liturgical striptease. His students roared in laughter, but the Vatican censured him for his iconoclastic disrespect. The man who was going to teach liturgical theology looked tough, stern, and forbidding. (I learned later that his father was a colonel in the Italian army.) From the podium he stared, literally stared, at each one of the 120 students. After this long ceremonial he asked, "And so, what is liturgy?" I have been asking the same question since that memorable afternoon of October 1965.

Liturgy can be defined in a variety of ways depending upon the aspect one wishes to stress. Every definition has a particular nuance representing an agenda such as active participation, inculturation, fidelity to rubrics, and so on. The liturgy is a rich complex—I should say a happy confluence—of theology, history, spiritual insight, and pastoral care. This explains why no single definition is able to capture its nature and purpose. Each definition has something to contribute to the holistic concept of the liturgy. Each is a partial answer to Marsili's question, "And so, what is liturgy?"

LITURGY IS SERVICE

It is a standard practice to examine the etymological root of the word "liturgy," which is derived from the Greek words *laos* (people) and *ergon* (work). In its pre-Christian usage the immediate meaning of the compound word *leitourgia* was public works or state projects on behalf of the people. Indirectly it also referred to the office that one undertook in the name of the state as a public servant. The consular service, which was an administrative division of the Roman government, could rightly be called a "liturgy." During the Hellenistic period the word acquired a broader meaning to include the work done by slaves for their masters or even the small acts of service one did for a friend. Liturgy was an occupation or function that a person performed for the welfare of others. Etymologically, liturgy means service. It is helpful to note that the Latin version of the *Apostolic Tradition* (3), attributed to Hippolytus of Rome, translates *leitourgounta* as *servientem.* The notion of service is essential to the definition of liturgy.

The use of the word "liturgy" has a long history. The Septuagint employs the word *leitourgia* as many as 170 times to designate the Levitic cult or the official worship of Israel. It is not easy to explain how a secular word came to be used for the sacred rites of Israel. Perhaps this had something to do with the classical meaning of the word, which referred to the official function held by State dignitaries, as I mentioned earlier. Certainly, the word fits the definition of the Levitic cult as a divine institution entrusted to Israel's public officials, the Levitic priests.

The words *leitourgia, leitourgein,* and *leitourgos* appear fifteen times in the New Testament with different meanings. In Romans 13:6 Christians are exhorted to pay taxes because the magistrates are *leitourgoi* of God. In consonance with the tradition of the Old Testament, Luke 1:23 refers to the priestly function of Zechariah in the temple as *leitourgia.* Hebrews 8:2 tells us that by his priestly sacrifice Christ has become the new *leitourgos* of the sanctuary. Hebrews ranks the priesthood of Christ on a level superior to that of the Levitic priesthood, which, being of the old covenant, has now become obsolete. In Romans 15:16 Paul calls himself "*leitourgos* of Jesus Christ to the Gentiles" because of his mission to preach the gospel to them. Acts 13:2 reports that in the Church of Antioch the prophets and teachers, among them Saul and Barnabas, *leitourgounton* (celebrated the liturgy). In all of these uses of the word *leitourgia* the notion of service is implied.

For the Churches in the East *leitourgia* signifies the sacred rites in general and the Eucharistic celebration in particular. The Liturgy of St. John Chrysostom, of St. Basil, of St. James, and of St. Mark means the Mass. The Latin Church, on the other hand, used terms like *officia divina, opus divinum,* and *sacri* or *ecclesiae ritus.* These are public acts of worship that should be distinguished from personal or private prayer. As public acts they entail ministerial service. The word *liturgia* for the celebration of the Mass did not appear in the Latin Church until the sixteenth century, thanks to renaissance writers like George Cassander, Jacques Pamelius, and Johannes Bona. For the other forms of worship the old Latin terms continued to be used. The word *liturgia* appeared for the first time in official Latin documents published during the pontificate of Pope Gregory XVI (+1846).

Those who perform the liturgy on behalf of Christ's faithful enter into what the ancient Romans called *servitium*, a word that described the condition of a servant. Liturgical ministers, whether clerical or lay, are servants, and the office they hold as they preside or assist at liturgical celebrations is a form of service. Clerical ordination and lay ministerial institution create service ranks in the Church, but they do not raise the sociological status of a person above the assembly. Rather, they designate the ordained or instituted person as minister, that is, servant. They give to the office holder the authority to serve but do not empower them to dominate. The distinction between service rank and sociological status becomes clearer as I pursue the topic. When clerical order is regarded as a career and a promotion to a higher status in the community, the liturgy loses its force as service and is subjected to the weakness of human power. The reminder of 1 Peter 5:2-3 to the elders of the Christian community is timely: "Tend the flock of God that is in your charge, exercising the oversight, not under compulsion but willingly, as God would have you do it—not for sordid gain but eagerly. Do not lord it over those in your charge, but be examples to the flock." *Apostolic Tradition* (no. 10) explains that "the clergy are ordained for the liturgy" or, in other words, for service in the Church.

Alas, it might appear to some that the ceremonial robes that presiders wear and the special treatment they receive when they perform their function gainsay their role as servants. But we know that beneath the "pomp and circumstance" of liturgical celebrations lies the solid foundation of ministerial service. If we keep in mind that Christ celebrated the original liturgy on Calvary in utter abasement, with his own blood as his only garment, we begin to have a more balanced approach to liturgical appurtenances. Surely we should dedicate to God what is noblest in our culture and national heritage. During the era of Constantine the lofty expression of worth and dignity was embodied by court ceremonials. For good or ill, the Church welcomed some of these into the liturgy. The result was the splendor and magnificence of medieval church architecture, richly illuminated Mass books, lavishly adorned vestments, precious vessels, and artistic furnishings. The ministers occupied the throne, donned rich vestments, and were treated in ways that were reminiscent of the imperial court. Yet deep down the ministers knew that they were servants and that the honor they received was not on account of their person but on account of their sacred role and the person of Christ and the community of the Church that they represented.

The liturgical rubrics that were borrowed from court ceremonials developed further, especially during and after the Franco-Germanic Period in the eighth century. The seventh-century *Ordines Romani*, the *editio princeps* of the Pontifical by Piccolomini and Burchard of Strasbourg in 1485, and the Ritual of Castellani in 1523, among countless others, reinforced the importance of rubrics and ceremonials in the celebration of the liturgy. The importance of rubrics took the lion's share in the study of liturgy. Until the early 1960s the word liturgy was synonymous with rubrics. The master of ceremonies was called liturgist. In seminaries the sacraments were treated under three different headings representing three aspects: systematic theology, moral theology, and liturgy, which meant knowledge of the rubrics. In a way, I found liturgy class entertaining because it was practical, as when we baptized a doll or sat in the confessional pretending to hear the confession of the professor. When I took the examination *ad audiendas confessiones* I was asked a question on the liturgy, since the examiner identified me as Benedictine. His question was: how many times do you genuflect before the Blessed Sacrament when you take and return the ciborium?

The liturgical movements of the nineteenth and twentieth centuries, featuring the Benedictine monks Prosper Guéranger and Lambert Beauduin, respectively, restored the original understanding of the liturgy as something theological more than merely rubrical. The etymological definition of the liturgy as a work of service to the people recovered the deeper theological and spiritual insights on Christian worship that prevailed during the patristic age.

There is a comforting attempt in some local churches, especially among the poor and developing countries, not only to work for the poor but also to live the life of the poor. The Church can work to improve the social, intellectual, and spiritual situation of the poor from the armchair position of the rich. But these local churches have chosen to share the poverty of their people. The economic situation of the community is a reliable gauge of the socioeconomic standing of the Church's ministers. Their option to be poor has an inevitable effect on the liturgy. Church buildings and liturgical ceremonials should fit the environment of poverty. Shanties, beggars, naked children scavenging for food, and the absence of basic commodities are the context in which the liturgy is celebrated by the community and are not to be regarded as eyesores offending the view of an imposing church. Liturgical ostentation in the midst of human poverty sends the wrong signal to those who can hardly make both ends meet. However, a word of caution is useful: the liturgy does not suffer the state of human destitution as a normal condition that must be helplessly accepted. The liturgy, even in the situation of poverty, should be a convincing sign to the community that while dignity in poverty and noble simplicity are exalted Christian values, all must work toward the eradication of human misery. The liturgy is the service, which the Church of the poor offers to the poor.

The Office of Readings for Saturday of the Twenty-First Week in Ordinary Time reproduces a homily of John Chrysostom, which I find quite acrid but inspiring at the same time. I quote some of the more striking passages: "Do you want to honor Christ's body? Then do not scorn him in his nakedness, nor honor him here in the church with silken garments while neglecting him outside where he is cold and naked. For he who said: This is my body, also said: You saw me hungry and did not feed me. A gift to the church may be taken as a form of ostentation, but an alms is pure kindness. Of what use is it to weigh down Christ's table with golden cups, when he himself is dying of hunger? First, fill him when he is hungry; then use the means you have left to adorn his table. What is the use of providing the table with cloths woven of gold thread, and not providing Christ himself with the clothes he needs? What if you were to see him clad in worn-out rags and stiff from the cold, and were to forget about clothing him and instead were to set up golden columns for him, saying that you were doing it in his honor? Would he not think he was being mocked and greatly insulted? I am not forbidding you to supply these adornments; I am urging you to provide these other things as well, and indeed to provide them first. Do not therefore adorn the church and ignore your afflicted brother and sister, for they are the most precious temple of all."

But even in communities that are wealthy the liturgy should not blend, and much less compete, with its affluent surroundings. Its building and furnishings, though noble and worthy of divine worship, always possess those countercultural qualities that speak accusingly against the irresponsible stewardship of earthly goods. In this connection I have sometimes explained the meaning of the minor rite of mixing Mass wine with water as a measure to temper the sourness of wine offered by the poor. Cyprian of Carthage (*Letter to Cecil*) explained that the wine represents Christ, while the water signifies the people. Hence, if water alone is placed in the cup, Christ is not offered at Mass to the Father. This was the line of argument he used against the sect called Aquarians. In their Eucharist the group used only water for fear of being detected by pagans by the smell of wine as they came out of their early morning Mass.

The text that accompanies the present rite is borrowed from Pope Leo the Great. The text speaks about our sharing in the divinity of Christ who shared in our human nature. It is a storehouse for the liturgical theology and spirituality of the Mass. But I am partial to the sociological interpretation I mentioned above. It is an eloquent and convincing symbol of the Eucharist that is offered by the poor in the service of the poor. Even in rich churches and prosperous communities the priest must pour water into the cup of wine to convey the basic option of the Church to serve the poor and be counted among the poor.

The espousal of the Church to the Roman Empire after the fourth century resulted in some undesirable offspring. One of them is the intrusion of the Roman sociopolitical system in the patterns of liturgical worship. Classic examples of such intrusion are the three ordination formularies in the Veronese Sacramentary composed most probably in the year 558 during the reign of Pope Pelagius I. Up until the reform of the ordination rite in 1968 the Latin Church had used the three formularies according to the major recensions found in the Veronese, Gregorian, and Gelasian Sacramentaries and the *Missale Francorum*. Some words that were appropriated from the sociopolitical system of Rome appear throughout the ordination prayers. Eminent among them are *dignitas, honor,* and *gradus.* From the point of view of semiotics, one can conclude that these words marshaled the ordination scheme based on promotion. It stands to reason that the Roman system profoundly influenced the Veronese view of the three ordination rites as three ascending stages of ecclesiastical ministry or career. With each of these ranks (*gradus*) correspond special dignity and honor. I have little doubt that the composer of these formularies endorsed the use of these three words to develop the theology and the design of the three orders.

For at least thirteen centuries the words "dignity," "honor," and "rank" resounded solemnly in cathedral churches as bishops, presbyters, and deacons were ordained. The constant repetition of these words has made a deep impression in the thinking of both clergy and people. In some countries even today the clergy are considered the elite of society who enjoy direct access to the powerful and the affluent. Before 1968, when the pontifical rites and insignia were simplified, we listened to statements such as this: "These rites provide a symbol of the honor by which the bishop's dignity is to be acknowledged in the Church." The image projected by the statement is a dignitary being served at the throne rather than a servant who kneels down to wash the feet of the people he was ordained to serve. The effort of the post-conciliar Church to eradicate, gradually and prudently, the imperial traces in the liturgy is one of the blessings of Vatican II. The chair of the bishop, for example, should not resemble a throne, the vestments should "symbolize the function proper to each ministry" rather than conjure up honor and dignity, and the throne of the bishop should properly be called *cathedra*, or the chair from which he teaches the assembly.

The present system will doubtless continue to prevail in the liturgy. It is a fact, however, that for many of the faithful the clerical insignia do not evoke anything imperial. They are instead the proper, though peculiar, attire for performing liturgical functions. Even the peculiar cap and gown worn by judges in court, or the academic gowns for that matter, do not appear entirely outlandish to most people. Today, who would associate the bishop's miter and ring with the Roman Emperor's paraphernalia? Do people trace the entrance procession—with the full complement of choir, magistrates, candle bearers, and thurifers—back to the imperial court ceremonials? The liturgy possesses the characteristic trait of conserving some of its symbols beyond their useful life span, because people generally enter the church to settle down and find peace in familiar surroundings and rituals. The inner longing for a fixed, established liturgical environment could very well be the reason why creativity after the sixth century had not been one of the salient qualities of the Roman rite.

But the real issue is not with chairs, vestments, and burning incense. The issue is with the frame of mind, attitude of the heart, and outward demeanor, especially of the ministers who were ordained to preside as servants of the community. Those who preside at the liturgy clothe themselves with the humility of Christ, the *leitourgos* of the new covenant, who came to serve, not to be served. Presiders are accorded signs of respect, not because of their person, but because of their office that embodies Christ's service of his people. When presiders are honored with incense, Christ and the Church are the ones being honored. When minor ministers bow to them, Christ and the Church receive their act of reverence. In the face of this truth presiders fade into insignificance: they are servants that decrease in order that Christ will increase in the estimation of the faithful. If they interiorize this their attitude will be one of embarrassment over the fact that the servant receives the obeisance that is due the Master. Clerical ordination is principally for the liturgy, that is, for the service of Christ's faithful.

Liturgy means service, and priests are ordained for the liturgy of the assembled community. Priest-presiders will do well to remind themselves that the liturgy is for the assembly, that the liturgy is people oriented, and that liturgical leadership is for the service of Christ's flock. A situation where the presider's leadership is put to the test is the schedule of liturgical services. In highly technological communities time, even in the case of the liturgy, is of the essence and all, including the presider, are expected to be punctual. This is not so in some societies where people do not count the hours by the clock. They quite simply note the passing of day and night by sunrise and sunset. If you ask the driver when the bus will start moving, his answer will be "when it is filled up." When you want to start the meeting at four, you announce that it will start at three. This cultural trait can be very mortifying for priests who were trained in the seminary to be time conscious.

I am not saying that the liturgy should be subjected to the disconcerting habit of latecomers. Yet it is useful to remind ourselves that the liturgy is people oriented. Take, for example, the rubric for the entrance rite of the Mass, which instructs that "when the people are assembled, the priest with the ministers proceed to the altar, while the entrance song is chanted." The Mass starts when the people are assembled, not when the clock shows it is time. For a couple of years I served a small farming village in the heart of Mindanao in the Philippines. The Sunday Mass, which was scheduled at nine in the morning, never started on time, in spite of frequent reminders about punctuality. One excuse for being late was that the majority came on foot from their distant homes with children and the aged. Every so often I had to remind myself that the Mass was for them and that it would be foolish to prove the importance of punctuality by starting the Mass in a half-empty chapel. The ability to hide one's irritation is, I think, one of the virtues every presider, as servant of the worshiping community, is expected to possess.

THE OFFICIAL WORSHIP OF THE CHURCH

Early Christian writers who used the word "liturgy" conserved its connotation as official worship. An example is the first-century book *Didaché* (15, 1), which, by the way, says that bishops and deacons also perform the *leitourgia*, as do the prophets and teachers. Note the word "also." According to the ranking system of *Didaché*, the itinerant prophets and teachers are listed ahead of bishops and deacons. Apparently they presided at the official worship of the community they were visiting. This probably has some reference to Ephesians 2:20: You are "built upon the foundation of the apostles and prophets, with Christ Jesus himself as the cornerstone." Together with the resident bishops, the itinerant prophets, who, unlike bishops and priests, were not necessarily ordained for a particular community, composed the Church leadership (Eph 3:5). They too were officials of the Church, and hence it is evident that the liturgies they performed were official worship. It is clear that the prophets' role of preaching included the function of presiding in worship.

Didaché and the third-century *Apostolic Tradition* are quite lenient with the form and style of the liturgical celebrations presided over by the prophets. At any rate, it was too early in the history of the liturgy to bother about liturgical norms and censures. The itinerant prophets of the early Church were the first charismatics. Today some pastors and liturgists are vexed by charismatic groups that, under the sway of the Spirit's capricious inspiration, disregard liturgical rubrics. As secretary of the Episcopal Commission on Liturgy, I was asked time and again to intervene or issue a memorandum to toe the line. Frankly, I would have nothing to do with special groups that claim the authorship of the Holy Spirit. Supposing the claim is true, I for one would dread to stifle the Spirit. Thus my answer did not always satisfy my listeners, who thought I was evading the issue. What I always said was to ensure that the regular schedule of parish liturgies should not be compromised; the members of the special groups should be encouraged to join the larger parish community at Masses on Sunday; and the Spirit should be allowed to blow where he wills. The liturgy as defined by the authority of the hierarchy is and remains the official worship of the Church, but we should be prepared for the possible promptings of the Spirit outside the normal and official structure of the Church.

Apostolic Tradition (10) notes that clerical ordination is on account of the liturgy (*propter liturgiam*) and spells out the chief function of the bishop, priests, and deacons. On the other hand, widows, virgins, and other minor ministers like lectors, acolytes, and subdeacons are not ordained through the sacramental hand-laying. They are simply instituted or declared as such. Women are instituted to the state of widowhood not *propter liturgiam* but *propter orationem*, that is, for unceasing prayer. They represent every Christian whose primary obligation is to pray without ceasing.

The two ancient documents emphasize the official character of Christian worship. They teach that the liturgy is an action performed by designated ministers for the Church and in the name of the Church. Although the faithful are the chief beneficiaries of these actions according to the classic dictum *sacramenta sunt propter homines* (sacraments are for the people), their active participation in the liturgy did not figure prominently in these documents. Perhaps this explains why for several centuries active participation was not regarded as a matter of serious consequence. Another probable reason was the waning interest of the faithful in celebrations where they sat as the mute audience of the clergy that performed in the sanctuary. As early as the sixth century, proxy participation was a conventional practice. In one version of the Roman Canon reproduced in the Gregorian Sacramentary there is a curious provision for those instances when the persons that offered the stipend were not present during the Mass. Roughly translated, the text reads: "Lord, remember your servants and all who stand here around (your table). Their faith and devotion are known to you. They offer to you—as we also offer on behalf of those that are not present here—this sacrifice of praise." When the word "official" was affixed more to the role of ministers and less to the community that should claim ownership of the liturgy, the liturgy became a clerical reserve. Some of the faithful must have thought that there was no need for them to be physically present because their material offering stood for them as kind of proxy.

Pope Pius XII's *Mediator Dei* defines the liturgy as "the public worship, which our Redeemer as head of the Church renders to the Father, as well as the worship which the community of the faithful renders to its Founder, and through him to the heavenly Father. In short, it is the worship rendered by the Mystical Body of Christ in the entirety of its head and members" (25). This definition has a remarkable bearing on SC 7, which describes the liturgy as "the whole public worship performed by the Mystical Body of Jesus Christ, that is, by the Head and his members" and as "an action of Christ the Priest and of his Body which is the Church."

The official character of the liturgy should not create the impression that it is the exclusive domain of the clergy. On the contrary, it is official because it is owned by the community of the Church and celebrated on its behalf. Clerical liturgy, which has no need of lay ministers and no regard for the assembly, is atypical, at least after the reform of Vatican II. I have heard about a presider that performed practically all the liturgical roles, including the ringing of the sanctuary bell at the elevation! I have been to a parish church where the priest who did not believe in forming and appointing regular lectors and servers went to the nave of the church before Mass in search of hapless readers and servers.

I am personally ill at ease with the celebration of the Mass in private to satisfy personal devotion or fulfill the obligation of a stipend. This type of celebration downgrades the value of the liturgy as public worship of the Church. It becomes an instrument to satisfy personal devotion or fulfill a canonical requirement. The practice of celebrating the Mass alone on a side altar as a daily act of devotion or for the intention of benefactors tends to forget the official character of the liturgy. I have no right, of course, to question and much less disagree with the retention of the medieval form of celebrating the "Mass without a Congregation." I presume that there is wisdom in such an odd decision, which I believe answers certain theological issues and pastoral concerns. It is useful, however, to take seriously the reminder of the General Instruction on the Roman Missal: "Mass should not be celebrated without a minister or at least some of the faithful except for a just and reasonable cause. In this case, the greetings, the remarks, and the blessing at the end of Mass are omitted" (254). Unfortunately, the phrase "just and reasonable cause" is ignored by those who have made solitary Mass the rule of prayer. It amuses me to imagine a priest saying the greeting, reciting the invitations, "Let us pray," and "Pray, brothers and sisters," and giving the blessing at the end of Mass in an empty chapel. In defense of solitary Masses someone pointed out that the Mass is celebrated in the presence of the heavenly beings and the souls in purgatory. Hence the priest is not alone and he has an assembly before him that is visible to those who have faith in the communion of the saints!

But the presiders and ministers are not the sole offenders. On the part of some of the faithful there is a lingering attitude of personal ownership of sacraments, especially the Mass celebrated for their intention. The announcement that "this Mass is offered for the intention of the donor" underscores the offering of the donor who is considered the principal beneficiary of the Mass. The practice goes back to the Middle Ages. During the recitation of the Roman Canon the names of benefactors were read aloud from a diptych. The liturgy of Vatican II retained the medieval text in the Memento of the Living, with the possibility of mentioning the names of those being specially prayed for. The Constitution on the Liturgy sets down the principle that "whenever rites, according to their specific nature, make provision for communal celebration involving the presence and active participation of the faithful, it is to be stressed that this way of celebrating them is to be preferred, as far as possible, to a celebration that is individual and, so to speak, private" (27). In the official worship of the Church we stand before God not as individuals but as a community. As official worship the liturgy is never exclusive and never private.

One welcome consequence of this conciliar principle in densely Catholic countries like the Philippines, where there is a shortage of priests, is the communal celebration of baptism, marriage, penance, and funerals. The so-called mass weddings, especially of those who have lived together for many years without the benefit of the sacrament, have become a regular affair. The participation of grandchildren carrying the wedding rings adds a human touch to the rite. In most parishes Advent, Lent, and town fiestas are marked by a communal rite of penance. Priests from neighboring parishes hear the confession of great numbers of penitents. Regarding funerals, I have had the occasion to celebrate a funeral Mass in a large parish in front of eight coffins. The usual wailing and outpouring of grief was noticeably restrained, due perhaps to some consoling thought that the bereaved were not alone. Members of different families have instantly created a grieving community where the pain of separation and loss was the unspoken language heard and understood by all.

The General Instruction of the Liturgy of the Hours (20–26) reminds all that "the liturgy of the hours, like other liturgical services, is not a private matter but belongs to the whole Body of the Church." It explains in terms of entrustment and commissioning the obligation of the clergy to pray the divine office: "Sacred ministers have the liturgy of the hours entrusted to them in such a particular way that even when the faithful are not present they are to pray it themselves. . . . The Church commissions them to celebrate the liturgy of the hours so as to ensure at least in their persons the regular carrying out of the duty of the whole community." Praying the Liturgy of the Hours in community, to which the faithful are invited, especially on Sundays and holidays, remains an ideal to be pursued "with every effort." Pastors are instructed to teach the faithful "how to make this participation a source of genuine prayer." The recitation of the Liturgy of the Hours in private should not weaken the official character of this liturgy.

To no avail have been the attempts to attract the faithful to the celebration of Lauds and Vespers in parish churches on Sunday. This would probably work in parishes where only one or two Masses are celebrated on Sunday, and the parishioners are willing to return to church at the sound of the evening bell. But in parishes where as many as seven Masses are celebrated every Sunday, not counting the Masses in far-flung villages, it would be excessive and futile to call the clergy and faithful to Lauds and Vespers. I assume that one other reason why attempts do not prosper is the faithful's perception that going to Mass on Sunday, which is their principal obligation, is their religious priority. When made to choose between Vespers and Mass, most will certainly choose the Mass. The Instruction directs the pastors to familiarize the faithful with the plan of the Liturgy of the Hours and the meaning of the psalms. That is a tall order! This is one instance when we can repeat the phrase "easier said than done." How I wish that the plan, not the length, of Lauds and Vespers were simpler and adjustable to different situations in the parish. All those antiphons and short responsories could have been kept for the monastic choir, and the shorter, more prayerful psalms could have been chosen to the exclusion of long and tedious ones.

I was told that the architect of the Liturgy of the Hours, Msgr. A-G. Martimort, was a fierce advocate of the monastic divine office. It is not surprising, then, that he used it as a pattern for the revised Roman Liturgy of the Hours. I had the privilege to sit with him in the meetings of the Vatican liturgy consultors and to invite him for lunch and coffee in our community on the Aventine. It was always delightful and refreshing to listen to his scholarly discourses that merited the approval of his proposals by the Congregation for Divine Worship. It was not out of jest but filial admiration that we called him "the little Napoleon." My younger colleagues and I could hardly hide our astonishment when like a bolt from the blue he declared, "after our generation there are no more liturgists"! How I wish I had the occasion and the courage to speak to him about shaping Lauds and Vespers for parishes where Sunday observance includes baptisms, marriages, funerals, blessings, and committee meetings. Frankly, I have no notion how Lauds and Vespers can be conveniently inserted in such a parish schedule. But if it could be done, I assume that the Liturgy of the Hours would be freed, like the other liturgical services, from the misconception that it is the clergy's personal obligation and does not stand as another form of worship that belongs to the whole Body of the Church.

The official character of the liturgy has great bearing on the spirituality of the priest as minister of liturgical worship. Liturgical ministry is that form of spirituality whereby the minister grows in holiness. The Document of the Second Plenary Council of the Philippines describes the spirituality of the priest in the framework of his ministry: "It develops in the ministry and through ministry. . . . The priest grows in holiness through the faithful performance of his ministry—the ministry of the word, the ministry of the sacraments, and the ministry of shepherding the community. . . . It is through his ministry that he will grow in pastoral charity and hence in perfection" (par. 535). A basic component of the spirituality of the priest is his liturgical-sacramental role of ministering to the assembly as presider. The liturgy nourishes his spirituality while he conducts the liturgy of the word, stands at the Eucharistic table, administers the sacraments and sacramentals, blesses and buries the dead, and prays the Liturgy of the Hours.

But to rush through liturgical celebrations in order to have time afterward for spiritual reading and private prayer misses the point about the priest's liturgical spirituality. There should be no dichotomy between personal prayer and liturgical ministry. Spiritual reading, besides the Office of Readings and private prayer, should of course never be absent from the daily routine of priests. However, these are at best regarded as personal preparation for the ministry of sanctification that they perform as liturgical presiders. I maintain that the liturgical prayer priests offer for the benefit of the faithful who receive the sacraments is at the same time their personal prayer. The sacramental formulas they recite are an expression of their faith that what they celebrate as ministers is the saving act of Christ. For them the words "This is my body, this is the cup of my blood" are their prayer for the assembly, that those who receive them may "become one body, one spirit in Christ." For them the words "I baptize you" and "I absolve you" are not mere liturgical formulas; they are their personal prayer that the persons baptized and absolved will receive the grace of these sacraments. Liturgical presidency is always an act of faith in the spiritual power of the sacraments. It is likewise an act of loving service to the faithful and a prayer of hope that the celebration will yield fruits of conversion and holiness.

Even in an ideal condition of prayerful environment the ministry of presiding carries with it a certain amount of distraction and anxiety, especially when the rites are complicated and things are done in a haphazard manner. In some churches that are not air conditioned, especially in the tropics, the atmosphere of recollection and tranquility could be quite a rarity. Priests may find themselves in a situation where they have to compete with outside and even inside noise. As a priest accustomed to the tranquil setting of monastic worship, I at one time considered the piercing cries of babies, the barking of dogs outside, and the persistent sound of honking horns reason enough to swear that I would not return to celebrate in that church again. Constant movements could also be annoying.

I remember one occasion when I brought an English monk for Sunday Mass in a parish church in the vicinity of Manila. In my judgment the flow of celebration was very smooth, and there was nothing I could say to improve the quality of presiding and participation. I asked him what aspect of the celebration impressed him most. He answered, "The nonstop rustle of the women's fans."

There are situations when priests might be tempted to perform the celebration with great haste in order to escape the noise, the heat, and the dust. Yet for priests these liturgical celebrations are the normal occasion to personally meet the Lord in the assembly. Under such uncomfortable circumstances they encounter Christ as they wash children in the life-giving water of baptism, recite the awesome words over bread and wine, pronounce the assuring words of absolution, solemnize the vows of wife and husband, anoint and comfort the sick, and bid farewell to the departed.

Sometimes priests may suffer the low tide or the cold chill of the spirit and the lessening in their hearts of the original ardor of Christ's love. It is a humbling experience for them to recite the Eucharistic Prayer and fail to have a glimpse of the cross and the resurrection under the veil of the sacramental words. It is a cause for concern for them when they absolve penitents and do not personally share in the joy of the merciful Father that welcomes back his lost sons and daughters. The feeling of being awkward and uninvolved is present when they bury the dead amid the sound of weeping and have tears neither in their eyes nor in their hearts. Priests experience the pain of anguish when they discover that while they lead the faithful to Christ, they lag behind.

And yet Christ loves his priests to whom he committed the ministry of the official worship of the Church. He is a sympathetic witness to the tears they shed as they struggle to be faithful and loyal to their ministry. When discouragement overpowers them and they turn away from the ministry, he joins them and walks with them on the road. When darkness sets in, they can always turn to him with confidence: "Stay with us, Lord." Stay with us and dispel our fears, dispel our doubts and insecurity. He explains the Scriptures to them that they may announce it to their brothers and sisters. He breaks the bread that they may share it with others. He breaks the bread that in turn they may continue to be broken for others. And in the course of life's ebb and flow, through the changes and chances of this world, priests can always look back to the many times he walked with them on the road, stayed with them at eventide, and sat and broke the bread with them. Were not their hearts burning within them as he spoke to them on the road and explained to them the Scriptures? As they sat at table with him, did they not recognize him in the breaking of the bread? And so they retrace their steps back to the Jerusalem of their priestly ministry, as each of them asks again and again: why does he love me so much?

LITURGY AND THE HISTORY OF SALVATION

It might come as a surprise to many that liturgy had not been my preferred field of specialization. After I was ordained my abbot, Bernardo Lopez, informed me that he was sending me to Rome to study liturgy. He explained that the community needed a master of ceremonies. With due respect to all masters of ceremonies, I must confess that being numbered among them never even crossed my mind. I pleaded with my abbot to allow me to study systematic theology instead and sit for a few subjects of liturgy. My plea fell on deaf ears. When I finally mustered the courage to say, "Suppose, I do not want to go to Rome?" his answer was curt: "You are going." To this day I have not regretted my act of obedience.

To my great relief the professors at the Pontifical Liturgical Institute dealt with rubrics only in connection with history and the meaning of the rite. The liturgical formation we received consisted of history, theology, patristic and medieval sources, textual analysis, and spirituality. Pastoral liturgy was understandably a weak course offering because the students came from different countries and pastoral situations. Professor Adrien Nocent used to remind us that if we mastered history and theology, the rest was common sense. What is pastoral liturgy? It is, he insisted, the pastor's utilization of common sense when he plans and celebrates the liturgy for the welfare of his people. But my conversion to the liturgy came about as I listened enthralled to Professor Salvatore Marsili's lectures on the relationship between God's plan of salvation and the liturgy. Perhaps his lectures could best be described as an outpouring of his profound spirituality. I remember the evening when the city of Rome experienced a severe power failure. It was during Marsili's class, and we decided to stay. We sat quietly, not minding the darkness in the hall as we hung upon his words.

To my mentor Salvatore Marsili, whom I revere as a liturgical theologian, I owe what I have been teaching my students about liturgical theology for the last thirty or so years. I can define the kernel of my teaching and research on liturgical theology in the three pair of words that I will call trilogy: salvation history and liturgy, paschal mystery and Pentecost, and anamnesis and epiclesis.

The trilogy can be drawn in simple lines. They consist basically of downward and upward movements. Salvation history is the downward movement: God descends to humankind. Liturgy, on the other hand, is the upward movement: humankind ascends to God. I visualize the two movements as a single line that descends and ascends. To quote the lapidary words of Marsili, "The liturgy is the final phase of salvation history." In salvation history God descends to earth so that in the liturgy we may ascend to the heavenly realm. Salvation history and liturgy are the two stages of God's continuing action of revelation and salvation.

The doctrine of divine descent and human ascent is the theme of a magnificent Christmas homily of St. Augustine, which is quoted in the Office of Readings (*Sermo 13 de Tempore*): "Of his own will Jesus Christ was born today, in time, so that he could lead us to his Father's eternity. God became human so that humans might become God. . . . Humankind fell, but God descended; humankind fell miserably, but God descended mercifully; humankind fell through pride, but God descended with his grace."

In the paschal mystery of Christ the same movements of descent and ascent are at work. God stretches his hand to rescue humankind from the fetters of death. The paschal mystery is God's descent in the person and death of Christ. It is the final manifestation of God in salvation history. The mystery of Pentecost, in turn, causes the paschal mystery to be present and effective in our time, so that by the power of the Holy Spirit humankind may ascend to the throne of grace. Daily, the liturgy embodies Pentecost: the liturgy is the continuing work of the Holy Spirit that plunges us in the stream of salvation history whence we rise up to the vision of our heavenly home. The paschal mystery and Pentecost, like salvation history and the liturgy, are one continuing movement of descent and ascent.

The liturgy itself is Christ's saving action. It represents the worship that Christ addressed to the Father when he obeyed his will by accepting death on the cross. This act of worship he now performs through the agency and ministry of the Church. I find no better way to explain this than by quoting the Constitution on the Liturgy: "To accomplish so great a work, Christ is always present in his Church, especially in its liturgical celebrations. . . . Christ always truly associates the Church with himself in this great work wherein God is perfectly glorified and the recipients made holy" (7).

Two basic liturgical actions constitute the Church's role as agent of Christ's worship. As it celebrates the liturgy the Church calls to mind the paschal mystery. Remembering is an essential trait of liturgical worship. Liturgists call it "anamnesis," a Greek word that is better left untranslated. After all, it is a technical term that will not be read to the assembly as part of liturgical prayer.

However, it is not enough to remember. The Church recalls and at the same time prays that what it recalls will become tangible reality. This prayer is called "epiclesis," another Greek word I do not dare to translate. Apropos I quote the words of the Constitution on the Liturgy: "Recalling thus the mysteries of redemption, the Church opens to the faithful the riches of the Lord's powers and merits, so that these are in some way made present in every age in order that the faithful may lay hold on them and be filled with saving grace" (102). The object of anamnesis is the paschal mystery. The object of epiclesis is the mystery of Pentecost. Anamnesis and epiclesis are the unbroken line of God's descent and humankind's ascent. The liturgy is salvation history, the paschal mystery, and the mystery of Pentecost. The efficacious presence of all these in the Church is made possible through liturgical anamnesis and epiclesis.

I believe it would be useful to dwell at some length on the notion of salvation history, paschal mystery and Pentecost, and the binomial anamnesis and epiclesis and to discuss how they relate to each other.

Salvation History

The *Catechism of the Catholic Church* (51–67) does not use the term "salvation history," but it amply discusses it as "The Revelation of God" or "God Coming to Meet Humankind." And rightly so, for what is salvation history other than the series of divine manifestations and revelations from the time of creation? The *Catechism* recalls the principal revelations of God, namely, in created realities, the covenant with Noah, the call of Abraham, and the formation of the people Israel. I am particularly gratified by the mention of "such holy women as Sarah, Rebecca, Rachel, Miriam, Deborah, Hannah, Judith and Esther who kept alive the hope of Israel's salvation. The purest figure among them is Mary" (64). In the fullness of time God spoke to us by a Son, Jesus Christ who is mediator and fullness of all revelation. "Christ, the Son of God made man, is the Father's one, perfect and unsurpassable Word. In him he has said everything; there will be no other word than this one" (65).

Salvation history is God's own history. God who dwells beyond the realm of history began to exist in history when he created the universe and became involved in human affairs. For those who believe, the *kosmos*, or celestial bodies, and the earth's natural environment are books that record the deeds of the Creator. The psalmist attests to it: "The heavens are telling the glory of God; and the firmament proclaims his handiwork" (Ps 19). In the Greek perception of the seasons, spring and summer are the *epidemìa*, or the time of the year when the gods reside on earth causing it to blossom forth. *Apodemìa*, on the other hand, is that time of the year when they withdraw from the earth. Their departure results in winter gloom and death of nature. For Christians seasonal changes do not symbolize the presence or absence of God. God is always present in the yearly "history" of the *kosmos*. The liturgy has no feast that bids farewell to God in winter and welcomes God back in spring. The Easter reflections of fourth-century Christian writers, such as Gregory of Nyssa, compare the soul that has abandoned God to a nature bereft of foliage. On the other hand, *chronos*, which is the succession of time indicating the passing of years, months, weeks, and day and night, is the historical moment when God descends to earth to play a major part in the unfolding of human history. The psalmist sings: "Day to day pours forth the speech, and night to night declares knowledge" (Ps 19). For Christians, as I noted earlier in this book, every human event is to be read and interpreted in the framework of God's history of inclusion in and exclusion from the affairs of humans.

It is not God who excludes himself or withdraws from our history. We humans are the ones that write the history of God's *apodemìa*.

When Christ became incarnate, God entered our cosmic time and inserted himself in our human history and, I should add, in our personal stories. God's saving deeds in the person of Christ took place in time. Historical time became the time of salvation; *chronos* became *kairós* or season of grace. Incarnation means that the words and works of Christ can now be historically recorded, because they happened in a given year, in a given month, in a given week, on a given day or night, at a given hour. By his incarnation Christ subjected himself to the flow of created time. His suffering and death are likewise grafted on historical time. Tradition has it that he submitted himself to the agony of the cross during the week when the Jews celebrated their Passover in memory of the historical exodus. Furthermore, we are informed that it happened at the equinox of spring, when it was full moon. The Synoptic Gospels note that Christ died at around three in the afternoon on a Friday. History and cosmos merged to provide the setting for Christ's celebration of the paschal mystery.

The liturgy recalls the mystery of Christ from the incarnation to his return in the context of an ever-present *hodie*, "today." The solemn invitation sung in Gregorian chant at the start of Christmas vigils always moves me: "Today Christ is born for us, come, let us adore him" (The English breviary strangely omits "today"). The mysterious word *hodie* mystically transports me to another sphere of time where I become a witness to the birth of God in human flesh. The Magnificat antiphon is emphatic in its use of *hodie*: "Christ the Lord is born today; today the Savior has appeared. Earth echoes the songs of angel choirs, archangels' joyful praise. Today, on earth his friends exult: Glory to God in the highest, alleluia." The *hodie* of the liturgical mystery pervades the homily of St. Peter Chrysologus, which is read at the Office of Readings after Epiphany: "Today the Magi find, crying in a manger, the one they have followed as he shone in the sky. Today the Magi see clearly, in swaddling clothes, the one they have long awaited as he lay hidden among the stars. . . . Today the Magi gaze in deep wonder at what they see. . . . Today Christ enters the Jordan to wash the sin of the world. . . . Today the servant lays his hand on the Lord. . . . Today the Holy Spirit hovers over the waters in the likeness of a dove. . . . Today Christ works the first of his signs from heaven by turning water into wine" (*Sermo* 160).

Hodie takes place in the framework of what is known today as the liturgical year, or more familiarly, the Church year, which the Lutheran

Pastor Johannes Pomarius introduced in 1589. The term "liturgical year," coined by Abbot Prosper Guéranger, entered the active vocabulary of the Roman Church in 1841. The early medieval books called it *ordo anni circuli*, the order of the yearly cycle (of feasts). In the Roman tradition the liturgical year follows a calendar year that is peculiar to the Western Church. It has its particular system of determining the beginning and end of the year, of reckoning the Easter month that consists of thirty-five days running from March 22 to April 25, of considering the fifty days of Easter as if they were one day, of declaring on Sunday that Christ ascended to heaven on this fortieth day, which in reality is the forty-third day, and of extending Sunday from the afternoon of the previous day to the midnight of the following day.

But we should not interpret these peculiarities as a form of isolation from the reality of human life and history. Just as Christ's paschal mystery was inserted in cosmic and historical time, so is the liturgical celebration of that mystery. Liturgical feasts are attached to the seasons of the year, traditional feasts of the people, the cycle of human work, and the political systems of nations. Through liturgical feasts the different aspects of the Christian mystery are woven into the fabric of the history and cosmic experience of humankind. The Christian people are given the assurance that Christ and the Church walk with them on their journey through life. The long and short of it is that the celebration of Christ's mystery is held in conjunction with the experiences of people in the course of the year. The liturgy does not isolate itself from what goes on in the world. It interplays with the academic year, the business year, the political year, the cause-oriented year, the years of struggles and hopes, and the years of war and peace. The liturgy interplays with these life situations in order to imbue them with the mystery of Christ. I would cite as basis for this the theological axiom "what was not assumed at the incarnation was not redeemed." The task of the liturgy is to ensure that nothing in human history and experience is excluded from the realm of Christ's saving work.

The Paschal Mystery and Hope

The other concept I would like to develop is the paschal mystery. The liturgical movement, the council, and the postconciliar reform of the liturgy have used every available means to propagate it. There was a time when the incarnation received paramount importance in liturgical rites. An example is the posture of kneeling at the Creed's "and he became man" and of genuflecting at the words "and the Word was made flesh" of the Tridentine second gospel. Until now many of the faithful still regard Christmas as the leading feast of the year, even if liturgically Easter ranks first. The postconciliar liturgy has tried to offset the disparity with a sweeping reform that would give greater prominence to the paschal mystery, defined as the suffering, death, and resurrection of Christ. Today is there any liturgical rite that does not in one way or another speak about the paschal mystery as the nucleus of the celebration? What do we proclaim at almost every Mass as the mystery of faith? "Christ has died, Christ is risen, Christ will come again." This acclamation is an ingenious attempt to relate the mystery of Christ's body and blood with his death and resurrection. The sacrament on the altar is the symbol and embodiment of his paschal mystery. Some people inquired whether it would be liturgically correct to have acclamations that are specific to the feast, like "Today Christ is born for us, come, let us adore him."

My liturgical formation at the Pontifical Liturgical Institute evidently focused on the paschal mystery, which permeated every class course, from history and theology to pastoral liturgy. Christmas was treated merely as one of the solemn feasts in the liturgical year. Fr. Burkhard Neunheuser, who was a disciple of Odo Casel, never tired of stressing the central position of the paschal mystery in the liturgy and spiritual life. His lectures and homilies invariably touched on it. Sometimes he would be carried away as he repeated again and again in a crescendo, *il mistero pasquale, il mistero pasquale!* (the paschal mystery, the paschal mystery!). Although his students and some of his colleagues thought it was a kind of liturgical barrage, we shared his conviction that since Christmas led to Easter, the paschal mystery must consequently occupy the preeminent post in the liturgy. When he returned to his monastery in Maria Laach, he never failed to send me greetings on my name day. I believe that he had a special devotion to my patron saint. It was he who recalled to me the epithet of the saint, which is his as well: *Intus monachus, foris apostolus* (a monk inside, an apostle outside). In February 2001, at the age of 98, he wrote: "I am still able to take part in the entire Opus Dei and do some small work like writing book reviews for the *Archiv für Liturgiewissenschaft*. I do not know how much time the Lord will still grant me, but I leave all to his mercy." I wrote back: "I am deeply touched by your kindness toward me. Year after year you unfailingly remember me, your student in Rome from 1965 to 1968. You even contributed an article for a Festschrift in my honor! I cannot thank you enough for what you do for me. You are 98 years old, yet you have not retired from serving the Lord as monk and liturgist. I am 61 and still learning so much from you about the liturgy. You continue to inspire me to remain zealous for the liturgical reform of Vatican II. I must admit that sometimes I become discouraged because of the liturgical stance being taken by our superiors beyond the Tiber." In 2003, a few weeks before he returned to the Father to celebrate the eternal Passover, he wrote me a card with the premonition that it might be his last.

The paschal mystery is an object of faith; it is a statement of love; and it is the source of hope. The third point is seldom treated in the liturgy, but I believe it merits special consideration.

On the tranquil Aventine Hill in Rome there is a house gate on which these intriguing words, in iron, are fastened beside a cross: *Sine spe sine metu* (without hope, without fear). Fr. Adrien Nocent informed me that the words were affixed by a priest who had been excommunicated with the category of *vitandus* (to be shunned). Whatever the true story was, the four words are a biting statement of rebellious despair on the part of someone whom the world would have expected to hope courageously against hope amid the trials of life. Sometimes despair can drive ordained ministers to rebel against authority, to seek fulfillment outside their ministry, and to abandon their commitment to Christ and the Church. Despair can put on many ugly faces, but the paschal mystery can be a source of solace and hope.

An active lay leader under pressure of unfair criticisms by both the clergy and fellow workers moaned: "I always knew that faith and charity are difficult, but now that I am experiencing the paschal mystery I have discovered that hope can be extremely trying." Indeed, it is in times of trial that hope comes alive in the life of the Church. Among early patristic writers hope was often associated with persecutions and harassments to which Christians were being subjected. In moments such as these writers like Tertullian, Origen, and Cyprian (*De carne* 5; *Hom. in Ier.* 20; *De religione* 16 and *De patientia* 1321) exhorted the faithful to remain steadfast in hope. A persecuted Church—should we not perhaps thank God that he allows it to continually be persecuted?—stands as a convincing symbol of hope. A Church at rest forgets hope. But the blood and bitter tears shed in the missions and the home front are able to nurture the virtue of hope.

Patristic writers also connected hope with trials that afflicted the Church from within. The presence of moral decadence, heresies, and discriminations urged them to preach not only about the need for conversion but also about the importance of hope. In the face of the division that rocked the Church of Corinth, the writer of the First Letter of Clement (27) recommended the practice of the virtue of hope. In moments of discouragement brought about by moral degeneration among Christians, the Shepherd of Hermas (6, 2; 8, 7) and Tertullian (*De paenitentia* 10) appealed to the necessity of conversion and hope. Heresies were also occasions for Ignatius of Antioch and Irenaeus of Lyons (*Ad Eph.* 21 and *Ad Magn.* 11; *Adv. haer.* 2, 28) to remind the faithful of their common hope in Jesus Christ. These are some examples of how hope accompanies the Church when it labors under the weight of the paschal mystery. As long as the Church remains the community of believers that experience the death of Jesus, the call to conversion and hope will continue to be heard in our churches, our homes, and our streets.

Tertullian wrote that the passion of Christ is "the one hope of the whole world" and his resurrection "the exemplar of our own" (*De carne* 5; *De resurrectione* 48). Our hope, he says, is fastened to the death and resurrection of Christ. As there is a *regula fidei*, or rule of faith, so there is a *regula spei*, or rule of hope, for every Christian. When we suffer with Christ we can have the unfailing hope to rise with him, because God has made the paschal mystery the pattern of his relations with his people. What God accomplished in Christ, he will accomplish in us. Such was the hope the early Church shepherded through the trials that beset it from without and within.

Among the early Christian writers who developed the theme of hope was Augustine. Hope is "the expectation of the future resurrection." According to him, the basis for such hope is none other than the example of Christ's resurrection (*Enarratio in Ps. 70, 11*). Yet as long as we are in the flesh we are subjected to corruption and must await the day of our resurrection *in patientia*, in suffering, after the example of the Crucified. Our awareness that our human nature is fallen shields us from presumption. At the same time, however, God's promise of a future resurrection, which he already fulfilled in Christ, safeguards us so that we do not yield to despair. Christians, Augustine concludes, are a people that God has called to live in hope (*Enarratio in Ps. 61, 20; Enarratio in Ps. 131, 19*). We proclaim that hope when we celebrate in the liturgy the blessed passion and the glorious resurrection of our Savior. For is not the liturgy the experience of hope anchored on Christ's paschal mystery? Is not the acclamation "Christ has died, Christ is risen, Christ will come again" our cry of hope? If Christ had not died for us, how can we even begin to love him? If he had not risen from the dead, then our faith is in vain and we are, among all the peoples of this world, to be pitied the most. And if he will not come again, what is there to hope for in this life and the next? For it is by his second coming, when the entire cosmos will be brought to perfection, that our hope will receive ultimate fulfillment.

In accord with tradition the liturgy connects hope with the future resurrection. Preface I for the Masses for the Dead declares that because Christ rose from the dead we are given the hope of a blessed resurrection after the earthly tent of our bodies shall have been dismantled. The ancient Preface for the Ascension, magnificent in doctrine and literary style, is a solemn announcement of the hope that one day the members of Christ's body will share the glory of their head: "Christ has passed beyond our sight, not to abandon us but to be our hope. Christ is the beginning, the head of the Church; where he has gone, we hope to follow." The object of hope, which is defined by these texts as blessed immortality, is not something we can possess or relish fully in this life. That is why we can only hope or look forward to what lies beyond the present world. Hope tells us that there is more to life than its earthly reality. The character of Christian hope as a joyful expectation is captured for us by the embolism to the Lord's Prayer at Mass: "As we wait in joyful hope for the coming of our Savior, Jesus Christ."

I remember distinctly one occasion when my discourse on hope was frowned on as something too otherworldly and utterly unconcerned with the changes and chances of this passing world. The liturgy, I was told, should finally be emancipated from the sanctuary with its smell of incense and burning candles. The doors and windows of the church should be opened to let fresh air in, or better yet, the liturgy should walk out of the church and settle in the real world. There was in fact a time when the Church's teaching regarding heaven and the afterlife was branded as opium that deadens our sense and appreciation of the sad, sometimes tragic, plight of humankind. The liturgical texts that I quoted above were dismissed as being irrelevant to our times. Some preachers focused their attention on the contemporary socioeconomic and political issues. Someone quipped rather harshly, "Stop hoping. Just do something. Act now!" A group of religious women with the best intention prepared a special lectionary with readings exclusively about social justice and political freedom.

Surely, we should not ignore the earthly city, for as the Constitution on the Church in the Modern World, which carries the Latin title

Gaudium et Spes (Joy and Hope) reminds us, "its progress is of vital concern to the kingdom of God, in so far as it can contribute to the better ordering of human society" (39). The Constitution exhorts that our expectation of a new heaven and a new earth should spur us to develop this earth, for it is here that the family of God grows and foreshadows in some way the age which is still to come. We are told that the "form of this world, distorted by sin, is passing away, and that God is preparing a new dwelling and a new earth in which righteousness reigns, whose happiness will fill and surpass all the desires of peace arising in the hearts of people." This is the reason why the liturgy continues to preach the hope of a blessed resurrection to those who place their trust in God's promise, who unite themselves with the passion of Christ, and who regard his resurrection as the paradigm of their own. This is why the liturgy, even at the risk of sounding quaint and outlandish, does not cease to celebrate hope and open the horizon of optimism.

The hope that emanates from the paschal mystery contradicts the purely materialistic view of human existence. The Christian hope nurtured by the liturgy has a countercultural quality: it critiques the current conception that material and technological progress is the final destiny of humankind; it affirms the existence of a life beyond. This kind of hope speaks loudly against the insidious premise that no moral law must interfere with the achievement of such progress; that poorer countries should practice artificial birth control and even abortion in order not to weigh heavily on the resources of developed countries; that our natural environment should be at the absolute disposition of industrial productivity. Hope cries out to warn us that human aspiration should not be contained within the bounds of this passing world. Finally, the kind of hope preached by the liturgy reminds the Church that while it cooperates in building the earthly city, it should not lose sight of its unique character as a pilgrim community with no permanent dwelling place here on earth. I would like to present this as the hope the Church is called to shepherd across the perils of hopelessness.

In Greek mythology the first woman on earth was Pandora. The gods endowed her with every attribute a woman could desire. Among the gifts was a box she was warned never to open. But her curiosity overcame her. She opened the mysterious box and every kind of evil flew from the box: hatred, murder, poverty, plagues, human sorrow. Realizing what had happened, she immediately closed the box. When her distraught husband Epimetheus came and learned what had happened, he opened it, and lo and behold, there flew out what had remained in the box: hope.

Anamnesis and Epiclesis

The third topic I wish to develop is the binomial anamnesis and epiclesis that constitute the liturgical action. The first refers to the ritual act of remembering the paschal mystery. The second is the prayer for the bestowal and gift of the Holy Spirit. They are inseparable acts and can readily merge into one. In the performance of a liturgical rite it might not be easy to distinguish where anamnesis ends and where epiclesis begins. For example, the rite of sacramental absolution whereat the priest lays his hands on the penitent and recites the formula is anamnesis and epiclesis at the same time. The paschal mystery is recalled and the Holy Spirit is simultaneously invoked for the remission of sin. Anamnesis and epiclesis reproduce ritually the nucleus of salvation history, which is the death of Jesus Christ that culminates in his resurrection and the gift of the Holy Spirit. Thus anamnesis relates to epiclesis in the same way as the paschal mystery relates to Pentecost. Just as Christ's death and resurrection culminates in the bestowal of the Holy Spirit, so the rite of recalling the paschal mystery concludes with the prayer for the gift of the Holy Spirit. It would not be an oversimplification to say that liturgical worship consists basically of the act of remembering the paschal mystery and the prayer for the descent of the Holy Spirit.

I have heard it said that when the Constitution on the Liturgy was being discussed in the council, a group of Eastern-rite bishops made the observation that the document did not give enough attention to the role of the Holy Spirit in the liturgy. Already as a student in Rome I felt that there was a kind of what I call "liturgical stereotyping": the Roman rite focuses on anamnesis, while the Eastern rites on epiclesis. The Roman Canon is a classic example. Its epiclesis does not mention the Holy Spirit. In fact it does not mention the Holy Spirit except at the doxology, which is probably not an original part of it. The additional Eucharistic Prayers in the Roman Mass solved the problem by inserting an epiclesis before consecration and another one before Holy Communion. The Eastern *anaphoras* contain only one and it is found after the consecration. This bothers Western theologians who cannot make out the logic of asking the Holy Spirit to consecrate what has already been consecrated by the words of Christ. After the council the *anaphora* attributed to Hippolytus of Rome, obviously not Roman in origin, was adopted by the Roman Church and became Eucharistic Prayer II. But it had to undergo a significant revision: it now has a double epiclesis.

Two of my mentors typified the distinct characteristics of the Roman and the Eastern rites. Salvatore Marsili will always be remembered for his lectures on anamnesis. Not surprisingly he named the handbook of the Pontifical Liturgical Institute *Anamnesis*. On the Eastern side was Emmanuel Lanne, cofounder of the Institute and a much respected ecumenical liturgist who left a mark in the World Council of Churches' celebrated document "Baptism, Eucharist, Ministry." From him I learned to appreciate the vital role of the Holy Spirit in salvation history and the liturgy.

Anamnesis, which is the Greek word for remembrance, is used by liturgists in a technical sense. It is not a purely mental exercise that can be done when one recollects or reflects. Private meditation on the passion of Christ does not pass as liturgical anamnesis, even if one does it in church before a crucifix. Liturgical anamnesis is a rite. I believe that such a notion can be traced back to Christ's command to "do this in my anamnesis" (Luke 22:19). In the original text to "do this" is to perform, reproduce, or re-create the actions he did at the Last Supper when, in the company of his disciples, he took bread, said a prayer of blessing, broke the bread, and gave the broken pieces to them. Anamnesis is the performance of a rite. In the liturgy the rite is carried out in words and gestures, and often with symbols or material elements. It is the way whereby the Church remembers the paschal mystery. Thus as the minister pours water on the person being baptized while reciting the baptismal formula, the death and resurrection of Christ are refreshed in the mind and heart of the liturgical assembly.

There is an important point I should make here. It is the common belief today that anamnesis causes the presence of the paschal mystery in the assembly. Thus, as the Constitution on the Liturgy teaches, the faithful are enabled to "lay hold on it and be filled with saving grace" (102). They do not regress to the past: the past reappears in the present because the commemorative rite of anamnesis is duly performed. I shall have occasion at a later time to elaborate on the concept of Christ's presence in the liturgy.

The action of remembering works two ways. We recall the *magnalia Dei*, the wondrous deeds of God in Christ. This is anamnesis. After reminding God, so to speak, about his saving work, we ask God to remember us, the Church, the human society, and the world at large.

This type of remembering is the prayer of intercession. We pray for God's blessing. It is called epiclesis, a Greek word for invocation or appeal addressed to the divinity. Liturgical epiclesis is a prayer wherein the Church calls upon God to send in the person of the Holy Spirit his blessing, love, mercy, and forgiveness. After reminding God about his saving works we can, with confidence, ask God in turn to remember. We pray that through the Holy Spirit God will do again and again in our day what he accomplished in ages past through Christ. Epiclesis is based on God's fidelity and consistency. God is faithful to his promises; God is consistent in unfolding his plan of salvation. Anamnesis leads to epiclesis, in the same way as the paschal mystery led to Pentecost. Epiclesis completes the action of anamnesis. Salvation history or God's descent to humankind shifts to the liturgy, which is humankind's ascent to God through Christ in the Spirit.

There was a debate among liturgical theologians on whether it is the Father that sends the Spirit through Christ, or Christ that sends the Spirit from the Father. Frankly, I regard the issue as quite academic and of little consequence. I recognize in it though the theological undercurrent of the *Filioque* controversy.

Emmanuel Lanne neatly distinguished two types of epiclesis in the Roman Mass. One is consecratory epiclesis, the other is communion epiclesis. In consecratory epiclesis the Church addresses the Father to make the gifts "holy by the power of your Spirit, that they may become the body and blood" of Christ (Eucharistic Prayer III). The communion epiclesis, on the other hand, is a prayer that "we, who are nourished by his body and blood, may be filled with his Holy Spirit, and become one body, one spirit in Christ." Similarly, we can speak of consecratory epiclesis in the case of baptismal water and chrism. According to Tertullian, "After God is invoked all waters attain the sacramental power to sanctify; for the Spirit immediately comes from heaven and rests on the water in order to make it holy. Once made holy, it acquires the power to sanctify" (*De baptismo* 4). Ambrose of Milan explains: "The priest delivers an invocation and prayer so that the font may be sanctified and the presence of the eternal Trinity may be at hand" (*De sacramentis I*, 5). In today's theological parlance I dare say that the baptismal water is raised to the dignity of a sacrament because of the Holy Spirit or the Trinity that dwells in the consecrated water. Physical contact with the water in the name of the Trinity brings about spiritual contact with the Holy Spirit. Christians are reborn in water and the Spirit. The other epiclesis similar to the communion epiclesis can be found explicitly or implicitly in the other sacraments and may be called confirmation, ordination, or marriage epiclesis. This type of epiclesis is for the benefit of those who receive the sacrament so that they may be configured to Christ, set apart for the priestly ministry, or become witnesses of Christ's enduring love for the Church.

The liturgical gesture used for epiclesis is hand-laying. It seems to have biblical precedent in James 5:14, which directs the presbyters to "pray over the sick." The Greek word connotes the action of stretching hands toward or over a person or object. The gesture is an integral element of the sacrament of confirmation and is essential to ordination. As regards the sacrament of penance, the one short sentence of the Constitution on the Liturgy is noteworthy: "The rites and formularies for the sacrament of penance are to be revised so that they more clearly express both the nature and effect of the sacrament" (72). It puzzled me that the council had only that to say about this sacrament in perpetual crisis. But looking over the Acts of the Council, I found out that "nature" means the social and ecclesial character of the sacrament, while "effect" refers to the restoration of the gesture of hand-laying to signify reconciliation. In grilled confessional boxes the gesture can hardly be called hand-laying. It appears more like hand raising, which some penitents mistake as the sign of the cross and a signal to leave the confessional.

At Mass the presider and concelebrants speak the words of consecratory epiclesis "with hands outstretched toward the offering" (General Instruction on the Roman Missal, no. 230). The rubrics instruct the concelebrants to extend their right hand toward the bread and toward the chalice, if this seems appropriate, while they pronounce the words of the Lord. The question arose whether the gesture was made by hand-laying in the style of epiclesis or by pointing the hand in a demonstrative manner to the elements that are being consecrated. Cipriano Vagaggini held the first, while A.-George Martimort, the second. The debate gathered momentum when the Ceremonial of Bishops clarified in a footnote that the gesture is done perpendicularly. Thomas Krosnicki thought the issue should be dismissed, since the gesture is after all done "if it seems appropriate." This reminds me of the never-ending debate among medieval theologians on the spiritual and corporal effects of the sacrament of anointing. An impatient Pope Benedict XIV shelved the discussion by declaring that it was both idle and unprofitable.

To conclude the discussion on anamnesis and epiclesis it might be relevant to speak about the way the two concepts work. At baptism the paschal mystery is recalled and made present. Through the washing with water the person who is baptized symbolically enters the tomb to be buried with Christ. Having died to sin and risen to a new life, the baptized receives the Holy Spirit of adoption whereby they become children of God. At confirmation the paschal mystery is commemorated by the rite of hand-laying and chrism whereby Christians receive the Holy Spirit of Pentecost that sends them into the world to be heralds of Christ. The Eucharist is the anamnesis par excellence of the paschal mystery. The presence of the Holy Spirit is invoked over bread and wine so that those who partake of them in Communion may become one body and one spirit in Christ. In the sacrament of penance the words of absolution sum up the theology of human sin and divine forgiveness. God is the father of mercies who has reconciled the world to himself through the death and resurrection of Christ and sent the Holy Spirit for the forgiveness of sins. Ordination is the special participation of the minister in the paschal mystery, which was Christ's supreme act of service to humankind in obedience to God's will. Ordination is stewardship of the divine mysteries. It is imparted to the minister by the Holy Spirit of leadership or the *Spiritus principalis*, or "governing Spirit" in the case of bishops. The sick are anointed with the oil of comfort so that as they patiently bear in their bodies the passion of Christ, they may experience the consoling presence and companionship of the Holy Spirit. Finally, in the rite of marriage the couple receives the Holy Spirit so that they may perform the task of imaging the paschal love of Christ for the Church, a love that cost him his life.

Similarly, anamnesis and epiclesis are the core of sacramentals and blessings, Liturgy of the Hours, and the liturgical year. They all celebrate the pervasive paschal mystery, which the corresponding anamnesis brings to life. At the same time, they represent the Church's prayer for the gift of the Holy Spirit who consecrates and makes holy the different occasions in the life of a Christian. In the Liturgy of the Hours the recitation of the psalms is the anamnesis of salvation history, which the Church interprets in the context of Christ's mystery. St. Ambrose, in the Office of Readings for Friday of the Tenth Week in Ordinary Time, has these penetrating words about the psalms: "In the psalms not only is Jesus born for us, he also undergoes his saving passion in his body, he lies in death, he rises again, he ascends into heaven, he sits at the right hand of the Father. What no human would have dared to say was foretold by the psalmist alone and afterward proclaimed by the Lord himself in the Gospel." In the course of day and night through the chanting of the psalms the Holy Spirit utters in our hearts words of praise and thanksgiving as we recall the life, mission, passion, and resurrection of Christ.

People sometimes ask me a question that tries to make rational sense of what I teach about the effect of epiclesis. I do not know whether to take the question seriously. It runs like this: "You have been telling us that the Holy Spirit is bestowed at every celebration of the liturgy. Is he given again and again? How do we figure that one out? Or is he given partially in some sacraments and fully in others, like the bishop's ordination?" I admit that I spent much time to formulate my answer. Perhaps the following explanation might clarify the matter. The basic feature of my answer is that our relationship with the Holy Spirit began at baptism and develops in other sacraments. Baptism establishes an enduring bond with the Holy Spirit of adoption whereby we call God our Father. In baptism the Holy Spirit lays hold on us for good. Nothing in heaven and under heaven can delete the imprint of our adoption as daughters and sons of God. Not even the most grievous sin can eradicate that reality.

Medieval theologians claimed that there was such a thing as permanent character imprinted by the sacraments of baptism, confirmation, and ordination. I believe in the permanency of our adoption, as far as God is concerned. We can disown God, but God will not disown those he has adopted by the working of the Holy Spirit. This, in my thinking, is what it means to "receive" the Holy Spirit in the sacrament of baptism. When we say that we again "receive" the Holy Spirit in the other sacraments, we mean that through them our relationship with the Holy Spirit takes on a new modality. In confirmation our baptismal relationship with the Holy Spirit evolves into participation in the Pentecostal mission of the Church. In the sacrament of penance the Holy Spirit we received in baptism heals and restores what we have broken because of sin. Even in the darkest moment of our relationship with God, God is the merciful father who awaits our return, the shepherd who searches for the lost sheep, the woman who sweeps the entire house in the middle of the night in search of a misplaced coin. When we break our relationship with God, God remains steadfast and sends the Holy Spirit with the mission to lead us back to him.

My answer is that we do not "receive" the Holy Spirit again and again or partially in some sacraments and fully in others. It is our fundamental bonding with the Holy Spirit through baptism that evolves, grows, and develops through the other sacraments that accompany us through life. I hope not to appear banal with this rather commonplace comparison. Nothing can change the reality of us being the children of our biological parents. But as we grow up, that relationship can evolve into friendship, business partnership, and other alliances. However, these changing modalities will always be rooted in the primary bond that unites parents and children. I realize that I am describing a reality that is too deep for words. The word of advice I offer my students is to ponder the mystery in the silence of the heart and discover its presence in the absence of words.

What, then, is liturgy? It is our daily ascent to the heavenly home. The journey begins at baptism from the womb of Mother Church and continues through the different phases of human life until we enter the womb of Mother Earth whence we commence our final passage to eternal life. Christian life is a constant anamnesis and epiclesis that take place in the yearly cycle of liturgical feasts, the weekly or daily Eucharist, the daily cycle of divine praises, and the celebration of the sacraments of life. Our journey through life is like the waves of the sea that roll back gently, at times violently, to the shore. I associate the lyrical first movement of Johannes Brahms' Symphony no. 4 with the waves of the sea that symbolize our return to the heavenly land. Marsili's homily at the funeral of his mother touched me immensely. He began by recalling that at baptism his mother received a lighted candle. She carried it lighted throughout her life, joining the myriad of the baptized marching in procession and lighting up the world. Then, Marsili concluded, one day God blew out her candle, because from then on God was going to be her light.

SACRAMENTALS AND BLESSINGS

To answer more comprehensively Marsili's challenging question "And so, what is liturgy?" it would be useful to touch briefly on the types of liturgical worship. The Constitution on Liturgy makes it clear that liturgical actions are those that the Church officially recognizes as constituents of its public worship. The Constitution devotes chapters and articles to the Mass, the sacraments, sacramentals and blessings, the Liturgy of the Hours, and the feasts in the course of the liturgical year. These are the official list of the types of liturgical worship of which the Church claims ownership. It is not necessary to develop here the theology of the sacraments, but it might be useful to treat at length the subject of sacramentals and blessings in relation to the sacraments and the liturgical year. It is a pastoral fact that for a large number of Catholics sacramentals and blessings occupy a prominent place in the exercise of religion.

In the twelfth century a certain philosopher and theologian by the name of Hugh of St. Victor (+1141) made a distinction between major and minor sacraments. According to this distinction, the major sacraments like the Eucharist and baptism were authored by Christ, while the minor sacraments like almsgiving, fasting and abstinence, and the blessing of persons, places, and things were instituted by the Church. These he called "sacramentals," a Latin diminutive meaning minor sacraments. However, I believe that such a distinction did not immediately enjoy universal acceptance. For the next two hundred years the word "sacrament" continued to be applied loosely to various religious practices of Christians.

In the fifteenth century the Council of Florence (1439–1445) made the dogmatic definition that Christ had instituted the seven sacraments that we know today. Consequently, many of those that were excluded from the list of the seven sacraments came to be known as sacramentals if they are objects, and blessings if they are actions like religious profession, funeral rites, and dedication of the church. Lutherans and some Methodists who believe that Christ explicitly instituted only two sacraments, namely, baptism and Eucharist, call the other five "sacramentals."

The Constitution on the Liturgy (60) uses the traditional definition of sacramentals, which the *Catechism of the Catholic Church* has adopted. The text reads: "The Church has instituted sacramentals. These are sacred signs bearing a kind of resemblance to the sacraments: they signify effects, particularly of a spiritual kind, that are obtained through the Church's intercession. They dispose the people to receive the chief effect of the sacraments and they make holy various occasions in human life."

It is curious to note that in the chapter on the sacraments and sacramentals the Liturgy Constitution does not reaffirm the teaching that Christ instituted the sacraments. I suspect that the framers of the Constitution had presumed that it was a generally known and accepted doctrine. Christ instituted the sacraments, while the Church instituted the sacramentals. The principal distinction between sacraments and sacramentals is their authorship. Both were instituted, which means that both were established as an institution or rule of life for the Christian people. Clearly, spiritual life should not be confined to the sacraments. Sacramentals also have a role to play in the life of the Church, although they do not have the importance and the degree of efficacy that the sacraments have. In my readings of the Acts of the Council, I came across a suggestion that sacramentals should be treated in a separate chapter. The conciliar commission answered that "by their nature sacramentals are intimately joined to the sacraments, and it is the practice to deal with both under the same heading."

The council's definition of sacramentals is taken almost entirely from the 1917 Code of Canon Law. But I point out one notable difference. While the Code refers to sacramentals as objects (*res* in Latin) or actions (*actiones*), the Constitution calls them sacred signs (*signa*), just like the sacraments. Sacraments are, of course, also objects and actions, but from the liturgist's point of view they are not just objects and actions: they are above all liturgical celebrations. The underlying reason for this is obvious. By calling sacramentals sacred signs, the Constitution in effect wants us to regard them not merely as some religious objects or private devotions but also as liturgical rites that are celebrated in the manner of sacraments.

Sacramentals resemble the sacraments, because like the sacraments they are in the category of signs that are performed as rites. I should like to think that the performative aspect of sacramentals accounts for the following provision of the Liturgy Constitution: "Sacramentals are to be reviewed in the light of the primary criterion that the faithful participate intelligently, actively, and easily" (79). If the faithful are expected to participate actively, it is evident that the Constitution regards sacramentals as liturgical celebrations. I realize that the definition of sacramentals as liturgical actions poses a practical difficulty. If sacramentals are performed in the manner of sacraments, are religious objects like holy water, rosary, scapulars, and medals sacramentals? My impression is that the majority of Catholics think of sacramentals primarily, if not exclusively, as religious objects. It will surprise them to know that the Constitution takes no notice of sacramentals as objects. It is evident that the overriding concern of the Constitution is to firmly establish that sacramentals are liturgical celebrations. Consequently, it skips the more popular conception of sacramentals as objects. However, its treatment of sacramentals is indeed rather lopsided in favor of sacramentals as actions, and even these are limited to blessings, consecration of virgins, religious profession, funerals, and burial of infants (SC 79–82).

I am indebted to my mentor, Cipriano Vagaggini, OSB, for much of my knowledge about sacramentals. His classic work *Theological*

Dimensions of the Liturgy (1976) allots a considerable number of pages to the definition and effects of sacramentals. Vagaggini lists three effects of sacramentals: first, actual grace and by means of it the recovery or increase of sanctifying grace; second, the prevention of diabolical influence on persons and things; and third, temporal graces for the spiritual good of the person. Any theologian would naturally ask: Do not the sacraments produce similar effects? What use do we have of sacramentals if they produce the same effects as the sacraments? Think, for example, of the sacrament of penance, which brings about primarily the recovery of sanctifying grace. For that matter, think of all the sacraments that increase and strengthen sanctifying grace as they ward off diabolical power. Perhaps this is the question the *Catechism of the Catholic Church* has in mind when it says that "sacramentals do not confer the grace of the Holy Spirit in the way that the sacraments do." Sacramentals, like the sacraments, confer also the grace of the Holy Spirit. The manner in which grace is conferred is what distinguishes sacraments from sacramentals. Basically the question is not what is conferred but how it is conferred.

It is official teaching that sacraments produce their effects *ex opere operato*, which is rather difficult to translate but not as difficult to explain, if we stick to St. Thomas Aquinas. In this matter I suggest that we do. Sacraments are actions of Christ and hence do not depend on the personal merit of the minister. In other words, if the rite is validly performed grace is conferred, provided the recipient does not put an obstacle to it by lack of faith and proper disposition. Sacramentals, on the other hand, produce their effects through the intercessory prayer of the Church or, in the thinking of St. Thomas Aquinas, *ex opere operantis Ecclesiae*. Thus when sacramentals are performed in the manner prescribed by the liturgical norms, they are actions of the Church. They embody the prayer of the Church for the beneficiaries of the sacramentals. But how effective is the prayer of the Church? Vagaggini offers a reassuring answer, which I believe is also the only valid answer. Because the Church is united with Christ, God answers its prayer as if it were the prayer of Christ. Ultimately, the efficacy of the Church's prayer rests on Christ himself. These are Vagaggini's words, which strike me as rather timid, for that was the humble, unassuming theologian he was: in the celebration of sacramentals "Christ as head of his members assumes responsibility before God, so to speak, for the performance of the prayer and the rite which he by special mandate has given power to the hierarchy to institute and to perform in his name as head of the Church."

Sacramentals bestow the person of the Holy Spirit who is referred to as the grace of our Lord Jesus Christ. Allow me to theologize. Like the sacraments, sacramentals establish and strengthen our relationship with the Holy Spirit. Baptism confers on us the Holy Spirit of adoption whereby we become children of God. The Eucharist fills our hearts with the Holy Spirit who transforms us into the Eucharist we eat and drink. Similarly, the sacramentals in their own way impart to us the person of the Holy Spirit that activates in us the effects proper to them. A chief effect of sacramentals is to foster in the faithful a genuine disposition to celebrate the sacraments worthily. Sacramentals lead to the sacraments and, I should add, flow from the sacraments. A couple of examples will help to clarify the matter. Baptism and Eucharist are the nucleus of the other sacraments. This explains why, except for the sacrament of penance, the other sacraments may fittingly be celebrated within Mass. Similarly, the sacraments are the nucleus of the sacramentals. Religious profession, for example, keeps close pace with the baptismal rite. On the other hand, the funeral rite alludes to baptism and the Eucharist. Sacred objects (the crucifix, holy water, incense, candles) and religious articles (rosaries, scapulars, and medals) remind us of the sacraments such as initiation and penance and of the feasts of saints in the liturgical year.

At the start of the postconciliar reform a monastery injudiciously introduced a liturgical novelty in the funeral Mass of a monk. The abbot and concelebrants, including me, wore red vestments. The aim, an intriguing display of liturgical scholarship, was to show the connection between the funeral rite and Good Friday and Pentecost, when red vestments are used. During Mass the organ boomed with joyful music and the church bells were festively rung to signify the resurrection. There was no place for sorrow. Smiles were publicly exchanged in the sanctuary. The offended family of the dead monk reprimanded the abbot for the humiliation and lack of good sense.

Sacramentals are woven into various occasions in human life that are not directly covered by the sacraments. This is one reason why the Church instituted sacramentals. The Constitution on Liturgy explains that "for well-disposed members of the faithful, the effect of the liturgy of the sacraments and sacramentals is that almost every event in their lives is made holy by divine grace that flows from the paschal mystery of Christ" (61). In traditional theology the seven sacraments correspond to the turning points in the life of a Christian, namely, rebirth, growth, community meal, love and union, servant leadership, repentance and forgiveness, and sickness. Christian life, however, is not made up only of turning points. We are all deeply aware of how complex Christian life is and that it is a mosaic of daily struggles, temptations, disappointments, successes, hopes, and joys. Sacramentals are meant to accompany the faithful in such circumstances, so that they may experience the presence of Christ and the Church in their daily lives. The funeral rite is not a sacrament, but can we dispense with burying our dead in the Christian way? Religious profession, unlike holy orders, is not a sacrament, but it is an eloquent symbol of intimate discipleship with the Lord. The blessings of homes and vehicles are not sacraments, but who among the ordinary faithful would like to live in a house that has not been blessed or drive a car that has not been washed with holy water, never mind what theology they have about such blessings?

The innumerable blessings that existed in the Middle Ages, many of which exist even today, are a remarkable demonstration of how the faithful value sacramentals. The 1984 *Book of Blessings* contains rites for the blessing of families, children, elderly people, new homes, libraries, offices, shops, gymnasium, animals, and fields. Its tenth-century predecessor, the Roman-Germanic Pontifical, has a wider range of blessings that covers practically anything that people use daily, like bathing soap, bread, cheese, milk, honey, and meat of animals. Alas, it also contains the blessing of instruments of ordeal that were used to determine the guilt or innocence of accused persons. The grotesque and cruel practice consisted of forcing the accused to walk on a blazing gridiron or throwing the person in a deep well. Emerging unharmed would be the proof of innocence.

Vagaggini distinguishes two types of sacramentals, namely, things and actions. He writes: "The sacramentals that are things are those that remain even after the action has taken place, such as holy water, blessed candles, blessed olive or palm branches, the ashes of Ash Wednesday." After the procession on Palm Sunday the palm branches are affixed on the doors of homes. Reasons vary, and some may even verge on superstition, but I reckon that the basic reason is the belief that the palms are sacred objects. These palms are burned to ashes to become Ash Wednesday sacramental. The triumph of Palm Sunday crumbles to the ashes of humiliation. The other type of sacramentals is constituted by actions. Such are the liturgical rites mentioned in the Constitution on Liturgy (arts. 79–82): religious profession, consecration of virgins, funeral rites, and burial of infants. After the council a good number of liturgical books for the celebration of sacramentals were published. Among them are the blessing of abbots and abbesses; the institution of lectors and acolytes; the blessing of holy oils, sacred vessels, vestments, and church bells; and the rite of crowning the image of the Blessed Virgin Mary.

A sacramental that is familiar and simple to perform is the sign of the cross. While the cross with the image of the crucified Lord is the basic Christian symbol that should be held in high honor, the sign of the cross is an action that is believed to possess divine power because of its composition, namely, belief in the Holy Trinity and veneration of the cross of Jesus Christ. The story is told that when rebellious monks placed poison in the wine cup of St. Benedict, he made the sign of the cross on it, and behold the cup was shattered to pieces! Bert Ghezzi's book *The Sign of the Cross* (2006) is a compelling work on the spiritual value of this sacramental. Filipino Catholics are wont to make the sign of the cross several times during the day: when they leave home, ride a public vehicle (I could not agree more to this particular practice), pass by a church or cemetery, encounter strange occurrences, see a lightning bolt, feel the earth quake, bathe in a pool, river, or sea, and step into the basketball court or boxing ring. Ghezzi would surely approve of such Filipino Catholic ritual. The author quotes the third-century writer Tertullian who encouraged making the sign of the cross at every occasion: "In all our travels and movements, in all our coming in and going out, in putting on our shoes, at the bath, at the table, in lighting our candles, in lying down, in sitting down, whatever employment occupies us, we mark our foreheads with the sign of the cross."

The *Catechism of the Catholic Church* includes in the list of sacramentals the rite of exorcism whereby "the Church asks publicly and authoritatively in the name of Jesus Christ that a person or object be protected against the power of the Evil One and withdrawn from his dominion" (1673). It is a liturgical rite that some consider old-fashioned and others, bizarre. At any rate, it is such a sensitive theological issue that the *Catechism* instructs that "before an exorcism is performed, it is important to ascertain that one is dealing with the presence of the Evil One, and not an illness." Ascertaining diabolical possession must be a knotty business, but I presume that the professional exorcist has all the instruments for it. The third-century book *Apostolic Tradition* directs the bishop to lay his hands on the catechumens to find out if they were under the spell of Satan.

The popular belief in diabolical inhabitation had profound influence on certain rites, such as the blessing of homes, food, groves and fields, and instruments of work. The medieval rite of house blessing, for instance, was not so much an act of praise and thanksgiving for God's gift of a home as a prayer to free it from the power of the Evil One. The sign of the cross, holy water, and blessed salt were believed to drive the devil away from such places and objects.

A word of caution might be useful at this juncture. People tend to forget that evil with its manifold manifestation often springs from within us, from our fallen nature. Baptismal exorcism prays for fallen nature's radical healing. There may be instances when an external force known as the Evil One takes possession of a person. However, the growing preoccupation about such occurrences rather than the awareness of the saving presence among us of the Spirit of adoption is bound to encourage superstition and a bleak attitude toward the world redeemed by Christ and inhabited by the Holy Spirit. Our battle against evil will go on because of our fallen nature that has been redeemed and is still in need of redemption. The "already" and the "not yet" are the perennial realities of Christian life.

Among the sacramentals that are actions the *Catechism of the Catholic Church* attaches special importance to blessings. It says: "Among sacramentals, blessings (of persons, meals, objects, and places) come first. Every blessing praises God and prays for his gifts. In Christ, Christians are blessed by God the Father with every spiritual blessing." Blessings are given to people, devotional objects, instruments of work, and places. The *Book of Blessings*, published by the Congregation for Divine Worship in 1984, has as many as forty-eight headings of such blessings. I limit my enumeration to the more significant ones. The blessing of persons includes the family, spouses on the anniversary of their marriage, children before baptism, engaged couples before marriage, women before and after childbirth, homebound elderly persons, the sick, and travelers. Places include new homes, offices, markets or malls, sports and civic centers, roads, bridges, ports, airplanes, ships, and the fields in time of planting and harvesting. Instruments of human development, such as aqueducts and energy plants as well as tools and larger implements people use in their work, are also blessed. The suitable time for blessing them is obviously on the memorial of St. Joseph the Worker. Animals for work or as pets are blessed on the feast of saints known for animal advocacy, like Francis of Assisi. Religious objects, such as holy water, images of saints, medals, scapulars, and rosaries, are likewise blessed.

Eminent among the blessings is the grace before and after meals. It is a Jewish religious ritual and is the ancestor of the Eucharistic Prayer. Jesus said grace at the Last Supper: "He took bread and gave you thanks and praise." The elaborate form of that prayer has come down to us as the Eucharistic Prayer. The grace we recite before meals is akin to the Eucharistic Prayer recited over the bread and the wine. In both prayers we praise and thank God for the gift of food and drink. The consecrated bread and wine on the altar nourish the life of the Christian community, while the food on the table unites the family and those that partake of it with gratitude and generosity. Contrary to medieval belief, the grace before meals does not expel evil power from the food and drink. The traditional and simple formula "Bless us, O Lord, and these your gifts" accompanied by the sign of the cross petitions God to bless us and our food. According to the *Catechism of the Catholic Church* and the *Book of Blessings*, the grace before meals is a prayer of praise and thanksgiving to God for the gift of food. I propose that every now and then we use a formula like this one: "We bless you, O Lord, for these your gifts, which we are about to receive from your bounty, through Christ Our Lord."

The Constitution on Liturgy affirms: "The liturgy means that there is hardly any proper use of material things that cannot be directed toward human sanctification and the praise of God" (61). Considering the long list of people and things that may be blessed, one could begin to think that there is nothing that cannot be blessed. Priests bless graduation hoods, diplomas and medals, pencils for the board examination, and sports trophies. But priests might find themselves in entangling and annoying situations where they are asked to bless houses of ill repute or objects that are used for superstitious and animistic rituals, like the blood of a chicken to be poured on the foundation of a new building. In such and similar instances priests will have to discern carefully and act with necessary prudence and pastoral care. I should mention that the *Book of Blessings* explicitly excludes the blessing of civic monuments and instruments of war. I suspect that civic monuments are not blessed because they depict national heroes and war scenes that are often purely political in inspiration. Regarding instruments of war, their exclusion is based on the Church's repudiation of armed violence. Soldiers are blessed as they set out for war; but, ironically, the Church expects their guns to keep the silence of the lambs. This liturgical norm can be a source of disaffection among Catholic soldiers because their instrument of combat is unblessed. It also embarrasses military chaplains whose pastoral ministry includes not only the spiritual welfare of combatants but also their safety during military encounters.

The rite of blessing can have a lasting effect on some persons, places, and objects. Virgins are consecrated for life; religious men and women are perpetually consecrated to the Lord; churches, shrines, and altars are reserved for sacred actions; and crucifixes, medals, and holy water retain their character as sacramentals after they are blessed. Such is the power of liturgical blessings. But let me add an important note: not all objects blessed become sacramentals. The car is not a sacramental, however abundantly doused with holy water. The most appetizing food on the table does not acquire the name "sacramental" after it has been blessed. However, and this is a significant "however," the blessing of people, places, and things creates a Christian environment. Everything that has received blessing becomes a constant reminder that Christ and the Church accompany us in our journey through life. We begin to view the things of this earth in the light of our heavenly goal. I should say that blessings transform the entire universe into a sacrament, that is to say, into an effective sign of God's presence among his people. I repeat the lapidary words of the Constitution on Liturgy: "The liturgy means that there is hardly any proper use of material things that cannot be directed toward human sanctification and the praise of God" (61).

It is quite easy for priests to please people and make them grateful. Many of the faithful do not expect more than a sign of the cross and a dousing of holy water on the object to be blessed. Some may even feel cheated if a mere trickle of water touches their home or vehicle. Because of the importance given to holy water, the proclamation of the word of God and the prayer of blessing are often relegated to a secondary role. The truth of the matter is that the liturgy of blessings consists essentially of the scriptural reading and the prayer of praise. It is the word of God that imparts divine power on the Church's act of blessing. There is no way we can circumvent the proclamation of the word of God. The prayer, on the other hand, praises God for his gifts and fatherly providence and implores God's constant help and protection. The prayer is often, though not necessarily, followed by the sign of the cross and sprinkling of holy water. I am aware that this is bad news to priests who are ambushed by the faithful after Mass with requests to bless religious objects, and the priests have to accommodate them by silently making the sign of the cross on the objects and sprinkling them with holy water.

The *Book of Blessings* even carries a solemn rite of blessing when there is a group of people gathered for the occasion like the blessing of a new house. The full liturgical rite consists of an introduction, reading from Scripture, homily, litany or intercessions, formula of blessing, and the application of liturgical signs like holy water and incense. For smaller objects like rosaries and medals, the rite is simpler: reading from Scripture and formula of blessing. For such type of blessing the reading from Scripture may be shortened, but not omitted. The formula of blessing, which is essential to the rite, must be said. The sign of the cross and sprinkling of holy water need not be performed, but what priest in his right mind would omit them?

Having said all this, I need to caution that not every blessing has to be a liturgical blessing. The simple sign of the cross on a person or object without the complement of God's word and prayer of praise is surely not a liturgical blessing, but I would not deny that it is a blessing. The Constitution on Liturgy reminds us that "the liturgy does not exhaust the entire activity of the Church" (9) and that "the spiritual life is not limited solely to participation in the liturgy." Christians are urged "to pray without ceasing."

To conclude, allow me to compare the sacraments and the sacramentals and blessings to a painting. The grand design that gives us the total picture is the sacraments. But the painting is also made up of hundreds of details that give color and texture to the picture. These are the sacramentals and blessings. The Eucharist and baptism are essential to the life of every individual Christian and of the Church as a whole. The other sacraments have their assigned roles in the life, ministry, and personal calling of individuals. They accompany the faithful in the major turning points and critical moments of life as they journey toward the heavenly home.

COMPONENTS OF LITURGICAL WORSHIP

To complete the answer to Marsili's question "And so, what is liturgy?" let me turn to the Constitution on the Liturgy that defines, describes, and designates the meaning and components of liturgical worship. Anamnesis and epiclesis are actions that are carried out using sacramental objects like water, bread, wine, and oil, while reciting fixed sacramental formulas and performing gestures like hand-laying. Furthermore, anamnesis and epiclesis are carried out in the framework of the council's teaching about the true nature of liturgical worship.

Word and Sacrament

Among the ritual components of the liturgy of sacraments and sacramentals the binomial "word and sacrament" stands prominently. It is the basis for the plan of liturgical celebrations, consisting of the liturgy of the word and the liturgy of the sacrament. In the case of the Mass, the General Instruction of the Roman Missal states that it "is made up as it were of two parts: the liturgy of the word and the liturgy of the Eucharist. These two parts are closely interconnected that they form but one single act of worship. For in the Mass the table both of God's word and of Christ's body is laid, from which the faithful may be instructed and refreshed" (28). In the case of the sacraments and sacramentals the standard plan of the celebration includes the word of God. Ideally there should be a liturgy of the word, consisting of reading from Scripture, homily, and intercessions. We should be able to speak of a liturgy of the word and a liturgy of the sacrament or sacramentals.

The Constitution on Liturgy articulates the necessity of the word of God in liturgical worship when it affirms that "before people can come to the liturgy they must be called to faith and conversion" (9), and the sacraments "not only presuppose faith, but by words and objects they also nourish, strengthen, and express it; that is why they are called sacraments of faith" (59). But as we know, faith and conversion are brought about by hearing the word of God. Hence the purpose of the liturgy of the word is to create and nourish the proper disposition of faith that is required by the sacrament. In addition to this the Constitution says that "it is from Scripture that the readings are given and explained in the homily and that psalms are sung; the prayers, collects, and liturgical songs are scriptural in their inspiration; it is from the Scriptures that actions and signs derive their meaning" (24). In its turn the liturgy of the sacraments and sacramentals confers on the word of God a ritual, visible form.

Thanks to the liturgical reform, we easily distinguish the two components of word and sacrament in most of today's liturgical celebrations. Word and sacrament are distinct parts but they form one act of liturgical worship. There should be no theological and liturgical disjunction of these two components any more than there should be no dichotomy between the priest's ministry of preaching and sacramental administration. After the council and as an upshot of liberation theology, thinking evolved that priests were ordained primarily for the ministry of preaching. There arose a disparaging distinction between the preaching priests that joined cause-oriented rallies and the sacramental priests that confined their ministry to the sanctuary and the confessional. The truth, of course, is that preaching culminates in sacramental administration. Christ first preached and afterward summed up his messianic ministry by celebrating his paschal mystery. The Synod of Bishops in 1971 made the timely reminder that the integral nature of priestly ministry requires the priest to preach the word and celebrate the sacraments: "a separation between the two would divide the heart of the Church to the point of imperiling the faith."

For the faithful the liturgical shape of word and sacrament expresses the basic truth that those who have listened to the preaching of the word and pondered it in their hearts should hasten to the celebration of the sacrament. On the day of Pentecost those who heard the word "were cut to the heart and said to Peter and to the other apostles, 'Brothers, what should we do?' Peter said to them, 'Repent, and be baptized every one of you in the name of Jesus Christ . . .'" (Acts 2:37-38). What takes place in the liturgy when the word of God is proclaimed first and the sacrament is celebrated afterward fittingly symbolizes the process of encounter between God and his people.

The Constitution on the Liturgy teaches that "in the liturgy God speaks to his people and Christ still proclaims his gospel" (33) and that Christ "is present in his word, since it is he himself who speaks when the holy Scriptures are read in the Church" (7). Let us take note of the phrases "God speaks," "Christ proclaims," "Christ is present in his word," and Christ "himself speaks." These are forceful words. Theologians tell us what they mean: when sacred Scriptures are read to the assembly gathered in worship, the proclaimed word becomes a sacrament of Christ. Several years ago the English translation of *Verbum Domini* was rightly changed from "This is the word of the Lord" to "The word of the Lord." Some lectors with a penchant for drama raised the Lectionary or, alas, the Book of Gospels as they intoned, "This is the word of the Lord," giving the impression that the book is the word of God. Good theology tells us that the sacrament of God's word is not the book but the action of proclaiming and listening. The reading of Scripture in the liturgy is a trustworthy sign that Christ is present and that he indeed speaks to the assembly. I would go so far as to say that he is as present in the word as he is in the consecrated host, as present in the proclamation of the word as he was when he preached to the people in the synagogues and the hillsides of Galilee.

The great theologian, Pope Paul VI, left no room for doubting the real presence of Christ in the reading of Scriptures. In the encyclical letter *Mysterium fidei* he expounded the doctrine that the Eucharistic or real presence should not lead us to think that the other presences of Christ in the liturgy are not real. The Constitution on Liturgy names several instances when Christ is present in liturgical worship: in the Eucharistic species, in the person of his minister, in the sacraments, in the proclamation of God's word, and in the assembly gathered for worship (7). Pope Paul VI affirmed all these to be real presences. However, in the Eucharist Christ's presence is par excellence. I should add that while the presence of Christ in the word is transitory, that is, while it is read, the Eucharistic presence is permanent. This should not be taken to mean that the presence of Christ in his word is less real because it does not enjoy the permanence of the Eucharist.

But the Scriptures are read not only as integral components of the liturgy but also as a form of encounter with Christ outside liturgical worship. The effect of one is not far from the other. For Christ speaks to us in the liturgy and outside the liturgy. It is told in the life of St. Augustine, that at the critical moment of decision between God and the sinful life Augustine was leading, he chanced upon the book of Sacred Scriptures. An inner voice urged him: *Tolle et lege* (Take and read). This event marked the turning point of his life. Through the words of Scripture Christ came to him and spoke to his heart. From that day on Augustine became another person.

Something that happened in the early 1970s, when I was chaplain of college students in our Benedictine school in Manila, remains deeply etched in my memory. One afternoon, unlike other afternoons, I found myself alone in the chaplain's office, which was frequented by students, I think because it was air-conditioned. Not knowing how to pass my unusual solitude, I reached for the Bible, opened it, and began to read John 14. As I read on, a student rushed in, and seeing the open Bible, said in what I detected was a mocking tone: "You're reading that book again. Close it, we need to talk." Annoyed by such impudence, I continued to read, pretending not to mind him. He insisted: "I said, close that book; I'm in serious trouble." More annoyed, I started to read aloud, not without anger in my voice: "Peace I leave with you; my peace I give to you. . . . Do not let your hearts be troubled, and do not let them be afraid." He sat down helplessly, and after awhile left without a word. My feeling as chaplain turned from anger to guilt: the young man needed to talk to me, and all I did was read the Bible to him, in anger. The next day he returned, sat down, and said: "Please, Father, please read those words again." I am quite certain that through the words I read from the Sacred Scripture, Christ spoke to the young man, in spite of him and in spite of me. His problem was still there, but the comforting word of Christ allowed him to view it in another light. After so many years the words of the young man still ring in my ears: "Father, please read those words again."

Other Components

Several other things may be cited for a fuller definition of the liturgy. Some of them will be treated at length in the other chapters of this book. Because of its complexity the study of the liturgy, especially certain celebrations like the Easter Vigil, can truly be daunting. My mentors used to compare the study of liturgy to entering a forest. They warned me not to stop at every tree but to have a picture of the entire forest. Having an eye for details is useful but not necessary. The problem that often arises is deciding which details are of primary importance and which ones can be safely placed aside for future leisurely investigation.

The trees I would stop at are those Bugnini lists in his posthumous work *The Reform of the Liturgy, 1948–1975*. He calls them the fundamental principles of the liturgical reform. The first is articulated by the Constitution on Liturgy 10, which is strongly influenced by *Mediator Dei*: the liturgy is *culmen et fons*. It is "the summit toward which the activity of the Church is directed; at the same time it is the fount from which all the Church's power flows."

The second is the principle of conciliar reform, which the Constitution repeats time and again as a refrain. The full, conscious, and active participation of all God's people in the liturgy is the principal aim of the reform and promotion of the liturgy. Active participation is the right and duty of the faithful "by reason of their baptism." The Constitution on the Liturgy 79 declares that intelligent, active, and easy participation by the faithful is the "primary criterion" to be observed when revising the rites of sacramentals.

The third principle is the timely reminder of the Constitution that "liturgical services are not private functions, but are celebrations belonging to the Church." They belong to the whole Body of Christ, although "they concern the individual members in different ways, according to their different orders, offices, and actual participation" (26).

The fourth is the principle of "substantial unity" of the Roman rite, which is mentioned by the Constitution in one of the paragraphs concerning inculturation (38). I take it that the word "substantial" is telling us that liturgical unity in the Roman Church should not be construed as absolute, rigid uniformity. The one Roman Rite can exist in different shapes and cultural forms, provided of course that such are pertinent and pastorally beneficial to the faithful. In short, there is a need to inculturate the liturgy or at least prepare liturgical rites that are particular to the local church. The Constitution, in fact, instructs the conferences of bishops to prepare without delay their particular rituals based on the typical edition of liturgical books: "these rituals are to be adapted, even in regard to the language employed, to the needs of the different regions" (63).

This brings us to the fifth component of the liturgical reform. The Constitution desires that the reform of the liturgy be carried out with all the seriousness that befits the tremendous mystery it contains. Careful theological, historical, and pastoral investigation should always be made into each part of the liturgy to be revised, in order "that sound tradition may be retained and yet the way remain open to legitimate progress" (23).

The complete definition of the liturgy includes music, art, and furnishings, for these are integral parts of the liturgical celebration. Although the liturgy can, strictly speaking, be celebrated without music, it is in the interest of active participation and the solemn form of divine worship to sing parts of the liturgy. Although the liturgy can make use of any decent and suitable space, it is fitting to celebrate it in the ambient of beauty, nobility, and dignity. I will have occasion to discuss this more fully in the other chapters of this work.

Chapter Three

To the Father, Through the Son, in the Spirit

The first time I met Abbot Ambrose Verheul I complimented him on his book *Introduction to the Liturgy*, the outline of which I followed for my course. He was abashed but he managed to declare detachedly, almost dismissively, "It is a good book." We met a couple of times in his Abbey of Mont-César, the monastery of Lambert Beauduin, to discuss a possible publications tie-up between his abbey and the Pontifical Liturgical Institute. Sadly, the project did not materialize. And so in 1983 Adrien Nocent and I started the Institute's periodical *Ecclesia Orans*. It was a dauntless act for an institute that needed to publish or else perish in the estimation of the liturgical academe.

The plan of this chapter follows closely the book of Verheul, but I have added to the content the result of my years of entanglement with the awe-inspiring mystery of the Blessed Trinity that is at work in Christian worship.

LITURGY IS ENCOUNTER WITH GOD

"And so, what is liturgy?" Verheul defines it as encounter between God and the worshiping assembly. The Latin etymology of "encounter" (*in* and *contra*) is not sympathetic to the use of this word in the liturgy, or theology, for that matter. Nor so are the different meanings English dictionaries give to it: a meeting between hostile factions; a sudden, often violent, clash such as a military encounter; an unexpected or chance face-to-face meeting; and a coming to the vicinity by a celestial being, as in the title of the film *Close Encounters of the Third Kind*. But after Edward Schillebeeckx's book was translated into English in 1971 under the title *Christ, the Sacrament of the Encounter with God*, hostility, violence, or chance meeting gave way to a new lexical use that stressed harmony, mutual respect, and love. Today there is a popular seminar program for married couples called Marriage Encounter.

The phrase "encounter with God" implies a number of things. Encounter is the personal act of the individual worshipers that together constitute the liturgical assembly. The assembly is not a mantle under which individuals can settle quietly with one's heart not being in the liturgical action that is taking place. The quality of community worship cannot be gauged merely on the surface of active participation. It suffers when the individual persons are not interiorly involved, when their hearts do not burn within them as they listen to the word of God, and when they do not perceive the presence of Christ in the breaking of the bread. In reality only God knows the true quality of liturgical worship, because God alone can read the heart and mind of each person. The tools for active participation are nothing more than external aids to bring to realization the individual person's encounter with God. After we have performed the liturgy to the best of our ability, we can only hope that it deserved full marks for "achieving human sanctification and God's glorification, the end to which all the Church's other activities are directed" (SC 10).

Our encounter with God in the liturgy is personal also inasmuch as we encounter the persons of the Holy Trinity. When Christians pray, they do not address a Supreme Being or Divine Entity: they pray to God who revealed himself as a Trinity of Persons. That is why liturgical worship is addressed to the three Divine Persons. The invocation "God" may give the wrong impression that we are calling upon some unnamed divine being, but in the liturgy "God" is the Father of Our Lord Jesus Christ. We address our worship to the Father, through Jesus Christ, in the unity of the Holy Spirit. The ancient doxological formula phrases this succinctly: *Ad Patrem, per Filium, in Spiritu Sancto*. The formula expresses the final phase of salvation history, which is the liturgy. It describes what takes place during liturgical worship: we ascend to God through the mediation of Christ and by the power of the Holy Spirit. The liturgy reverses the descending action of God that saw him send his Son and the Holy Spirit upon humankind. The formula embodies the Church's understanding of revelation as a series of divine missions.

Our inkling of faith about the Holy Trinity springs from the pages of the New Testament: the Father sent the Son into the world to redeem it, and after the Son had accomplished his mission the Father sent through the glorified Son the Person of the Holy Spirit. The liturgy retraces this path of salvation history as it lifts us up to the Father through Christ in the communion of the Holy Spirit. Thus the formula depicts the divine working *ad extra*, outside the mystery of the Trinity's inner life that is the object of theological speculation. According to it, the Father eternally generates and so loves the Son that from their love there proceeds the person of the Holy Spirit. The eternal generation of the Son and the eternal procession of the Holy Spirit explain why they are equal in power and majesty. I should go no further. What I wish to point out is that such ennobling speculation is actually based on the external working of the three Persons. Generation and procession are theological constructs built on the *ad extra* missions of the Son and the Holy Spirit.

The original Trinitarian doxology that we still use at the conclusion of the Eucharistic Prayer is "Glory to the Father, through the Son, in the Holy Spirit." It is the ascending line that emerges from salvation history's descending line. Liturgy historian Josef Jungmann explains in his work *The Place of Christ in Liturgical Prayer* why the words of this doxology were modified to what we commonly use today: "Glory to the Father, and to the Son, and to the Holy Spirit." He blames the adherents of the Arian heresy that capitalized on the phrase "through the Son" to confirm its doctrine that as mediator the Son was indeed inferior to the Father. To safeguard the integrity of orthodox belief the sagacious solution was to declare the equality of the three Persons by the use of "and" before the Son and the Holy Spirit. Jungmann examined over one thousand collects in the Roman sacramentaries. He found sixty-four addressed to Christ. He noted that seventeen of these were originally addressed to God (the Father) but were later made to refer to Christ simply by changing the conclusion "through Christ" to "you live and reign with God the Father."

The unfortunate consequence of the Arian controversy is that the Trinitarian doxology no longer evokes salvation history and its continuing realization in the liturgy. The current formulation has stripped liturgical worship of the sense of relationship with the three Divine Persons. It predicates equal glory to them, but as a liturgical prayer it does not make me feel enfolded by the Holy Spirit and clutched by Christ the Mediator as the sacred rite lifts me up to the bosom of the Father. The present doxology is beyond doubt theologically accurate, but is it liturgically befitting? I do not, of course, even suggest that we revert to the ancient doxology. I console myself with the thought that at least the doxology of the Eucharistic Prayer escaped revision and thus retains the original formula.

GLORY TO THE FATHER

Who is the Father? This was the topic a group of religious superiors addressed many years ago at a roundtable discussion that I facilitated.

I assumed that the topic was chosen because of what the figure of the Father meant to superiors. The first to speak was a theologian who read an excellent paper on the Person of God the Father. The next was a superior who spoke with simplicity and without theological pretensions about his personal experiences involving the Father. It was a prayerful and moving meditation. To the astonishment of all, the theologian who had spoken earlier disclosed between sobs that he had written and preached many times about the Father but never felt him in his life. The discussion left a profound mark on my liturgical consciousness. At least three times a day at Mass and the liturgy of Lauds and Vespers we call God by name as Jesus taught us to do. The prayers, with relatively few exceptions, are addressed to the Father. But how many of us experience the person of the Father as Jesus did at least analogously?

The Bible has different names for God. In the Old Testament God is generally called *El*, which simply means God. In order to distinguish God from pagan gods and idols, the Hebrew people called God *Elohim*, the "God of gods" or the "Supreme God." When God revealed himself to Abraham, he named himself *El-Shaddai*, the "Almighty God." Finally, when God spoke to Moses, he revealed his ineffable secret name, which is *Yahweh*, meaning "I am Who I am." The Hebrew people consider this name so sacred that although they write it, they do not dare to utter it but read it as *Adonai*, or Lord.

In the New Testament God is known by the name that Jesus often used when he spoke to God or about God: Abba, Father. This name expresses intimacy between God and Jesus who is believed to be the Son God sent into the world. It thus confirms the doctrine that God begot a Son in eternity whom he sent into the world. The name of God as Father is the mode of expression that Jesus chose in order to explain in human language that God begot him before all ages. It is the culmination of the many revelations in the Old Testament about who God is. Jesus revealed that God is Father using the human imagery of parenthood. But he declared that "no one knows the Son except the Father, and no one knows the Father except the Son and anyone to whom the Son chooses to reveal him" (Matt 11: 27). Jesus has chosen to reveal God to us in a language we can understand, but I believe we should not be so presumptuous as to imagine that our intellects have captured the being of God. At the end of the day we should admit that our knowledge of God as Father is not so much a matter of the intellect as a perception of the heart when it addresses God in prayer and experiences his parental care.

Through the use of parables Jesus unveiled the true nature of the Father. They are Jesus' answer to the question, "Who is the Father?" The parable of the prodigal son is rightly a parable of the compassionate Father (Luke 15:11-24). Jesus used moving words to describe the encounter between the welcoming father and his returning son: "But while he was still far off, his father saw him and was filled with compassion; he ran and put his arms around him and kissed him" (Luke 15:20). Jesus told this story to describe what goes on in the heart of God when wayward children return to him. God ignores and forgets the evil they have committed. The parable seems to tell us that God has no memory of our sins, that God does not harbor grudges, and that God understands, where we fail to understand, our weaknesses. The story reminds us of two other parables. The first is about the shepherd who leaves the ninety-nine sheep to go after the one that is lost. "When he has found it, he lays it on his shoulders and rejoices" (Luke 15:5). The other is about a woman who, having lost a silver coin, lights a lamp and sweeps the entire house and seeks diligently until she finds it (Luke 15:8). In the first of these two parables what strikes me is the image of God who leaves the ninety-nine for the sake of one. What shepherd would risk so much? In the second parable what astonishes me is the impatience of God who would not wait until morning to search for what was lost.

The model of the Christian's encounter with the Father is Jesus himself, whose entire being was oriented to the Father. He frequently made the revelation that he came from the Father and would return to him after completing his mission on earth (John 14:12; John 16:10, 28). The Fourth Gospel describes the death of Jesus using the Passover typology: "Now before the festival of the Passover, Jesus knew that his hour had come to depart from this world to the Father" (John 13:1). Jesus' death is the antitype of the exodus of the Israelites from Egypt to the Promised Land through the sea. Christ crossed the water of death as he made his exodus, or passage, from this world to the Father. Water is a polyvalent symbol of life and death. But if the Jewish Passover was the type of Jesus' return to the Father, this in turn is the type of the Christian's passage from the earthly city to the City of God. Baptism is the antitype of Christ's death and resurrection, of his return to the Father. Inspired by Romans 6:3-5, St. Ambrose explains to his neophytes: "In this faith you died to the world, you arose to God, and as if buried in that element of the world [water], dead to sin you were revived to eternal life" (De Mysteriis 4:21).

The best essay I have read about God the Father is in the *Catechism of the Catholic Church* (239). When we speak of God as Father, the *Catechism* wants us to bear three things in mind. First, "by calling God 'Father,' the language of faith indicates two main things: that God is the first origin of everything and transcendent authority; and that he is at the same time goodness and loving care for all his children." Second, "God's parental tenderness can also be expressed by the image of motherhood (Is 66: 13), which emphasizes God's immanence, the intimacy between Creator and creature." Do we miss the mark when we predicate to God the human qualities of a perfect mother? Do we overshoot the mark when we address God in liturgical prayer as "Father and Mother"? Rembrandt's famous painting of the parable of the prodigal son portrays the face of a man whose hands are those of a woman. Third, "the language of faith draws on the human experience of parents, who are in a way the first representatives of God for man. But this experience also tells us that human parents are fallible and can disfigure the face of fatherhood and motherhood. We ought therefore to recall that God transcends the human distinction between the sexes. He is neither man nor woman: he is God. He also transcends human fatherhood and motherhood, although he is their origin and standard: no one is father as God is Father." That Jesus called God his "Father" does not mean that God is a male person. That we employ masculine vocabulary when we speak about God does not mean that God is a man. The *Catechism* also cautions us that when we call God "Father," we should not too easily compare him to human parents. Some of them could be abusive and irresponsible toward their offspring. Indeed, no one is father as God is Father, and no one is mother as God is Mother.

The tradition of the Roman liturgy requires that the so-called presidential prayers be addressed to the Father following the example of Christ's prayer. Latin Africa, which closely followed the liturgy of Rome, made a ruling on this point in the Synod of Hippo in 393: "When we stand at the altar, let our prayers be always addressed to the Father." In the Roman liturgy the Eucharistic Prayers and most of the collects, prayers over the gifts, and prayers after communion are directed to the Father. Since the general intercessions are the prayer of the assembly as priestly people, Roman tradition directs them to the Father, as Christ the High Priest himself would. But some models of these intercessions in the Roman Missal are addressed to Christ. Other textual elements of the liturgy like hymns and litanies such as *Kyrie eleison* can have other addressees, including the angels and the saints.

When Pope John Paul II rallied the Christian world to prepare for the new millennium, he declared a year in which the faithful were to be stirred up to a more profound awareness of the person and work of God the Father. My perception is that the project produced positive results inasmuch as the liturgical assemblies at which I presided sang the Lord's Prayer with greater reverence and devotion. Prayers before meetings were increasingly addressed to the Father, sometimes in the style of the collects for Mass. However, the group that had been promoting the feast of God the Father seized the occasion. Treading on the heels of the awakened devotion, the group became tiresome with its demand that a feast of God the Father be instituted and that I had to work for it. The clamor for a liturgical feast in honor of God the Father is not new. In the eighteenth century Cardinal Giuseppe Tomasi (+1713), whom liturgists remember for compiling and editing several medieval missals, dismissed the idea as something quite superfluous and not in keeping with the meaning of the liturgical year.

Let us keep in mind that every day at Mass and in the Liturgy of the Hours prayers are addressed to God the Father. This is a continuing act of the Church to honor and praise God for his marvelous works. What is the sense of instituting a day in the year to honor God the Father when the whole year belongs to him? Besides, all liturgical feasts are Christological: they are the anamnesis of Christ's mystery, an anamnesis that the Church directs to God the Father. The group argues that while there is a feast of the Holy Spirit, there is none to celebrate the Father. As a matter of fact, however, there is no feast of the Holy Spirit. Pentecost commemorates the day when Christ sent the Holy Spirit upon the apostles. It is Christological feast. The paschal mystery culminates in the mystery of Pentecost. There is no convincing reason why a liturgical feast should now make God the Father the object of its anamnesis.

THROUGH CHRIST OUR LORD

Per Christum Dominum nostrum (through Christ our Lord): this is how the Roman Church traditionally concludes its prayers to the Father. Medieval sacramentaries, which are the forerunners of our Roman Missal, always affix the phrase *per Christum* or simply the preposition *per* as conclusion to orations and prefaces. The phrase stands for the role that Christ played in salvation history and in its continuing realization in the liturgy. In a way it embodies the two aspects of liturgical worship, namely, Christ as sacrament and Christ as mediator.

Christ the Sacrament

Christ is the sacrament of the Father. When God breached the chasm that separated the divine from the human in order to reveal himself, he did so gradually at different times and in different ways. He first manifested himself to our first parents, then to Noah, Abraham, Moses, and the prophets. Hebrews 1:1-2 sums up the story of God's manifold revelations as it points to the person of Christ as the final and definitive revelation of God: "Long ago God spoke to our ancestors in many and various ways by the prophets, but in these last days he has spoken to us by a Son." The statement that Christ is the sacrament of the Father is another way of saying that he is the revelation of God. In his human form Christ revealed the person of the Father, whom no one had ever seen (John 1:18). His incarnate body, his words, and his actions removed the veil that hid the Father from our sight. That is why he assured his disciples that those who have seen him have seen the Father, because "I am in the Father and the Father is in me" (John 14:9, 11). Colossians 1:15 calls him "the image of the invisible God." The Greek *eikón* (image) alludes to Christ as a portrait, as the image of the Father in a mirror. In the human form of Christ we "see" the invisible God as in a mirror and we get an intimation of who God is.

Jesus painted for us the human face of God. He "humanized" God. The incarnation means that the Son of God took on a human flesh; but it also means that the divine attributes adopted the human mode of expression. When he preached love, compassion, and forgiveness Jesus revealed that God is love, compassion, and forgiveness. When he cured the sick Jesus showed that God is the origin of life. When he welcomed little children to his embrace and defended the rights of women Jesus made known to the Jewish leaders that God upholds the equality of all. When he endured violent death on the cross Jesus brought to light God's "weakness" for his creatures: what folly moved God to sacrifice his Son for his rebellious servants? "In the days of his flesh, Jesus offered up prayers and supplications, with loud cries and tears, to the one who was able to save him from death, and he was heard because of his reverent submission" (Heb 5:7). When Jesus was pained at the sight of those afflicted by diseases and tormented by injustice, he gave away the mystery of God that had been hidden in ages past: in the human nature of Jesus, God could feel pathos; he could suffer. The sentiments of the man Jesus effectively translated the sentiments of God. God is not unfeeling, apathetic, distant, or indifferent. Nothing could be more reassuring, nothing more comforting.

After Christ's ascension his human body is no longer visible to our eyes. The economy of the sacraments has superseded the economy of God's revelation in Christ's flesh. We live in the age of sacraments, the sacraments that the Church celebrates under different ritual forms. In his second Homily on the Ascension, Pope Leo the Great explains what happened after the ascension: "Our Redeemer's visible presence has passed into the sacraments. Our faith is nobler and stronger because sight has been replaced by a doctrine whose authority is accepted by believing hearts, enlightened from on high. . . . Throughout the world women no less than men, tender girls as well as boys, have given their life's blood in the struggle for this faith." Faith must have been very difficult to profess after hearing strange declarations of Jesus, such as his saying that he was the bread that came down from heaven. Faith must have been nagged by doubt at the sight of Christ nailed to the cross. It was surely more difficult to believe the naked, stark reality than the sacrament that veils that reality. I have often asked myself, if I had been there when they crucified my Lord, would I have been at the foot of the cross or would I have joined the jeering mob? The thought boggles the mind. But the good news is that the sacraments have dispensed with the reality, or better have veiled the reality, so that faith comes more easily. In the words of Pope Leo, "our faith is nobler and stronger because sight has been replaced by a doctrine whose authority is accepted by believing hearts, enlightened from on high."

This brings me to the delicate issue of apparitions and private revelations. The Eucharistic miracle of Lanciano, a town south of Rome, is said to have taken place in the eighth century to confirm the faith of a Basilian monk who doubted the real presence. After the words of consecration the host was changed into live flesh and the wine into live blood. In the 1970s and '80s the flesh and blood were subjected to clinical analysis that concluded that the flesh is real flesh consisting of the muscular tissues of the heart and that the blood is real blood. I am of course in no position at all to cast doubt on the authenticity of the miracle. When I asked Adrien Nocent what he thought about it, he answered with a sneer, "It is another religion." It was his way of calling attention to the essentials of the faith: the Church, the sacraments, the word of God. These provide our spiritual life with necessary and sufficient sustenance. Anything else, he claimed, was like the icing on a cake that merely makes the cake attractive. But what, I persisted, if you found blood in the cup after consecration? He replied: "I'll have my doctor check my eyes." What Christ entrusted to the Church was the sacrament of his body and blood, not their physical form. I cling to the teaching that as long as the Eucharistic species have the appearances of bread and wine I am under obligation to believe in the real presence. The short and long of it is that after the ascension of Christ our encounter with him normally takes place in the framework of the sacraments. I conclude with the *Catechism*'s authoritative words: "Throughout the ages, there have been so-called 'private' revelations, some of which have been recognized by the authority of the Church. They do not belong, however, to the deposit of faith. It is not their role to improve or complete Christ's definitive Revelation, but to help live more fully by it in a certain period of history" (67).

The word "primordial" is often attached to the title of Christ as sacrament of the Father. It states that Christ was the first and the only one to reveal the person of the Father and that the fullness of God's revelation resided in him. According to the *Catechism*, "Christ, the Son of God made man, is the Father's one, perfect and unsurpassable Word. In him he has said everything; there will be no other word than this one" (65). The word "primordial" echoes St. Augustine's teaching that "there is no sacrament other than Christ" (*Epistle* 187). All other sacraments are so called in a derivative fashion. The Church and the sacraments draw their meaning and efficacy from the one primordial sacrament that is Christ. They are called sacraments because Christ works in and through them.

Christ the Mediator

"For there is one God; there is also one mediator between God and humankind, Christ Jesus, himself human, who gave himself a ransom for all" (1 Tim 2:5). Christ as sacrament relates to salvation history; he is God's descent in person to the world. On the other hand, Christ as mediator relates to humankind's ascent to God. Mediator, or intermediary, is a highly technical word. The repetition of the word "one" links Christ with God. The letter says in effect that the mediator is no less than God himself in the person of Christ. Intermediation between God and humankind is a divine act. It stands to reason that since the offence committed is against God, no human being can make satisfaction for it: only God can. In the thinking of 1 Timothy 2:5 Christ's mediation was an act of ransoming or purchasing a captive, a slave, or a criminal by the sacrifice of his life. Hebrews 10:11-14 connects Christ's mediation to his priestly office: "Every priest stands day after day at his service, offering again and again the same sacrifices that can never take away sins. But when Christ had offered for all time a single sacrifice for sins, he sat down at the right hand of God. . . . For by a single offering he has perfected for all time those who are sanctified." Romans 5:10 teaches the same thing: "While we were enemies we were reconciled to God through the death of his Son." In Christ, mediation and priesthood, reconciliation and sacrifice are correlative concepts. Christ mediated as the priest of the new covenant.

Why did Christ's single offering effectively reconcile, while its forerunners, repeated again and again, failed? The answer is because Christ's mediation was a divine act that matched and indeed exceeded the infinite gravity of the human offence against God. I am reminded of that difficult passage of Romans 5:20: "Where sin increased, grace abounded all the more." It is difficult because it is humanly irrational; it is difficult because it does not adopt the pattern of human thinking and sentiment. God's thoughts are not our thoughts. Where we condemn, God forgives; where we bring the offence to our graves, God absolves and forgets. God has no memory of our sins, and unlike humans never learns his lesson. Mediation is a divine act and it overshoots the mark. When God loves, he loves to folly.

After stating that no less than God mediated, 1 Timothy 2:5 turns its attention to the other side of the coin. The God that mediated is the human being Jesus Christ, or to soften the impact of such a contradictory statement, I can say that God carried out the act of mediation in the human body of Jesus. Hebrews' reference to the prescriptions of Leviticus 17 sheds some light on the sacrifice of the cross: "Under the law, almost everything is purified by blood, and without the shedding of blood there is no forgiveness of sin" (Heb 9:22). Scholastic theologians assured us that God could have remitted sins by a single word, but he willed otherwise. God heightened the divine drama of forgiveness by the most unexpected turn of events. God sent his only Son into the world, becoming a human being in everything except sin, in order to shed his blood for the remission of sins. Hanging on a cross between heaven and earth, the Son of God performed the liturgy of mediation, dismantling the barriers that separated God from humankind. All this sounds familiar, for that is what preaching has done. But familiarity should not breed indifference or cause the loss of awe and wonder at what God has done.

As there is no sacrament other than Christ, so there is no mediator other than him. The technical understanding of mediation as a divine act in the person of the human Jesus excludes the application of the word to any human being. No one but Christ is God, no one but Christ is God-Man, and no one has definitively reconciled humankind with God. However, as the name "sacrament" is derivatively given to the Church and its sacraments, the name "mediator" is sometimes conferred on saints. The Blessed Virgin Mary is called mediatrix. The Constitution on the Church makes a statement on the matter that I confess I had a problem taking seriously at first. It says: "The Blessed Virgin is invoked by the Church under the titles of Advocate, Auxiliatrix, Adjutrix, and Mediatrix. These however are not to be so understood that they neither take away from nor add anything to the dignity and efficacy of Christ the one Mediator" (62). If the title *mediatrix* takes away nothing from and adds nothing to the efficacy of Christ's mediation, is not its use idle and confusing? I should think not, if the title is taken in the context of her special role in God's plan. By consenting to be the mother of the God-Man Jesus she paved the way to Calvary. In this sense, she can be called mediatrix, not as if she had redeemed us, but because she allowed herself to be a principal player in the unfolding of God's drama of salvation. At any rate, we should use this Marian title with necessary caution.

In the liturgy the figure of Christ the mediator stands clothed in the robes of his priestly office. According to the Constitution on Liturgy, "the liturgy is considered as the exercise of the priestly office of Jesus Christ" (7). When we speak of Christ's presence in the liturgy, we ascribe it to his priestly role. He is present in liturgical worship as the high priest; when the Church baptizes, he baptizes as the priest of the new covenant; when the sacrifice is offered through the hands of the priest, he offers now what he as priest offered on the altar of the cross; when the word of God is read, he speaks as the preacher-priest; when the assembly gathers as a priestly people, he is present as the High Priest among those to whom he has given a share in his priesthood through baptism.

Through Him, with Him, in Him

The classical conclusion of the presidential prayers of the Roman rite is *Per Christum Dominum nostrum* (through Christ our Lord). The opening prayers for Mass almost always make an anamnesis of God's wonderful deeds, recalling especially the life and mission of Christ. In the strength of the anamnesis, or confident that God will do once again what he did in the past, we formulate our petition and conclude invoking the mediating power of Christ. The Latin *per*, which bears several meanings, has the same sense as its Greek counterpart *dià* used with the accusative case, signifying the assistance or instrumentality of a person in having something done. We lift our voices to God through Christ who causes them to reach the throne of God. This recalls Christ's declaration (John 14:13) that he will do whatever we ask in his name. As we shall have the occasion to discuss later in this work, the word "Lord" is loaded with meaning. It should not be replaced with such endearing but theologically less appropriate expressions as "big brother" or "super friend." Christ is invoked as the glorified Lord, *Kyrios*, because he bestows the Holy Spirit. Just as Pentecost completed the paschal mystery, so epiclesis concludes our anamnesis. The bestowal of the Holy Spirit is the fruit of liturgical worship, and this happens through Christ our Lord.

The longer version of "through Christ our Lord" is kept in the doxology that concludes the Eucharistic Prayer: "Through him, with him, in him." The last two segments elaborate the first. They enrich our appreciation of Christ's mediation by instilling in us a sense of personal relationship with him. The preposition "through" resonates with good theology, but it can sound rather impersonal. The Latin conjunction *cum* (with) on the other hand is relational. With Christ, that is to say, in his company, we approach God in prayer. The third segment ("in him") is somewhat difficult to explain because the Latin ablative with which it is used can refer to space (the person of Christ encompasses us or he keeps us before his eyes) as well as to time, situation, or personal relationship. This is a preposition that frequently occurs in the Pauline literature, and I sense that the liturgy took it from there. Personal relationship defines Christ's act of mediation. In the liturgy we encounter not only the Father but also the person of Christ who accompanies us in our journey ("with him"), enfolding us in his embrace ("in him").

The prayer of St. Ambrose is memorable: "Christ, you have shown yourself to me face to face; in your sacraments I encounter you" (*Apologia David* 12). To see Christ as large as life is more than anyone could bargain for. The Easter *Exsultet* or Proclamation, which has literary and poetic affinity to St. Ambrose, goes many steps ahead: "What good would life have been to us, had Christ not come as our Redeemer? O happy fault, O necessary sin of Adam, which gained for us so great a Redeemer!" If we were given a choice between the Paradise that did not know Christ and this present world where we can delight in his company, would we not choose misery rather than bliss? St. Paul's words are inspired: "For him I have accepted the loss of everything, and I look on everything as so much rubbish if only I can have Christ and be given a place in him" (Phil 3:8-9). To know Christ intimately is all there is to human existence: "Life to me is Christ." Rightly, then, the *Exsultet* exclaims with poetic indulgence, "O happy fault, O necessary sin of Adam." For had there been no sin, there would not have been a need for a Redeemer, Christ would not have come into the world, and we would not have known him. But what would life be without Christ?

Christ the mediator is robed in glory as on the day of his transfiguration and as the high priest that ceaselessly intercedes for us at the right hand of the Father. His glory should not, however, make us insensitive to the pain and humiliation that he endured during his passion. We can ask ourselves what went into the mind of God that he decided not only to become human but also to be subjected to degradation as if he were a common criminal. He who created the universe by the power of his word could have freed humankind from the fetters of sin by simply uttering a word of forgiveness. But he chose to die on a cross. What God is this that emptied himself of his awe-inspiring majesty and on the cross appeared humbler than the very creatures he had formed from the clay of the earth? What God is this who so loved the human race that he willed to share the ruthless reality of being exposed to pain and death? When he was nailed to the cross he embraced the thousand pains and the thousand deaths to which each of us is continually subjected. Christ the mediator was not a stranger to our earthly condition.

IN THE UNITY OF THE HOLY SPIRIT

"When the Son completed the work with which the Father had entrusted him on earth, the Holy Spirit was sent on the day of Pentecost to sanctify the Church unceasingly, and thus enable believers to have access to the Father through Christ in the one Spirit. He is the Spirit of life, the fountain of water welling up to give eternal life. Through him the Father gives life to humankind, dead because of sin, until he raises up their mortal bodies in Christ" (LG 4).

The Holy Spirit in the Liturgy

The solemn doxology that concludes the Eucharistic Prayer elaborates the ancient formula "Glory to the Father through the Son in the

Holy Spirit." It also develops the simple form "in the Holy Spirit" by inserting the word "unity": "Through him, with him, in him, in the unity of the Holy Spirit, all glory and honor is yours, almighty Father, for ever and ever." Liturgists, including my mentors, were not unanimous in their interpretation of "unity." Some of them read it in conjunction with the Trinitarian belief: the Holy Spirit is one and in unity with the Father and the Son. The structural analysis of the Latin text does yield such a conclusion: *Per ipsum, et cum ipso, et in ipso, est tibi Deo Patri omnipotenti, in unitate Spiritus Sancti, omnis honor et gloria per omnia saecula saeculorum.* The positioning of the Holy Spirit after the Father is a semiotic arrangement that relates the three Divine Persons to one another. With due respect to my mentors, I have to admit that I am of two minds about such an interpretation. It is what the structure of the text says, but it does not present the Holy Spirit in relation to Christ's mediation. The Holy Spirit seems removed from or uninvolved in the unfolding of the liturgical prayer to the Father through Christ.

There are others who hold that the solemn doxology should be read in the light of the Holy Spirit's action among the faithful: united with the Holy Spirit, or encompassed by him, we glorify the Father through Christ our mediator. I recall that Jungmann affirmed as much. I do not claim that this interpretation is in perfect harmony with the syntax of the text, but it is nearer to the mark that I propose about the role of the Holy Spirit. We ascend to God through the mediator Jesus and in the strength of the Holy Spirit that dwells in us or in whom we dwell. I am not certain if the English translation consciously adopted this interpretation. Because of the placement of the phrase "in the unity of the Holy Spirit" after "through him, with him, in him," the English text says in effect that it is in the unity of the Holy Spirit that we raise to God the sacraments of Christ's mediating sacrifice. I came across the following passage from St. Hilary (*On the Trinity*, Book 2, 1) that is read in the Office of Readings on Friday before Pentecost. It describes the Holy Trinity in the context of its external working and somehow throws light on the role of the Holy Spirit in salvation history and the liturgy: "There is one Creator of all things, for in God there is one Father from whom all things have their being. And there is one only-begotten Son, our Lord Jesus Christ, through whom all things exist. And there is one Spirit, the gift who is in all."

In a previous chapter I discussed under the heading of epiclesis the role the Holy Spirit plays in the liturgy. How do liturgical texts express it? In the baptismal rite epiclesis occurs at the blessing of the baptismal water. The first formula, which is a revised version of the sixth-century Gelasian Sacramentary, is prefaced by a lengthy enumeration of biblical types that foreshadowed the water of baptism: the water of creation, the great flood, the Red Sea, the river Jordan, and the water that flowed from the side of Christ. The prayer concludes its anamnesis with these words of epiclesis: "We ask you, Father, with your Son, to send the Holy Spirit upon the water of this font." Baptism is not by water alone but by water and the Holy Spirit that inhabits the water. Around the year 220 Tertullian wrote: "After God is invoked all waters attain the sacramental power to sanctify; for the Spirit immediately comes from heaven and rests on the water in order to make it holy. Once made holy, it acquires the power to sanctify" (*De Baptismo* 4). *Apostolic Tradition* requires the blessing of the baptismal water: "A prayer should be said over the water" (chap. 21). St. Ambrose is also a witness to this liturgical tradition: "The priest delivers an invocation and prayer that the font may be sanctified, and that the presence of the eternal Trinity may be at hand" (*De Sacramentis* I, 5). Hand-laying ordinarily symbolizes the descent of the Holy Spirit. As the minister recites the words of epiclesis, he is instructed to touch the water with his right hand. The gesture, which is taken from the twelfth-century Roman Pontifical, has unfortunately replaced the more graphic gesture of hand-laying.

In the sacrament of confirmation epiclesis takes place before chrismal anointing. As the minister lays his hands on the candidates he asks God to "send your Holy Spirit upon them to be their Helper and Guide." The text enumerates the different gifts of the Holy Spirit: wisdom and understanding, right judgment and courage, knowledge and reverence, and wonder and awe in God's presence. The hand-laying is done before anointing, the rite that constitutes the sacrament. Chrism plays such a principal role that confirmation is sometime called chrismation. The author of the fifth-century *Jerusalem Catechesis*, speaking about this oil, writes: "Beware of thinking that this holy oil is simply ordinary oil and nothing else. After the invocation of the Spirit it is no longer ordinary oil but the gift of Christ, and by the presence of his divinity it becomes the instrument through which we receive the Holy Spirit" (21). Regarding the gesture of hand-laying, Pope Paul VI explains that it "is still to be regarded as very important, even if it is not of the essence of the sacramental rite" (Apostolic Constitution "Divinae consortium naturae"). Adrien Nocent, an expert on the liturgy of confirmation, noted that while the introduction to the rite joins anointing with hand-laying (a double action of the right hand that I have difficulty visualizing), the rubrics instruct the minister to simply dip his right thumb in the chrism and trace the sign of the cross on the forehead of the candidate. This was one example he included among the reformed rites of Vatican II that needed to be further reformed.

The role of the Holy Spirit in the Eucharist figures prominently in liturgical discussions about the meaning and effect of epiclesis. I confine myself to a brief comment on the English rendering of the Latin epiclesis: *Haec dona, quaesumus, Spiritus tui rore sanctifica* in the second Eucharistic Prayer. *Rore* (from *ros*) means dew. It is a picturesque description of the fecundating action of the Holy Spirit on bread and wine; but the phrase "dew of the Spirit" is surely befuddling. Was this the problem ICEL tried to solve by the simple sentence: "Let your Spirit come upon these gifts to make them holy"? The revised ICEL translation drafted by the Advisory Committee is more literary, but it also evades the problematic "dew": "Therefore make holy these gifts, we implore you, by the outpouring of your Spirit." The proposed inculturated Order of Mass for the Philippines that was submitted to Rome way back in 1976 approaches the question of epiclesis from another angle using the Tagalog word for the bird's action of brooding (*lukob*). The intention is to convey the idea of the vivifying and transforming action of the Holy Spirit on the bread and wine and the assembly. Gerard M. Hopkins employs the imagery in his poem "God's Grandeur": "And for all this, nature is never spent; / There lives the dearest freshness deep down things; / And though the last lights off the black West went / Oh, morning, and the brown brink eastward, springs— / Because the Holy Ghost over the bent/ World broods with warm breast and with ah! bright wings" (Appendix of Hymns and Poems, in Liturgy of the Hours).

The epiclesis in the sacrament of penance is embedded in the formula of absolution: "God, the Father of mercies, through the death and resurrection of his Son has reconciled the world to himself and sent the Holy Spirit among us for the forgiveness of sins; through the ministry of the Church may God give you pardon and peace." Nocent commented that the formula of absolution could have ended there because it says all there is to say, but the declarative statement "I absolve you" was kept to keep canonical dispute at bay. Hand-laying accompanies the formula. This is an implicit desire of the council, as we can glean from its decree that "the rites and formularies for the sacrament of penance are to be revised so that they more clearly express both the nature and effect of the sacrament" (SC 72). As I noted elsewhere, by "nature" the council meant to stress the social and ecclesial character of the sacrament, and by "effect" it wanted to restore the ancient gesture of hand-laying to signify reconciliation. The ancient Gelasian Sacramentary (no. 353) compares the penitent's tears of repentance with the baptismal water of rebirth. The Holy Spirit is the author of both miracles of conversion, baptism being the first and penance, the second. On Holy Thursday the ancient rite of reconciling public penitents began with the deacon's solemn, touching address directed to the bishop: "The acceptable time has come, Venerable Pontiff, the day of divine propitiation and human salvation has arrived. We increase because of those who will be reborn; we grow because of those who are reconciled. Water washes as do tears (*lavant aquae, lavant lacrimae*)."

In the rites of ordination the gesture of hand-laying is considered an essential element of the rite. The third-century *Apostolic Tradition* (2), which is the source of the formula for Episcopal ordination, directs the ordaining bishop to lay his hands on the candidate "that the Holy Spirit may descend on him." The epiclesis reads: "Pour out now upon this chosen one that power which is from you, the governing Spirit, whom you gave to your beloved Son, Jesus Christ, the Spirit whom he bestowed upon the holy Apostles . . . " The phrase "governing Spirit" (*pneuma hegemonikón, Spiritus principalis*) has a curious history. It is taken from the Greek translation of Psalm 51:14 that the Latin Vulgate adopted. The original Hebrew has "spirit of obedience" to God's will. Somewhere later in the prayer of ordination there is mention of the "Spirit of the high priesthood" that complements the authority of the bishop as leader. At ordination the bishop receives the Holy Spirit that enables him to govern and sanctify the flock of Christ. *Apostolic Tradition* replaced the Veronese Sacramentary's ordination prayer, which the Roman Church had used since the sixth century. Someone irreverently suspected that a fashion designer had a hand in it because of its compulsion for the "adornments of glory," "dignity of robes," "pontifical glory," "radiance of gold," "sparkling jewels," and "diverse workmanship," which of course symbolize the interior character of the bishop.

The 1968 Rites of Ordination retained the Veronese formulas for the ordination of priests and deacons. The epiclesis for priests is a prayer to "renew deep in them the Spirit of holiness" so that as they assist the bishops in the ministry they may show forth in their lives the pattern of all righteousness and the example of daily conversion. The epiclesis for the deacons reads: "Lord, we beseech you: send forth upon them the Holy Spirit, that they may be strengthened by the gift of your sevenfold grace to carry out faithfully the work of the ministry." It is difficult to interpret the meaning of "sevenfold grace." The number seven can signify abundance of God's blessings. It can also mean the seven virtues enumerated in the prayer: deacons are enjoined to cultivate unfeigned love, concern for the sick and poor, unassuming authority, purity of innocence, spiritual discipline, good example, and clear conscience. But the phrase can refer as well to the person of the Holy Spirit who is bestowed on the deacons as their companion and guide.

The epiclesis for the anointing of the sick is found in the blessing of the oil. It is similar to the blessing of the baptismal water: "Graciously listen to our prayer of faith: send the power of your Holy Spirit, the Consoler, into this precious oil, this soothing ointment, this rich gift, this fruit of the earth." The presence of the Holy Spirit is invoked upon the oil so that it may be "a remedy for all who are anointed with it." The title given to the Holy Spirit in the sacrament of anointing is Paraclete, the Consoler who gives strength and comfort to the sick. The blessed oil is the sacrament by which the Holy Spirit accompanies the sick in their struggle with pain and anxiety, gives them moral and psychological strength to bear their suffering bravely as Christians, and supports them in their fight against the sickness. Accompanied and comforted by the Holy Spirit, the sick regain peace of mind and bodily well-being. Modern medicine discovered that mental peace and physical tranquility contribute immensely to the recovery of health. Should it surprise us that some patients with terminal cases recover after receiving the sacrament? The epiclesis is symbolized by hand-laying done in silence before the anointing. As a prayer it is integrated in the sacramental formula: "Through this holy anointing may the Lord in his love and mercy help you with the grace of the Holy Spirit."

The *Catechism of the Catholic Church* summarizes the role of the Holy Spirit in the liturgy: "When the Spirit encounters in us the response of faith which he has aroused in us, he brings about genuine cooperation. Through it, the liturgy becomes the common work of the Holy Spirit and the Church. . . . In this sacramental dispensation of Christ's mystery the Holy Spirit acts in the same way as at other times in the economy of salvation: he prepares the Church to encounter her Lord; he recalls and makes Christ manifest to the faith of the assembly. By his transforming power, he makes the mystery of Christ present here and now. Finally the Spirit of communion unites the Church to the life and mission of Christ" (1091, 1092).

The *Catechism* teaches that in the "sacramental dispensation of Christ's mystery the Holy Spirit acts in the same way as at other times in the economy of salvation." It confirms the thinking, which is really a belief, that the liturgy as "the common work of the Holy Spirit and the Church" extends in our time *per ritus et preces* (through rites and prayers) the deeds of God in salvation history, that the paschal mystery culminates in the mystery of Pentecost, and that anamnesis concludes in epiclesis. It is a mouthful, but I reckon that the subject requires no less.

The following pages deal with the part the Holy Spirit played in the life and mission of the historical Jesus and subsequently after the ascension in the life and mission of Christ's mystical body that is the Church. The Spirit that animates the Church is the same Spirit that inspired, led, and empowered Jesus while he was on earth. To develop this topic I adopt the final verse of the New Testament hymn in Philippians 2:11: "Every tongue should confess that Jesus Christ is Lord, to the glory of God the Father." This statement is the heart of the Christian creed. Jesus is a name; Christ and Lord are titles. They stand for the three chief mysteries of Christ, namely, incarnation, messianic mission, and death and glorification.

The Holy Spirit and the Incarnate Word

"Jesus Christ is Lord." The Word-made-flesh received the name Jesus, the name by which he was to be known and manifested to the world as the Son of God. I found this passage from St. Cyril of Alexandria in the Office of Readings for Thursday after Epiphany: "Though he is the Son of God the Father, begotten of his substance, even before the incarnation, indeed before all ages, yet he was not offended at hearing the Father say to him after he had become man: You are my Son; today I have begotten you" (*Commentary on John*, Book 2). The New Testament attributes the mystery of the incarnation to the Holy Spirit, the power of the Most High that covered Mary with its shadow (Matt 1:18-20). Christians everywhere and of every denomination hold the incarnation by the power of the Holy Spirit as a basic tenet of faith, even if they interpret it with different nuances: "He was conceived by the power of the Holy Spirit."

In my musings I have time and again posed this question to myself: which of these two is the cornerstone of our Christian belief, the incarnation or the resurrection? St. Augustine has a saying (*Sermo*

374, On Epiphany) that has struck me: *Plus est facere hominem quam resuscitare.* The sense, which I render freely, is "it took more to make Christ a human being than to raise him from the dead." Although St. Paul pointed out that Christ and his cross are a scandal to the Jews and a stumbling block for pagans, the truth is that it is more difficult, even with God's grace, to believe that God the eternal Spirit took on a human flesh and became like us in all things, sin excepting. Familiarity with the doctrine of the incarnation has in more ways than one dulled our sense of amazement and wonder. Every Sunday when we recite the crucial article of faith "and he became man," do we pause to ask ourselves what kind of doctrine is this? We delight in the image of a Child peacefully asleep on the lap of his mother, but has it crossed our mind that humanly speaking this entire story is simply unbelievable, like the fables of old when the gods roamed the earth in human form? But by God's grace we believe, and our faith is the pride and joy of our lives as Christians.

If we believe that God became human, we should expect that God did embrace all the consequences that ensue from being human, save sin, which is a denial of everything that is God. If we profess that Jesus took on our mortal flesh, should it bewilder us that he died? What is more bewildering though is not that he died, but that he chose to die on a cross like a common criminal. Now that should overwhelm us. And if God could die, should it astonish us that he was raised back to life? Everything we read in the gospels about the human Jesus is the consequence of God's primordial decision to be a human being. In all this we perceive the pervading presence of the Holy Spirit who worked behind the scenes conducting the course of the divine drama. When the Holy Spirit enveloped Mary with his fecundating energy, he set in motion the events that led to the manger, the home at Nazareth, the streets and lakeshores where Jesus preached and performed miracles, the Hill of Calvary, and the tomb of his burial and resurrection.

But what might God's scheme be in the mystery of the incarnation? I found an interesting answer in a homily of St. Augustine assigned to the Office of Readings on Saturday before Epiphany: "Of his own will Christ was born for us today, in time, so that he could lead us to his Father's eternity. . . . The Lord who had created all things is himself now created, so that those who were lost would be found. . . . Humans fell, but God descended; humans fell miserably, but God descended mercifully." In words that reverberated in the church where he was preaching, he delivered the stunning message: "God became man so that humans might become God!" (*Sermo* 13). The incarnation is God's "humanization," or descent. In what does our "divinization," or ascent to God, consist? St. Ambrose has the answer: "If the coming of the Holy Spirit upon the Virgin resulted in conception and birth, there is no doubt that the Spirit, coming upon the font or upon those who receive baptism, brings about rebirth" (*De mysteriis* 9). St. Ambrose is a master in the use of typology. The Virgin is the type of the Church; her womb, the font of baptism; and the conception and birth of Christ, the rebirth of Christians. In both type and antitype the figure of the Holy Spirit stands dominantly as the artificer and the *digitus Dei* (finger of God). Both the incarnation and sacrament of baptism are the work of the Holy Spirit. It was he that designed and carried out God's descent; it is he that actualizes our ascent.

Blessed Isaac of Stella's homily, which is reproduced for Friday of the Fifth Week of Easter, elaborates the teaching of St. Ambrose: "By the Spirit, from the womb of the Virgin, was born our head, the Son of Man; and by the same Spirit, in the waters of baptism, we are reborn as his body and as children of God. And just as he was born without any sin, so we are reborn in the forgiveness of all our sins" (*Sermo* 42). Those who wish to hear a stunning doctrine that must have been as astounding a novelty in the fifth century as it is today should read Didymus of Alexandria. In his treatise *On the Trinity* (Book 2) he calls the Holy Spirit our parent! The first time I came across the passage I thought the drafters of the Office of Readings should have known better the controversial language of Didymus and should have selected passages that are not theologically debatable. The Holy Spirit is called by many names and given many titles. But parent? And yet after I reflected on it, it dawned on me that it is a perfectly orthodox manner of describing our relationship with the Holy Spirit whom we profess to be the Lord and Giver of Life. Commenting on John 1:12-13, Didymus writes: "We are conceived twice: to the human body we owe our first conception, to the divine Spirit, our second. . . . All who believed in Christ received power to become children of God, that is, of the Holy Spirit, and to gain kinship with God. To show that their parent was God the Holy Spirit, he adds these words of Christ: I tell you solemnly that without being born of water and the Spirit, no one can enter the kingdom of God."

The Mission of Christ in the Spirit

Jesus is the name of the Incarnate Word. Christ is his title as God's Anointed. Jesus is called the Christ, the Anointed One, the Messiah.

The three titles signify one and the same thing: God sent his Son to accomplish the work assigned to the Messiah. When the disciples of John the Baptist inquired of Jesus whether he was the Messiah, Jesus first healed the sick before giving them this answer: "Go and tell John what you have seen and heard: the blind receive their sight, the lame walk, the lepers are cleansed, the deaf hear, the dead are raised, the poor have good news brought to them" (Luke 7:22). The Messiah was anointed, that is to say, consecrated or set apart for a particular mission. The English "anoint" is derived from the Latin *inunguere* (to smear with oil). Conscious of his mission, Jesus announced in the synagogue that the words of Isaiah 61:15 had been fulfilled in his person: "The Spirit of the Lord is upon me, because he has anointed me" (Luke 4:18). To the assembly gathered in Cornelius's house Peter addressed these words: "God anointed Jesus of Nazareth with the Holy Spirit and with power . . . he went about doing good and healing all who were oppressed by the devil, for God was with him" (Acts 10:38). As the Anointed One, Jesus was entrusted with the three duties of the Messiah, namely, to preach the Good News, heal the sick, and free those enslaved by evil powers.

But unlike the kings and prophets of old, Jesus was anointed not physically with oil but with the Holy Spirit. The ceremony took place at the Jordan when John baptized him. "When Jesus had been baptized, just as he came up from the water, suddenly the heavens were opened to him and he saw the Spirit of God descending like a dove and alighting on him. And a voice from heaven said, 'This is my Son, the Beloved, with whom I am well pleased'" (Matt 3:16-17). His baptism marked the moment of his formal inauguration as Messiah. It was the start of his public ministry. That the Holy Spirit descended on him signified that he had been vested with the power and wisdom required by his role as Messiah.

The phrase about the Spirit descending and alighting on Jesus like a dove has always intrigued me. Honestly, pictures and images of the Holy Spirit in the form of a dove amuse me. The image depicting the dove with its two feet joined together as if in prayer is particularly diverting. Such images sometimes cause me to raise the theological question whether the Spirit was "incarnated" too, at least temporarily. St. Gregory of Nazianzus wrote this curious statement: "The Spirit descended in bodily form like the dove that so long ago announced the ending of the flood and so gives honor to the body that is one with God" (*Oratio* 39). I do not want to play the exegete, but it seems to me that the Greek text does not say that the Spirit descended in "bodily form." The Greek adverb *oseí*, which is the crux of interpretation, does not imply anything bodily. It means "just as if" or "as though." I would venture to say that the Spirit descended in the manner of a dove alighting to rest.

As early as the second century the Gnostic sect of Valentinians considered the baptism of Jesus his public manifestation as Son of God. In Eastern tradition the feast of Epiphany on January 6 commemorates the baptism of Jesus. The date evokes the cosmic drama of winter when the light begins to prevail over darkness. Coming up from the water, Jesus shone as the light of the world. The Roman Church, on the other hand, has a special feast for the baptism of Jesus, because Epiphany centers on the visit of the Magi that heralded the universality of Christ's earthly mission. The preface for the feast of the Baptism of the Lord captures the meaning of the Eastern Epiphany: "Your Spirit was seen as a dove, revealing Jesus as your servant, and anointing him with joy as the Christ, sent to bring to the poor the good news of salvation." Likewise, the antiphons for Lauds and Vespers of the Roman Epiphany retain the original meaning of the feast. The antiphon for *Benedictus* construes Epiphany as the wedding day of Christ and the Church: "Today the Bridegroom claims his bride, the Church, since Christ has washed her sins away in Jordan's waters; the Magi hasten with their gifts to the royal wedding; and the wedding guests rejoice, for Christ has changed water into wine, alleluia." The antiphon for *Magnificat*, like the one for *Benedictus*, expands the theme to include the miracle at Cana and the baptism in the Jordan: "Three mysteries mark this holy day: today the star leads the Magi to the infant Christ; today water is changed into wine for the wedding feast; today Christ wills to be baptized by John in the river Jordan to bring us salvation."

Here I would like to pursue the method of parallelism. The Holy Spirit who was the author of Christ's incarnation is also the author of our divine adoption. The same Spirit that had anointed Christ in the Jordan anointed the Church on the day of Pentecost and now anoints every Christian with the oil of confirmation. On the day of his baptism Jesus received the title Christ; on the day of Pentecost the Church from every nation was manifested to the world as the sacrament of the Messiah with the mission to preach and baptize; on the day of confirmation the baptized receives the title Christian, sharing with Christ the role of Messiah. The Constitution on the Church says: The Church, "established in this last age of the world, and made manifest in the outpouring of the Spirit (at Pentecost), will be brought to glorious completion at the end of time" (2). I should admit that I do not find direct references in the liturgy of the Baptism of the Lord that allude to Pentecost and confirmation. But I am not disheartened. The idea I pursue is just too beautiful to be discarded for lack of liturgical documentation. My thesis is: just as the sacrament of confirmation renews the experience of Pentecost, so Pentecost for the entire Church and the sacrament of confirmation of individual Christians refresh the meaning and purpose of baptism in the Jordan. All three (baptism of Jesus, Pentecost, and confirmation) embody the mission of the Messiah to preach, heal, and liberate.

Some of the more suggestive symbols of the Holy Spirit are the dove, tongues of fire, and oil of chrism. The author of the *Jerusalem Catechesis* explains that "the oil of gladness with which Christ was anointed was a spiritual oil; it was in fact the Holy Spirit himself, who is called the oil of gladness because he is the source of spiritual joy" (21). Basing himself on Christ's promise of the living water welling up into eternal life (John 7:38), St. Cyril of Jerusalem (*Catechesis* 16) identifies the living water with the person of the Holy Spirit. According to a former colleague, Crispino Valenziano, the dove represents the element of wind over the waters at the time of creation; fire symbolizes enlightenment through baptism; and oil accompanied by hand-laying recalls the anointing by the Spirit. From the time of Tertullian, Easter Vigil was esteemed as the meaningful time for baptism. However, Pentecost was deemed to be appropriate. I presume that the reason is because of the two symbols of the Holy Spirit at Pentecost: water (baptismal washing) and fire (Holy Spirit). Valenziano, who initiated me into the world of cultural anthropology, claimed that water and fire are two interchangeable elements. Water enlightens and fire cleanses. I had initial misgiving about such confusion of ideas, but when I read a passage from Didymus of Alexandria in the Office of Readings for Monday of the Sixth Week of Easter, I was lost for words. It was amazing to discover that cultural anthropology dates back to patristic times. Didymus wrote: "We need the Holy Spirit to perfect and renew us, for spiritual fire can cleanse us, and spiritual water can recast us as in a furnace and make us into new persons" (*On the Trinity*, Book 2).

Pentecost Sunday often fills me with melancholy, knowing that the following day will be Ordinary Time. Pentecost brings the curtain down on the drama of Easter and it does so with such finality that no echo remains. Cardinal Augustinus Meyer, who as Rector of

Sant'Anselmo on the Aventine had taken me under his protective wings as a student from the Far East, enjoyed arguing with me about the liturgical reform. One of his laments was the slashing of Pentecost to one day. The octave days, he said, should have been retained. I replied lamely that the entire week before Pentecost talked of nothing else but the coming solemnity and that the traditional fifty days of Easter meant fifty days. But sometimes I tend to agree that the sudden ending does not allow what sounded like a powerful wind from heaven (cf. Acts 2:2) to reverberate across the liturgical year. The antiphon for *Magnificat* concludes magnificently the celebration of the fifty days of Easter: "Today we celebrate the feast of Pentecost, alleluia; on this day the Holy Spirit appeared before the apostles in tongues of fire and gave them his spiritual gifts. He sent them out to preach to the whole world, and to proclaim that all who believe and are baptized shall be saved, alleluia."

The Spirit of the Glorified Lord

"Jesus Christ is Lord." Lord is the title of Jesus whom God exalted on the day of his humiliation. Jesus is *Kyrios*, Lord, because as he breathed his last he bequeathed to the nascent Church the Holy Spirit he had received from the Father at his incarnation and baptism. John 19:30 narrates the death of Jesus differently from the Synoptics, which merely state that he gave up his last or simply that he died. In typical metaphoric and symbolic manner John says, "He bowed his head and gave up his spirit." The Greek phrase is *parédoken tò pneuma*, literally, he handed over the Spirit by way of tradition (*parádosis*). The last breath of Jesus was not only unto death but also unto the bequeathal of the Holy Spirit, his gift to the Church his bride. Or probably more correctly we can say that he died bestowing his Holy Spirit on the Church. St. John Chrysostom pointed out that the water and blood that flowed from the pierced side of Jesus were symbols of the baptism and Eucharist. "I said that water and blood symbolized baptism and holy Eucharist. From these two sacraments the Church is born: from baptism, the cleansing water that gives rebirth and renewal through the Holy Spirit, and the holy Eucharist" (*Catechesis* 3). St. John Chrysostom elucidates further: "Since the symbols of baptism and the Eucharist flowed from his side, it was from his side that Christ fashioned the Church, as he had fashioned Eve from the side of Adam." St Augustine (*Enarrationes* in Ps. 138) says as much, and the Constitution on Liturgy has owned his typology: "For it was from the side of Christ as he slept the sleep of death upon the cross that there came forth the wondrous sacrament which is the whole Church" (SC 5).

Good Friday is the birth of the Church from the pierced side of Jesus. Upon the cross, which was the new tree of Paradise, the new Adam espoused the new Eve and lavished the bridal gift of the Holy Spirit on her. Christ gained his bride by sacrificing his life: he loved her and sanctified her by water and the word (Eph 5:25-26). The wedding at Cana foreshadowed the wedding feast on Calvary where water and blood flowed freely to nourish the new people of God. The Church was the woman of Genesis; the woman whom Jesus gently reminded that his hour had not yet come; the woman his Mother represented as she stood bravely at the foot of the cross; the woman to whom, in the person of his mother, he entrusted his beloved disciple and all his future disciples.

On Calvary the Holy Spirit was fully at work as director of the play that unfolded the divine plan of salvation. The Holy Spirit was bequeathed, the Church was born, and the sacraments flowed from his pierced side. On the altar of the cross the sharing of the broken bread and the common cup at the table of the Last Supper received its full meaning as Supper of the Lamb slain for our redemption. The cross that marks the place of the Eucharist will always call attention to the awesome mystery of Calvary. We break bread and drink the cup with joy mingled with tears, because the Eucharist is the sacrament of his passion and death. And the Holy Spirit continues to direct the drama whose final act will be celebrated in the eternal banquet of heaven.

Jesus Christ is Lord. He is the *Kyrios* who sends forth the Holy Spirit to the Church. He had to go, that is to say, suffer death, so that the Holy Spirit the Paraclete might come (John 16:6-7). In the Gospel of John the mystery of Pentecost took place on Calvary; it was on the cross that Jesus gathered the new people of God and poured out on them the gift of the Holy Spirit. This seems to be the meaning of Jesus' declaration: "And I, when I am lifted up from the earth, will draw all people to myself" (John 12:32). Lifted on the cross, Christ was exalted and declared Lord by God.

Christ's glory brings us back to the day of his humiliation. On Good Friday Pilate exclaimed as he presented Jesus to the people: "Behold the man!" Yes, behold the man who on the cross revealed himself as the Creator and Savior of the human race. It was on the world's first Friday when God formed the human race from the clay of the earth, and it was on Good Friday when he redeemed it with his blood.

Behold the man who saved humankind on the tree of the cross, that humankind which fell into disgrace by the tree of Paradise. From his pierced side flowed water and blood: water to cleanse us from the filth of sin and blood to give to us a share in his divine life. As he gasped for breath he remembered to give to us a mother whom we could cherish, a mother who would cherish us as brothers and sisters of her crucified Son: "Here is your son," he said to the woman; "and here is your mother," he told his beloved disciple. Amid tears and the torment of execution he still found words of comfort for a repentant sinner: "Today," he promised him, "you will be with me in paradise." Amid insults and scorn by his tormentors, he still responded generously with a prayer for forgiveness: "Father, forgive them, for they do not know what they are doing."

Christ's death and burial completed God's descent to earth. At the incarnation the Word descended into the womb of Mary, pure and immaculate, but human nonetheless. At his birth he was laid in a manger in Bethlehem, the house of bread, to signify that he came to be broken and shared like bread, but what was more humbling than to be laid in a manger for lack of a cradle? Christ was relentless in pursuing his plan to descend to the lowest recesses of existence. After the crucifixion his body was laid in a tomb; it touched the earth, the final station that awaits all created life. But Christ went farther down: he entered the netherworld. He descended to hell. I do not nuance the word "hell." Christ went down to hell, because it is where humankind and each of us dwell. Life indeed can be hell for many of us, and Christ descends to our hell to raise us up from there. He came down to earth alone, but he did not return to heaven alone. He brought with him the throng of all those he had redeemed.

An anonymous second-century writer dramatized Christ's descent to the netherworld where the patriarchs and entire humankind awaited his coming. Oriental icons depict the scene vividly. Christ descends with the swiftness of an eagle and seizes the hand of Adam, lifting him on high. The icon is named *anástasis*, resurrection. Christ rose from the dead not by ascending but by descending. The proof that he had returned to life and that he had completed his work of redemption was his descent to the realm of the dead. The anonymous homilist gives the following account that the Church reads on Holy Saturday: "He has gone to search for our first parent, as for a lost sheep. Greatly desiring to visit those who live in darkness and in the shadow of death, he has gone to free from sorrow the captives Adam and Eve, he who is both God and the son of Eve. . . . The Lord approached them bearing the cross, the weapon that had won him the victory. . . . He took him (Adam) by the hand and raised him up, saying: Awake, O sleeper, and rise from the dead, and Christ will give you light."

The great and life-giving drama, where God unfolded his plan of salvation through Christ, was scripted, inspired, and directed by the Holy Spirit.

Chapter Four

In the Holy Church

"The Church is called catholic or universal because it has spread throughout the entire world, from one end of the earth to the other. . . . It is most aptly called a church, which means an 'assembly of those called out,' because it 'calls out' all humans and gathers them together. . . . So the psalmist says: I will give thanks to you in the great assembly, O Lord; in the mighty throng I will praise you." This is a passage from a catechetical instruction by Cyril of Jerusalem, which is in the Office of Readings for Wednesday of the Seventh Week in Ordinary Time. I find it particularly relevant to our topic because it defines the nature of the Church as the assembly that God has gathered from every corner of the world. Having been called out by God, it now calls out and gathers the entire world, so that as a great assembly of all the peoples on earth it may give God thanks and praise. The Church is "called out" and "calls out"; it is gathered and gathers.

THE WORSHIPING COMMUNITY

When I teach about the ecclesial aspect of the liturgy, I do exegesis of the classic biblical hymn in 1 Peter 2:9-10: "You are a chosen race, a royal priesthood, a holy nation, God's own people, in order that you may proclaim the mighty acts of him who called you out of darkness into his marvelous light." I should preface this with the admission that my exegesis is not the standard way of handling biblical texts. I do not mind if it is deemed amateurish. As a liturgist I have a point to make about the nature of the Church as a worshiping community, and I find solid support for this in the hymn, if it is explained liturgically. Basically the hymn transfers three Old Testament titles of Israel to the new people of God. The Church is now a chosen race (Isa 43:20), a royal priesthood, or body of priests (Exod 19:16), and a holy nation, or people set apart for God (Exod 19:6). So far I base my exegesis on William Dalton's commentary (*The New Jerome Biblical Commentary*). From here on the liturgist in me would beg indulgence for proceeding on a different route.

Dalton interprets the phrase "that you may declare the wonderful deeds," which God accomplished in the death and resurrection of Christ, to mean "Christian witness to the gospel." He explains that the succeeding phrase "called you out of darkness into his marvelous light" refers to the call of converts from paganism. I do not doubt his sound exegesis. But I wish to recall that we are dealing with a baptismal hymn that alludes to an Old Testament type. As Israel was called out of Egypt to worship God in the desert (that was Moses' excuse to Pharaoh to allow the Israelites to leave Egypt), so through baptism the Church was called from darkness into God's marvelous light to proclaim as a worshiping community the wonderful works of God in Christ. It is easy to connect "darkness" to the darkness that covered Egypt prior to the exodus of the Israelites to the land of light in the Middle East. The word *ekklesía* (Church) is alluded to in verse 9 by the Greek *ek skotous kalesantos* (called out of darkness). God called and gathered the Church into an assembly summoned to worship. *Ekklesía* carries the notion of a public assembly that is summoned regularly to discuss the affairs of the state. In a word, public or liturgical worship is essential to the definition of the Church. I take it that the drafters of the Constitution on Liturgy used this premise to affirm the primacy of the liturgy in the life of the Church.

The Constitution on the Liturgy 10, which has the hallmarks of its drafters, is a source of gratification for us liturgists: "The liturgy is the summit toward which the activity of the Church is directed; at the same time it is the fount from which all the Church's power flows. For the aim and object of apostolic works is that all who are made children of God by faith and baptism should come together to praise God in the midst of his Church, to take part in the sacrifice, and to eat the Lord's Supper." For some theologians who still regard liturgy as a compendium of rubrics, this statement is bewildering and inordinate. In the early years after the council a colleague in a school of theology where I was teaching harassed me as if I had authored the conciliar statement: "It's another example of your pretentious *panliturgism*," a word he coined to ridicule the progress of the liturgical reform. Another statement in Liturgy Constitution that caused some people to raise their eyebrows is simply astonishing: "Every liturgical celebration, because it is an action of Christ the Priest and of his Body which is the Church, is a sacred action surpassing all others; no other action of the Church can equal its effectiveness by the same title and to the same degree" (7).

I have entitled this chapter "In the Holy Church," a phrase the third-century *Apostolic Tradition* (chaps. 7, 8, 9, 21) appends to the Trinitarian doxology: "Through your Son Jesus Christ, through whom be glory and honor to you, Father and Son and Holy Spirit, in your holy Church, both now and through all ages. Amen." Ephesians 3:20 authorizes the inclusion of the Church in doxological formulas: "Glory be to him whose power, working in us, can do infinitely more than we can ask or imagine; glory be to him from generation to generation in the Church and in Christ Jesus for ever and ever. Amen." The first time I came across this type of doxology in a liturgical document I became a zealous promoter of attaching "in the holy Church" to doxologies. I advocated its inclusion in the "Glory be to the Father" and to the grand Eucharistic doxology. The assembly stared at me questioningly and concelebrants frowned at me for apparently making the Church a member of the Trinity. It was a dead loss. Clearly, according to *Apostolic Tradition*, it is in the midst of the Church that liturgical worship, which centers on giving glory to God, is celebrated. Earlier in the first century *Didachè* (chap. 9) used the word "Church" in the context of the liturgical assembly: "As this broken bread was scattered over the hills and then, when gathered, became one mass, so may your Church (*Ekklesía*) be gathered from the ends of the earth into your kingdom." The grains of wheat that were gathered from the hills to become one bread paint the image of the Church that was gathered from every part of the world to become one bread, the body of Christ.

CHRIST AND THE PRIESTLY PEOPLE

The classic definition of the liturgy was formulated by Pope Pius XII in his Encyclical Letter *Mediator Dei*: Liturgy is "the public worship which our Redeemer as head of the Church renders to the Father, as well as the worship which the community of the faithful renders to its Founder, and through him to the heavenly Father. In short, it is the worship rendered by the Mystical Body of Christ in the entirety of its head and members" (25). The definition has two parts. The first presents a picture of Christ, in accord with the imagery employed by Hebrews 8:1-2, as the eternal High Priest who is seated at the right hand of God, ministering in the heavenly sanctuary. The Encyclical Letter calls him Redeemer and head of the Church. These are relational titles. They tell us that having returned to the heavenly realm, Christ now stands before God in his role as Redeemer and head of the Church. His death on the cross was his supreme act of worship. In heaven it takes the form of supplication for the people he redeemed. In the words of Romans 8:34, Jesus Christ who died and rose from the dead is seated at the right hand of God, interceding for us. The worship he began on earth continues in the heavenly courts. Hebrews 5:7 describes that earthly worship: "In the days of his flesh, Jesus offered up prayers and supplications, with loud cries and tears, to the one who was able to save him from death." The liturgy that he performed once for all on Calvary he now celebrates at the right hand of God.

I would like to believe that the heavenly liturgy is Christ's continuing anamnesis of his paschal mystery before the throne of God and for which the entire host of heaven ceaselessly chants divine praises and blessings. Guesswork, I would caution, can lead to fantasy and reverie. When we deal with heaven, sometimes the best thing to do is to close the eyes of our intellect and believe that the reality surpasses all our imaginings.

The Constitution on Liturgy has a more graphic and lyrical description of worship in heaven: "Christ Jesus, High Priest of the new and eternal covenant, taking human nature, introduced into this earthly exile the hymn that is sung throughout all ages in the halls of heaven. He joins the entire human community to himself, associating it with his own singing of this canticle of divine praise" (83). The Constitution envisages a kind of movement from the cross to the heavenly courts and back to earth. There is a continuity of movement. What Christ does in heaven reflects what he did on the cross, and what we do on earth reflects what happens in heaven. There is something quite musical and poetic about it, like the final movement of a symphony that recaptures the preceding movements.

An important teaching of the Constitution is on the role or ministry of the Church: "For Christ continues his priestly work through the agency of his Church, which is unceasingly engaged in praising the Lord and interceding for the salvation of the whole world. The Church does this not only by celebrating the Eucharist, but also in other ways, especially by praying the divine office" (83). Here the Constitution visualizes heaven as a place where everybody sings for all eternity. Christ himself is said to sing the canticle of praise. I theorize that the subject of his song is the paschal mystery that he presents to the Father in an eternal anamnesis. I detect in this article the hand of Benedictine monks. I was informed that the monks of Solesmes contributed to its drafting. They epitomize the musical quality of liturgical worship by their daily choral chanting. I remember Marsili's wise advice to those who find the chanting of the Liturgy of the Hours burdensome. In heaven, he affirmed, there are no longer biblical readings, no more Eucharist, no more sacraments, and no more sacramentals and blessings. All that remains is the chanting of the divine praises that the Liturgy of the Hours echoes on earth. That being the case, he advised that we practice now what we shall be doing in heaven.

The belief that the earthly liturgy echoes the heavenly is the heart of liturgical theology and spirituality. It assures us that Christ is still actively engaged in the care of the people for whom he shed his blood. It likewise gives us the hope that the curtain will not close on the drama of salvation until humankind shall have joined Christ at the right hand of God. The words of Hebrews 6:19-20 are very comforting: "We have this hope, a sure and steadfast anchor of the soul, a hope that enters into the inner shrine behind the curtain, where Jesus, a forerunner on our behalf, has entered." Christ's continuing supplication for us and our sure hope of glory find resonance in the liturgy of Christ's ascension. The first preface of the solemnity reassures us that when Christ ascended to the heavenly realm, "he has not abandoned our human condition but has filled us with hope that where he, our head, has gone before us we, his members, shall follow after." The second preface tells us that Christ was taken up to heaven in the sight of his disciples "to claim for us a share in his divinity."

The second part of Pope Pius XII's definition of the liturgy deals with the role of the Church. The liturgy is "the worship which the community of the faithful renders to its Founder and through him to the heavenly Father." This seems to say that the Church addresses its worship directly to the person of Christ. He is the object and subject of the Church's worship. In the liturgy we speak to him and about him. It is his person that we meet in faith and whose presence we experience *per ritus et preces*. I should point out, however, that the Encyclical Letter is not entitled *Mediator Dei* for naught. Christ is the mediator of liturgical worship. The Church does not approach God directly: that, indeed, would be presumption. As we saw in the preceding chapter of this work, the Church addresses its prayer to God through the mediation of Christ. God gazes upon the assembled community and recognizes the image of the Son. Likewise, God beholds the Son and discovers the face of the worshiping Church.

The double definition of the liturgy as worship of Christ and worship of the Church should not cause us to imagine that there are two kinds of liturgy. It is not in keeping with *Mediator Dei* to think that

Christ performs the heavenly liturgy, while we perform the earthly. *Mediator Dei* speaks of one and the same action of Christ at the right hand of God to which the Church gives an earthly shape and appearance. The liturgy we celebrate embodies the heavenly worship of Christ. If not for this, what value would our liturgical celebrations have? It would be as ineffective as the daily sacrifices of Hebrews 10:11-14: "Every priest stands day after day at his service, offering again and again the same sacrifices that can never take away sins. But when Christ had offered for all time a single sacrifice for sins, he sat down at the right hand of God. . . . For by a single offering he has perfected for all time those who are sanctified." According to the Encyclical Letter, the liturgy "is the worship rendered by the Mystical Body of Christ in the entirety of its head and members." On the cross, as Christ worshiped God, he wedded the Church and associated her inseparably with his act of worship.

The doctrine of the Mystical Body is plainly linked to the biblical imagery of Christ and the Church as bridegroom and bride. The great liturgical theologian Odo Casel puts this succinctly in his book *The Mystery of Christian Worship*: "Bridegroom and bride, head and members act as one." The reality of the Mystical Body is achieved through the union of Christ, the bridegroom, and the Church, his bride. In the words of the Constitution on Liturgy, "Christ always truly associates the Church with himself in this great work wherein God is perfectly glorified and the recipients made holy. The Church is the Lord's beloved Bride who calls to him and through him offers worship to the eternal Father. . . . In the liturgy the whole public worship is performed by the Mystical Body of Jesus Christ, that is, by the Head and his members" (7).

The Constitution, rephrasing Pope Pius XII, defines the liturgy as "an action of Christ the Priest and of his Body which is the Church" (7). Time and again I have been asked who does what. It is an innocuous if not artless query from students who want clear-cut definitions of terms. How does one explain the assertion that there is one action with two agents? As the definition stands, Christ and the Church seem to be on the same footing, and that could be quite confusing. Can Christ dispense with the Church or at least reduce its role to something less consequential? And who are referred to in the word "Church"? In my years of teaching I have cautioned students about assuming that definitions are final and definitive. No definition is exhaustive, and here is an example of a definition that still leaves much to be defined.

At any rate, the Constitution is unequivocal in its declaration that the liturgy is the exercise of Christ's priesthood. But to accomplish it visibly he assigns a particular role to the Church. That role is ministerial. The Constitution describes the Church's role with phrases such as "through the hands of the priests," "when a person baptizes," "when the holy Scriptures are read," and "when the Church prays and sings." It is the Church (or, more specifically, the ministers and the assembly) that gives to Christ's invisible action a form that is perceptible to the senses.

Such a role is indispensable. Without the ministry of the Church there can be no liturgy: there can be no baptism, no Eucharist, no sacraments, no sacramentals, and no Liturgy of the Hours. No person is baptized without the Church's minister. The Eucharist is not celebrated without the ordained minister. By the mystery of the incarnation God bound himself, as it were, to the ministry of the Church. In the economy of the incarnation God became dependent on the Church, like the Child of Bethlehem who was dependent on his mother. When liturgical ministers, both ordained and lay, perform their roles, Christ must be filled with gratitude! His saving sacraments need human hands and voices. The power of his word, proclaimed in the assembly, needs the ministry of readers. After his ascension and in the present economy of salvation, Christ has need of the Church! On Calvary he saved humankind without the Church; in the liturgy he associates the Church to himself in order to continue what he began on the cross. Without the visible and tangible rites of the Church that we call liturgy the priestly office of Christ would remain invisible and inaccessible. In the words of Odo Casel: "Without it [the liturgy], the mystery of Christ could not become a reality age after age, from one generation to another."

CHRIST'S PRESENCE IN THE CHURCH

What I have been discussing so far is premised on the belief that Christ is present when the assembly performs the liturgy. The opening paragraph of article 7 of the Constitution develops this theological premise. Christ did not merely author the sacraments and consent to the institution of sacramentals. As their subject and agent he is present in the celebration of the rite. The Constitution explains this presence in great detail: "To accomplish so great a work, Christ is always present in his Church, especially in its liturgical celebrations." What are these liturgical celebrations? In the first place, the Eucharist, where he is present not only in the Eucharistic elements but also in the person of the priest through whose ministry he now offers what he formerly offered on the cross. He is present also in the sacraments, "so that when a person baptizes it is really Christ himself who baptizes." He is present when the word of God is proclaimed in the assembly "since it is he himself who speaks when the holy Scriptures are read in the Church." He is present when the Church prays and sings, for he promised to be in the midst of two or three gathered together in his name.

Surely Christ does not preside at the Eucharist, nor does he immerse in water the person who is baptized. These are the external, visible actions whose subjects are the Church's ministers. I am appalled by pictures of Christ celebrating the Mass and distributing Holy Communion with small white hosts. I am disconcerted by the claim that the Last Supper was the first Mass. I have misgivings about the statement that the Mass is the sacrifice of the cross. In my thinking it is an invalid shortcut of a theological doctrine. The Mass is not the sacrifice of the cross that happened once for all and cannot be repeated. Rather, it is the sacrament of the Last Supper and sacrifice of Christ. Abridging the statement by leaving out the sacrament, perhaps to simplify matters, is courting the perils of theological imprecision. The Last Supper and the sacrifice of the cross were the historical actions of Christ. The Mass, on the other hand, is their liturgical, sacramental, and visible manifestation, which the priest performs *in persona Christi* (in the person of Christ) as presider of the assembly.

I am aware that what I am saying can also be appalling and disconcerting for some people. But do we not too readily call the table for the Mass an altar, the presider a priest who offers the unrepeatable sacrifice, and the consecrated bread and wine the body and blood of Christ? Surely such statements are theologically incontestable. Would it not be rather contrived to announce to the communicant: "The sacrament of the body of Christ"? The truth, however, is that the form or shape of the Mass as sacred meal copies the Last Supper and hence is held on a table. But because the Mass is an anamnesis of Christ's sacrifice on the cross, the table is also called altar. I should note that the table should appear as a dining table and not an Old Testament altar of sacrifice. I hope I make sense when I say that theologically the presider is a priest, but liturgically the priest is the presider of the assembly at the Lord's Supper. Christ the High Priest does not preside at the celebration of the Mass, but he continues to offer to God, through the ministry of the presider, what he once offered on the cross.

The celebration of the Mass is liturgy; the Supper and sacrifice it represents are the nucleus of salvation history.

Through baptism Christ claims for himself the baptized he has saved by his death, but it is the minister who performs the rite. The Augustinian saying that "when a person baptizes, it is really Christ himself who baptizes" is a crux of interpretation. Surely Christ does not pour the water and utter the baptismal formula. How can he then be said to baptize? One of my students tried to depict what he thought Augustine meant by painting the baptizing priest with Christ's hand interlocked with his. It really was more of a cartoon than a theological representation. It dawned upon him that certain theological concepts defy any attempt to do a facsimile. A plausible interpretation is that Augustine identifies the ministry of the Church with Christ's saving work. Thus he could affirm that it is Christ who "baptizes," who redeems the person through the baptismal ministry of the Church. This is not just a question of semantics. It is a striking affirmation that Christ is personally present and at work when the Church celebrates the liturgy. Pope Leo the Great expressed his keen sense of Christ's presence, when he wrote: "All that the Son of God did and taught for the world's reconciliation is not simply a matter of past history. Here and now we experience his power at work among us" (*Homily 12 on the Passion*).

Odo Casel makes a helpful distinction between mystery and liturgy: "Mystery means the heart of the action, that is to say, the redeeming work of the risen Lord, through the sacred actions he has appointed. Liturgy, corresponding to its original sense of people's work or service, means rather the action of the Church in conjunction with the saving action of Christ." Mystery is not to be equated simply with salvation history. In Casel's thinking mystery is the salvation history that Christ unfolds *per ritus et preces* of the Church. Casel cautions, however, against too pronounced a distinction, as if the word "liturgy" did not apply to the action of Christ and "mystery" to that of the Church. He explains that "when the Church performs her external rites, Christ is inwardly at work in them; thus what the Church does is in truth mystery." Similarly, the saving action that Christ accomplishes through the rites of the Church is in reality liturgy.

There are several ways a person, event, or thing can be present besides being physically at hand. A loved one can be present in the heart of the lover; an event can be present in the memory of those who experienced it; and a thing can be present in the mind or intellect. Such presences, though not physical, are real, because they exist as a matter of fact in the heart, memory, or intellect. They are not tangible, but it does not mean that they are false and nonexistent. They are not figments of the mind, because they exist as realities outside the mind. When the conciliar constitution affirms that "Christ is always present in his Church, especially in its liturgical celebrations," to which celebrations does it refer? The Constitution on the Liturgy names the instances when Christ is believed to be present: in the celebrations of the Mass, the sacraments, the word of God, and the divine office. He is present when the word of God is proclaimed in the assembly and "when the Church prays and sings" (7). These affirmations underline the presence of the risen Christ as he exercises through the ministry of the Church the priestly office that he assumed during his earthly life.

The other question is: how is Christ present in all the liturgical actions of the Church? Pope Paul VI, in the Encyclical Letter *Mysterium fidei*, provides the answer: "The presence of Christ in the Eucharist is called real not by exclusion, as if the other presences are not real, but par excellence." In an article entitled "La Liturgia presenza di Cristo" (*Anamnesis* I) Marsili makes a masterly study of the pope's doctrine, which he develops in four points. First, the pope acknowledges other real presences of Christ outside the Eucharistic bread and wine. Second, the Eucharistic presence, in contrast to the other presences, involves a "substantial" change in the consecrated bread and wine. It is permanent. On the other hand, the other presences, because they are bound to the liturgical action, are transitory. Christ is present while the word of God is read; he is present while the sick person is anointed; and he is present while the Liturgy of the Hours is prayed. Third, the other presences in the liturgy are to be understood in analogy with the Eucharistic presence. There is no difference between one and the other as far as the reality of Christ's presence is concerned. They are all real presences. Fourth, the real presence of Christ in the liturgy is best understood in the context of his saving work. The liturgy is the continuation of that work. In a word, Christ is as present in the assembly; the presider *in persona Christi*; the sacraments, sacramentals, and blessings; and the divine office as he is in the consecrated bread and wine. Obviously, the intensity with which that presence is felt will be dependent in part on the assembly's perception of faith and devotion. A person or object can be physically present yet remain on the periphery of one's focus of attention. Christ can shine brightly through liturgical prayers and symbols, but the heart and mind may possibly be concerned with other realities of life. The doctrine of the real presence, especially outside the Eucharistic bread and wine, requires the vivid awareness that in every liturgical rite Christ appears as large as life.

The conciliar constitution extends the doctrine of real presence, though in a more guarded way, to the "mysteries of redemption." In the observance of Sunday and the feasts the liturgical year unfolds the entire mystery of Christ from his "incarnation and birth until his ascension, the day of Pentecost, and the expectation of blessed hope and the Lord's return" (102). Here the Constitution gets rather close to accepting Odo Casel's controversial doctrine on the real presence of Christ's mysteries in the liturgical feasts. In Casel's thinking the birth of Christ comes to life as an event during Christmas liturgy. That is why the Church sings: "Today Christ is born for us, come let us adore him." There is realism in this as there is in one of Augustine's Good Friday homilies: "As we recall the passion of Christ, we see him, as it were with our eyes, nailed to the cross." Save for the cautious phrase "in some way made present," the Constitution does not cast aside Casel's mystery theology. On the contrary, it makes good use of it to enrich the faithful's experience of Christ in the course of the liturgical year. The text reads: "Recalling thus the mysteries of redemption, the Church opens to the faithful the riches of the Lord's powers and merits, so that these are in some way made present in every age in order that the faithful may lay hold on them and be filled with saving grace" (102).

THE LITURGY AS EPIPHANY OF THE CHURCH

I once asked an audience what impressed them most during the Sunday parish liturgy. The question was quickly answered: the burning candles, the crucifix, the imposing altar. Someone frivolously chanted: the priest! It took some time before I received the answer I was looking for: the assembly. As we enter the church on Sunday what should impress us first and foremost is the gathering of people from all walks of life, old and young, rich and poor, all united in common worship.

The Liturgy Constitution affirms that "the preeminent manifestation of the Church is present in the full, active participation of all God's holy people in these liturgical celebrations, especially in the same Eucharist, in a single prayer, at one altar at which the bishop presides, surrounded by his college of priests and by his ministers" (41). The Constitution is evidently inspired by Ignatius of Antioch's ecclesiological model in which the bishop represents God the Father, the presbyters the college of apostles, and the deacons Jesus Christ the servant (Trallians 3). In his letter to the Smyrneans he writes: "Where the bishop appears, there let the people be, just as where Jesus Christ is, there is the Catholic Church" (8). Article 41 of the Constitution is patterned on the Ignatian monarchical model where the bishop is the chief *leitourgos*. He convokes the local Church to the liturgical gathering and causes it to be an epiphany of the universal Church. That is why it exhorts all to "hold in very high esteem the liturgical life of the diocese which centers around the bishop, especially in his cathedral church."

As a rejoinder the Constitution on the Church teaches that when the bishop presides, Christ is present and "the one, holy, catholic, and apostolic Church gathers together" (LG 26). The Constitution pursues the subject when it declares that "in any community existing around an altar, under the sacred ministry of the bishop, there is manifested a symbol of that charity and unity of the Mystical Body." Among the epiphanies of the Church, the Eucharistic celebration is where the presence and authority of the bishop are most felt. Day after day his name is mentioned in the Eucharistic Prayer, in accord with the celebrated statement of Ignatius of Antioch: "Let that celebration of the Eucharist be considered valid which is held under the bishop or anyone to whom he has committed it. Let no one do anything touching the Church apart from the bishop" (Smyrneans 8). Priests may quarrel with their bishop, but there is no way they can circumvent the mention of his name in the Eucharistic Prayer.

The liturgical assembly takes on the personality of the *Ekklesía* when its bishop presides. Although the gathering, not the venue, constitutes the *Ekklesía*, the cathedral church is the conventional place where the epiphany in its fullness takes place. More importantly, the local assembly presided over by the bishop is, in the words of the Constitution on the Church, the gathering together of "the one, holy, catholic, and apostolic Church." I explain this mystifying doctrine saying that the liturgical assembly is the concrete, here-and-now manifestation of the universal Church, which is in reality a conceptualization of the unity that exists among all the local Churches. An audience did not take kindly to what I asked in a desperate effort to make myself clear: "Have you ever seen the Universal Church promenading in the park? But you can see it gathered in a liturgical assembly where the bishop presides."

The Constitution on Liturgy addresses the question about parishes and how they manifest the Church: "But because it is impossible for the bishop always and everywhere to preside over the whole flock in his Church, he cannot do other than establish lesser groupings of the faithful" (42). Among these, the parishes are the most notable for two reasons. First, "they represent in a certain way the visible Church as it is established throughout the world." In union with the bishop they also become "in a certain way" the visible manifestation of the one, holy, catholic, and apostolic Church. Second, the parishes are "set up locally under a pastor who takes the place of the bishop." The Decree on the Ministry and Life of Priests resonates this: "In a certain way the priests make the bishop present in every gathering of the faithful" (5). Likewise, the Constitution on the Church teaches: "Associated with their bishop in a spirit of trust and generosity, priests make him present in a certain sense in the individual local congregations of the faithful" (28).

Article 42 concludes with an exhortation: "The liturgical life of the parish and its relationship to the bishop must be fostered in the thinking and practice of both laity and clergy." In the fourth century there arose the practice, especially in Egypt, of reading the so-called festal letters of the bishop on the celebration of Easter. In some countries today bishops and the conference of bishops regularly send pastoral letters that are read on Sunday in place of the homily. These pastoral letters are often cause oriented and represent the Church's stand on certain political, environmental, and socioeconomic issues that afflict the country. Availing themselves of the modern means of transportation bishops can regularly visit parishes to administer the sacraments of confirmation and ordination. I admiringly give the thumbs-up to a bishop of a hinterland diocese who visits on horseback far-flung villages that take two days to reach. Villagers are not only comforted; they are also encouraged to hold on to their faith in the face of aggressive proselytizers who take advantage of the absence of the shepherd of the flock.

In the fourth century the Roman Church introduced the practice of sending the *fermentum* to parishes or *tituli*. The *fermentum* was a piece of consecrated bread that the pope sent to parishes in the city on Sundays. Marcel Metzger gives helpful information about the practice in an article in *Handbook for Liturgical Studies* III. In the year 416 Pope Innocent I sent a letter to the bishop of Gubbio to explain the meaning of the practice: "As to the *fermentum* which we send on Sundays to the diverse *tituli*: all our churches are within the walls of the city. On Sunday, as their priests are not able to join us because of the people entrusted to their care, the *fermentum* from our Eucharist is therefore sent to them by acolytes so that they will not consider themselves separated from communion with us, especially on that day." It would appear that in the eighth century the practice evolved into the rite of mixing the *fermentum* in the chalice before communion, as it is still done today, except that the priest breaks his own host. There is eloquent symbolism here. The *fermentum* signifies the unity of the parish with its bishop. Not having historical tools at their disposal, some medieval theologians resorted to an allegorical interpretation of the rite of the *fermentum*. According to Thomas Aquinas, it symbolizes the resurrection of Christ when his body and blood were united again after they were disjoined by the separate consecration of bread and wine. The practice of the *fermentum* so vividly captures the image of the local Church as one worshiping community, that I have suggested its revival. Perhaps on Holy Thursday and other occasions when the clergy join the bishop for the Eucharist, the *fermentum* could be brought home to the parish and the faithful catechized about the unity of the Church.

The Liturgy Constitution exhorts further that "efforts also must be made to encourage a sense of community within the parish, above all in the common celebration of the Sunday Mass" (42). In 1786 the ill-fated Synod of Pistoia ordered that Sunday Masses be celebrated only in parishes, except in the case of cloistered nuns. The Synod, which was two centuries ahead of its time, has striking similarities with the liturgical reforms of Vatican II: the use of the vernacular, more ample biblical readings at Mass, obligatory catechesis of parents and godparents before the baptism of children, the importance of parish liturgy, and restraint on devotional practices. This should not come as a surprise, because its designer, Bishop Scipione da Ricci, had availed himself of the same liturgical documents that the drafters later used for the Constitution on Liturgy. The fragmentation of parishes into small semiprivate chapels and the practice now prevalent in some cities of celebrating Sunday Mass regularly in commercial centers or shopping malls sadly impair the sense of parish community. Time and again people try to justify the practice by citing pastoral convenience, which is really a lame excuse. But when pastoral convenience is just another word for the pervasive "pastor's convenience," I think that any attempt to rectify the matter is a pie in the sky.

The liturgy is the epiphany of the Church. To make this a reality the faithful should claim ownership of their ecclesial community. I notice marked improvement in participation and the composition of the general intercessions when people are conscious of belonging to the one, holy, catholic, and apostolic Church gathered in worship. This happens in cities as well as in small and poor communities living far from each other. People begin to think universally and globally, even if there are vexing local issues they need to address in prayer. In a small congregation where I presided at Mass several years ago the general intercessions turned into occasions to announce birthdays, minor illnesses, the demise of the community's pet dog, and to petition God urgently to send fine weather during the community outing. With patient catechesis on the meaning of being Church I was able to achieve a degree of success in changing this.

There are two Latin axioms I often employ to develop the sense of ownership in the Church. One is *sentire cum Ecclesia* and the other is *sentire esse Ecclesiam*. Many are familiar with the first, but not with the second. Roughly translated, *sentire cum Ecclesia* means to have the same mindset as the Church. This attitude is typified by a cheerful and ready acceptance of what the hierarchy teaches and commands. It is powered by faith and obedience. *Sentire esse Ecclesiam*, on the other hand, means having a sense not only of belonging to the Church but also of being able to claim ownership of the Church and be responsible for it. When Pope John Paul II visited our college on the Aventine Hill in June 1987, I had the rare privilege to deliver a short address to him. My good friend Magnus Löhrer, a dogmatic theologian whom I greatly admired, introduced me to the concept of *sentire esse Ecclesiam*, which I had not hitherto considered. As I discoursed on it, I could sense a faint, complacent smile on the face of the Holy Father. In the four or five times I had a word with him he addressed me as professor, and I took that to mean that he agreed with the axiom *sentire esse Ecclesiam*. The other speech I delivered in his presence was in October 1984 on the occasion of the convention of national liturgical commissions. The topic was liturgical inculturation. Unfortunately, my paper was edited backstage, so I ended up making "safe" statements that must have bored him to tears.

The epiphany of the Church in the liturgy is reinforced by the hierarchical order observed during the celebration: a presider assisted by various ministers and an assembly with the primary role of active and conscious participation. Such a feature of hierarchical order distinguishes the liturgical assembly from acephalous gatherings that dispense with elected or appointed leadership and corresponding roles and thus can sometimes give birth to individualism. There is no need to be apologetic about the hierarchical nature of the liturgy, as there is no need to be on the defensive when questions are raised about the existence of a hierarchical order in the Church.

Hierarchical celebrations seem to be the practice of the Church in Jerusalem, which was governed by the resident apostle James with his council of elders or Sanhedrin. Revelation 4:24 infers this form of liturgy presided by a bishop who is surrounded by twenty-four elders (the Greek is *presbyteroi*). Ignatius of Antioch advanced the cause of hierarchical liturgy and made it a norm: "All should respect the deacons as they would Jesus Christ, just as they respect the bishop as representing the Father and the priests as the council of God and the college of the apostles. Apart from these there is nothing that can be called an *Ekklesía*" (*Trallians*, 3). But hierarchical order does more than point to the need for order within the worshiping community. It underlines the Christian concept of leadership, which is exercised primarily in the liturgy.

Let me return to an earlier discussion regarding the ministry of the clergy according to the teaching of *Apostolic Tradition*: the clergy are ordained *propter liturgiam*. When ordained ministers exercise their role as leaders of the liturgical assembly, they realize fully the task for which they have been ordained. At the same time, it is in the liturgy that the faithful are eminently served by the clergy. The other word for hierarchical order is servant leadership. It pertains to the nature of the Church, and it is the chief duty of the hierarchy to prove that it is not an empty word. When the priest kneels humbly before the faithful to wash their feet in silence, he convinces the world that hierarchy and servant leadership are one and the same. In short, the liturgy should project the image of a Church gathered under the leadership of the bishop, who is surrounded by his clergy, who minister to the people entrusted to their pastoral care.

Viewed from a sociocultural standpoint, the liturgical assembly is the epiphany of the universal fellowship of the faithful. In it we witness the convergence of men and women, each one with a personal history and pursuit in life, and mostly strangers to each other. Yet for the duration of the liturgy they allow themselves to be called sisters and brothers and to experience together the sense of community, a community that is transitory and yet recurring, personal in one sense and yet anonymous in another. Unity is experienced at its deepest level, because the assembly breaks the barriers of race, social status, and ideology. The liturgical assembly symbolizes the community of faith where the poor sit with the rich, the ignorant with the learned, the social outcast with the respectable class, and the nameless with the celebrities. The reformed liturgy has thus rightly eliminated the practice of reserving seats in churches and giving special treatment to particular persons. In a word, the liturgical assembly invites human society to make a collective effort to affirm human equality, eliminate social injustice, and promote true fellowship among all. In this sense the liturgical assembly, like a prophetic symbol, will always contain an element of counterculture. It will always protest against the rugged individualism of society and nations, against racial and social discrimination, against social injustice, and against political and economic domination. It is indeed the epiphany of the Church "to those who are outside as a sign lifted up among the nations, under which the scattered children of God may be gathered together, until there is one sheepfold and one shepherd" (SC 2).

THE CHURCH AND PLACES OF WORSHIP

My first visit to the Holy Land was truly memorable. As the plane circled around Tel Aviv, I got a panoramic view of the city and its environs. The thought that sprang in my mind was, "He had been here." I admit I was seized with emotion, but that quickly left me when the suspicious immigration officers battered me with repeated interrogations as if I had committed a crime. When I visited the holy sepulcher early the next morning, I had the singular privilege of being alone. I knelt by the tomb and repeated the same words, "He had been here." It was only when a hooded Orthodox monk stretched out the collection box toward me that I returned to harsh reality. I spent several days by the sea of Tiberias. Walking by the lake, I read the gospels, and lo and behold, their stories began to jump out of the pages. He preached here; he took the boat here; he walked on the water here; he calmed the storm here. Once more I said, "He had been here." But I woke up to reality when a Palestinian woman approached me and asked for one of the cigars I was smoking.

For several years after that I returned year after year to give liturgy conferences in Tiberias. It is amazing that I formed a theology of the holy places amid the ongoing hostilities between Israelis and Palestinians and, to some degree, the lack of ecumenical understanding among the various Churches there. These places had been made holy by the presence and the activities of the Incarnate Son of God. No amount of political and religious conflict can eradicate their holiness. He had been in these places, and they will always serve as points of reference when Christians in any part of the world gather as a community of worshipers in order to experience his saving presence.

I propose that the theology of the places of worship should begin with the mystery of the incarnation. By his incarnation God, who exists beyond time and history, broke into cosmic time and into human history. God, who does not inhabit space, began to occupy space. Jesus, the Word made flesh, stayed in the womb of a human mother, was born in the little town of Bethlehem, and was laid in a manger. And after he died, he was laid in a tomb, thus completing the human cycle that starts in the womb and ends in the tomb. He spent his early years in the town of Nazareth. At the age of twelve he journeyed on foot across Palestine for the Passover festival in Jerusalem. He was baptized in a river, roamed the streets of cities and the countryside, climbed hills and mountains, and crossed the lakes. He ate his last supper with his disciples in a room we call today the Cenacle. Finally, on a hill called Golgotha he offered once for all to the Father the supreme sacrifice. When God became human he occupied space, sanctified it, and made it a place of encounter with the divine.

Christians have always made use of places as their meeting place with God. For Christians the original meeting place with God was the open space of a hill outside the Holy City of Jerusalem, outside the sacred temple, outside the holy of holies. There, a place for executions, a place made unholy by the shedding of human blood, Jesus hung on a cross between heaven and earth, reconciling God and humankind. The place of abomination became the holiest space where true worship was offered. From then on what was profane became sacred, because "he had been there."

A place is holy not because it has blessed walls, not because it has a sanctuary and an altar, not because it has a cross and sacred images. A place is holy because Christ dwells there. A school gymnasium, an open park, a space in a shopping mall or airport or prison compound can become holy when Christ finds a place there—he who at his birth was laid in a manger, since there was no place for him in the inn, and who complained that he did not even have a stone on which to lay his head. In a word, the presence of Christ in liturgical celebrations explains why there is no space that cannot be considered suitable for worship.

The theology of liturgical space allows us to connect places of worship with the earthly places visited by Christ. Thus any place designated for worship, whether permanently or for the occasion, evokes the houses, streets, hilltops, fields, desert places, and lakesides where Christ preached the word, defended the weak and oppressed, healed broken spirits, cured bodily illnesses, and performed miracles. As he was present in those places, so he is present now in our place of worship. Of the places where he was present three hold special significance for our liturgy. The first is the Cenacle where he ate the final meal with his disciples; the second is the hill where he offered the eternal sacrifice; and the third is the tomb where he rested before rising from the dead.

In his risen body Christ no longer occupies material space. He now dwells in the "space" of the assembly, which he claims as his body. The worshiping community is the space that Christ inhabits. And where that community worships, Christ is present and his presence sanctifies the place where the community is gathered. As the presence of Christ made holy the places in Palestine, so his presence sanctifies the places where Christians gather for worship. It is the presence of Christ in the worshiping assembly that transforms space into a meeting place with God. To the question, "Where can I find God," we often offer an easy, practical answer: "Go inside a church and there you will find God." A better answer, however, is, "Go and join the community at worship and there you will meet God." For God dwells not in empty buildings made of wood and stones but in the hearts of the faithful who gather to sing God's praises.

It seems to me that our sole justification for constructing church buildings and other places of worship is that the community assembled in them bears the presence of Christ who promised to be in the midst of two or three gathered in his name. In this sense, is it warranted to claim that the worshiping community is the "extension" and the presence of Christ's glorified body? Can we affirm that the liturgical assembly is the visible form of Christ who is the true temple of God? In other words, can we call the worshiping community the sacrament of Christ's risen body? But what a sacrament that is! For the earthly sacrament is a dull, opaque image of the dazzling glory of Christ's body. Think of the personal circumstances of the assembly, their passion and apathy, and the heavy burdens they carry in their hearts. That is the living sacrament we house in the sacred space we call church.

Why, then, do we need to build churches and dedicate them with a solemn rite? The answer is not exactly theological; the answer is practical. The faithful need a covered and sometimes walled space where they can meet in order to celebrate the liturgy, especially the Lord's Supper. They need a building to protect them from the elements and to experience a certain closeness that generates community spirit. For this they also need suitable spaces for the table, the presider and ministers, and the assembly. Such space is demanded not by the building itself but by the nature of the Eucharistic celebration. That is why, outside the church edifice, even in congested rooms, suitable space will always be needed for the table, the presider and ministers, and the assembly.

Following the example of Jesus who celebrated the Last Supper in the Cenacle or dining room, early Christians celebrated the Eucharist at home, as the Acts of the Apostles informs us. Wealthy Christian converts donated their spacious homes for the use of the community, especially when it gathered for Sunday worship. Such places came to be known as *domus Ecclesiae*, or house of the Church. These were the houses that Christians owned or sometimes even rented and to which they gave the name "church." *Ecclesía*, or "gathering," is the name Christians called themselves, for indeed God assembled them out of darkness into his marvelous light. Thus the church edifice became the symbol of their identity as a worshiping community. The Constitution on the Church (6) points out that the community is in fact the house of God, the household of God, the dwelling place of God, and God's holy temple. This living temple made up of people is symbolized by the places of worship. According to the Constitution, the liturgical space is both a place of assembly and an image of the community that God gathers together. It should not come as a surprise that eventually the building was simply called church. *Domus Ecclesiae* (house of the Church) became *domus ecclesia* (house church).

Since the church building symbolizes the Church community, it stands to reason that over the centuries the faithful made efforts to make their churches truly representative of their status and dignity as children of God. Depending on the material resources of the community, church buildings can be expensive projects. Excessive expenditures can sometimes even take precedence over the Church's work of charity and evangelization. St. Jerome did not mince his words when he spoke against such excesses: "The true temple of Christ is the soul of the believer; adorn it, clothe it, offer it gifts, receive Christ into it. Of what value is it to make walls gleam with jewels while Christ dies of hunger in the poor?" (*Letter 58*, 8). We should, of course, heed such reminders, but we should not neglect the material temple, which without being extravagant should be noble in its beauty and simplicity. It should be worthy of the sacrament of Christ's risen body, the priestly people of God. I still remember the lectures on liturgical space that Virgilio Noè gave at the Pontifical Liturgical Institute. At that time I found it odd that churches were called space, but thanks to him my theology of church buildings acquired the basic premise that by his incarnation Christ shares our space.

We know that the dream of some pastors is to build or renovate parish churches, while that of some bishops is to construct or enlarge the cathedral. It seems that the newly appointed pastor or bishop often has something to improve or correct in the existing edifices. I sometimes entertain the unkind thought that they might be building a monument *ad perpetuam rei memoriam*, after the example of popes who had their names inscribed on the façade of monumental churches. Money can certainly come from wealthy patrons, but sometimes at what cost to the renewed liturgy, especially when norms have to be accommodated to the whim of the donors?

Church edifices reflect the nobility and dignity of the Christian community. For this reason, the faithful desire to own a church that can make them proud. However, the care given to church buildings should in a relative way be accorded to other places outside the church where people gather for the liturgy. The Eucharist is the community's celebration of the Lord's Supper, regardless of whether it is held in a cathedral or a stadium. Ultimately, what matters is not the edifice but the liturgical celebration. Outside churches and oratories the table for the Eucharist should be worthy, the vessels deserving of the sacraments of Christ's body and blood, the liturgical books becoming, and the vestments appropriate. The reason is because places outside a church building attain the dignity of a liturgical space when the liturgy is celebrated there. Like church edifices, they become the image and symbol of the *Ekklesía*. During the liturgical worship these places are not less hallowed than a dedicated church. The assembly should be able to say, "He is here," because we are here. It is the presence of Christ in his body the Church that confers holiness to the space. It is the Eucharist celebrated there that sanctifies the place. It is God's word proclaimed and preached in a football field that makes the place a liturgical space. It is the assuring words of reconciliation that turn a classroom bench into a liturgical meeting place between God and the penitent.

There is a mistaken notion among some people that when the liturgy, including the Eucharist, is celebrated outside the church building, we need not worry about liturgical propriety regarding vessels, vestments, and books. Such attitude projects the wrong view that the Eucharist outside the church, especially in shopping malls and prisons, is less noble than the Eucharist celebrated in churches or cathedrals. It is always useful to remember that the worth of the liturgy does not rest upon the place where it is celebrated but upon the presence of Christ in his community.

I had the occasion to participate in a Sunday Mass in an airport, which is under the ecclesiastical jurisdiction of a rather wealthy diocese. To my chagrin the priest used a leaflet for the readings, which he devoutly kissed after the gospel. The Sacramentary was a worn-out book that antique dealers would be eager to buy. The chalice was a miniscule of a vessel and the ciborium was an orange-colored plastic container. The table was so low that the priest had to stoop to read the Eucharistic Prayer. It crossed my mind that his parish probably had all the appropriate vessels and furnishings, but that he had reasoned that, after all, this was just a Mass in an airport, so why bother to bring the good things reserved for a church?

A great number of liturgical celebrations are normally held inside a church. Popular devotions, on the other hand, may be held either inside or outside the church. As a matter of fact, several popular devotions are performed at home or in the open. Think of the rosary, novenas, street and fluvial processions, and religious dramas. In this way these devotions bring the faith outside the confines of sacred spaces and thus sanctify the places that are commonly regarded as secular and profane. However, it is not quite accurate to consider the liturgy as a church-contained celebration. While it is true that the Eucharist and most sacraments are normally held in church, it is also true that there are many other liturgical celebrations that are normally performed outside the church. The church building is not the only venue for liturgical worship.

The Jewish tradition, which the Christians inherited in some measure, used the Jerusalem temple, the local synagogues, and the homes as venue for worship. Some Jewish religious sects even baptized their proselytes in rivers. But the focal point of the yearly Passover meal and of the weekly observance of welcoming the Sabbath was the home. This domestic tradition left its mark on Christian worship. The Eucharist was originally celebrated at home, and priests normally visited the sick at home. The practice of celebrating the anointing of several sick people in church is a novelty in liturgical history. In the early centuries Christians were married at home. After the ceremony they presented themselves to the bishop to receive the nuptial blessing *in facie ecclesiae*, or in front of the church building. The third-century *Apostolic Tradition* mentions several blessings that were held at home, such as the blessing of the lamp at evening and of meat and cheese for Easter. It is odd that in a reverse way the Liturgy of the Hours, which had been originally celebrated inside the church by clergy and faithful, is now more often prayed by priests in the privacy of their room.

A number of liturgical rites presuppose a venue outside the normal places of worship. Such rites are not less liturgical, although they do not possess the value the Church attaches to the Eucharist and the sacraments. Yet it would be a mistake to ignore their significance and importance for the day-to-day lives of individuals. Liturgical blessings are an example of such rites. For many of the faithful, blessings are more closely allied to their spirituality because they respond more directly to their daily needs. Blessings effectively accompany the faithful in those particular situations where the presence of the sacraments is only subtly evoked. Moving into a new home or inaugurating a new shop can rekindle baptismal fervor, but that is easier said than done. The blessing given by parents to their children and the prayer before family meals are liturgical actions that can recall the Eucharist, but more often they remain in the periphery of liturgical awareness.

A statement from the Constitution on Liturgy, which deals with the use of material things in Christian worship, can fittingly be read in the context of the use of space: "The liturgy means that there is hardly any proper use of material things that cannot be directed toward human sanctification and the praise of God" (61). There is no proper use of space that cannot be directed toward human sanctification and the praise of God. If the Incarnate Word was laid in a manger and made the manger a powerful symbol of his presence among us, there is no reason why we should put up an impregnable wall that separates the sacred and the profane. If the Savior celebrated the most sacred act of worship on the most profane instrument of execution on the abominable Hill of Calvary, there is no reason we should despise the poverty and secular character of a place as venue for our worship.

Having affirmed a theological premise regarding the potential sacredness of space, for which statement I hope not to be accused of profanity, let me repeat that the liturgical norm requires decency, propriety, and nobility for any place in order to be used as a liturgical space. While every place belongs to God, not every space is appropriate for the celebration of worship, unless it is first freed from the encumbrances of superstition and indecency and transformed into an environment that is suitable for liturgical worship.

What, then, is the theology of liturgical space? By his incarnation Jesus Christ made holy the places where he preached God's word, where he healed and comforted the sick, where he freed people oppressed by evil power, where he ate his meals with his disciples and friends, where he died, was buried and rose again, and where he appeared to his disciples after the resurrection. Liturgical space is that suitable and fitting place where the body of Christ now gathers day after day, Sunday after Sunday to preach, heal, liberate, and celebrate the saving mystery of his death, burial, and resurrection.

WHERE TO FIND THE CHURCH

I asked earlier where we can find the Church. Over the years I have asked that question and received elusive answers. A social action worker proudly gave me a tour of the newly built houses and community center in a rural area and proclaimed, "This is the Church." A history professor summed up his course with perplexing advice: "If you want to experience what it means to be Church, read its history." After explaining a new Encyclical Letter a theologian intoned: "This is the voice of the Church." I do not question the validity of such statements, but they did not satisfy me. I continued searching for an answer. I found it in the assembly of the faithful gathered for worship.

With gratitude I recall my Dominican mentors, who during my four years of philosophy and four years of theology at the University of Sto. Tomas in Manila sowed in my soul the difficult virtue of loyalty to the Church as the only way to know Christ. They taught me many things, things from the time of Adam and Eve to the time of the Last Judgment. Many of these I have forgotten or perhaps conveniently chosen to forget. But what has taken root is loyalty to the Church's doctrine about Christ. They inspired me to cling to a Church that before the Second Vatican Council had appeared to me like a fussy old maid, quite removed from contemporary issues.

I was studying theology when the council was in session. New horizons were being explored, but sad to say, I was receiving confused signals. The Church seemed to me to have suddenly decided to be youngish and fashionable and behave like a liberated person. To this new type of Church my Dominican mentors struggled to be loyal. They faced a tortuous paradigm shift from Thomas Aquinas and the

Council of Trent to Yves Congar and Vatican II. Not heeding their stern warning, I secretly read Yves Congar, Karl Rahner, Hans Küng, and Edward Schillebeeckx. They enthralled my inquisitive mind.

Throughout those agitated times my mentors remained loyal, firmly anchored in the changing Church. In the process they taught me that it did not matter whether the Church was old or young, for in reality the Church has always been both ancient and new, like its Lord who is the same yesterday, today, and forever. Just stay inside the boat, they advised, and hold on for dear life, especially when the boat rocks mightily. And sometimes, believe me, even for some clergymen, it takes an act of faith to accept everything that the Church preaches officially from the pulpit and to remain loyal and unquestioning. Such intellectual loyalty can be very trying indeed, especially when a contesting inner voice whispers: "It's absurd, irrational, and old-fashioned." But my mentors assured me that there was no other way, and I believed them.

The study and celebration of the liturgy unveiled for me the mystery of the Church at worship. Searching for it and discovering it in the liturgy is, I am vain enough to say, what I have always tried to impress on my students. A teacher for so many years, I have lost count of my students in Rome, where I taught for seventeen years; at Notre Dame University, where I lectured for a couple of summers; and in various theological schools in the Philippines. My first doctoral student at the Pontifical Liturgical Institute was Wilton Gregory, who defended his dissertation with such brilliance he brought the house down. In his foreword to my Festschrift he wrote: "Anscar always motivated his students to love and to trust the wisdom of the Church. Like pioneer thinkers before him, he sensed that liturgical development would not always be met with a warm welcome. He has been proven right in a number of ways. Still, he has always found reason to hope." I remember fondly my student and friend Gerald Shirilla, who encouraged me to submit to Paulist Press my first title, *Cultural Adaptation of the Liturgy*. He now celebrates the liturgy before the heavenly throne.

Several of those that I had the privilege to mentor are still in my active address book. To name a few in the United States: Mark Francis and Keith Pecklers (I am in their debt for graciously editing a Festschrift in my honor entitled *Liturgy for the New Millennium*), Michael Witczak, Dominic Serra, Jan Michael Joncas, Sharon McMillan, and Cassian Folsom. Folsom succeeded me as president of the Pontifical Liturgical Institute, where I had served for twelve years. In his contribution to my Festschrift he recalls how the Abbot Primate of Sant'Anselmo Victor Dammertz was taken aback by my announcement that the Philippine bishops had required my services to found a liturgical institute at home. I left Rome in 1990 but returned in 1993 at the insistence of Abbot Jerome Theisen, who appointed me pro-president for four additional years. Folsom summed up my career in Rome by quoting my answer to his question of why I did everything I was doing: "Because I love the Institute."

In addition to my former students in the United States, there are a number in the Philippines who are also now my colleagues: Genaro Diwa and Virgilio Hernandez (they continue to support with extraordinary dedication and generosity the programs of Paul VI Institute of Liturgy), Romulo Valles and Julius Tonel (both are now the chief *leitourgoi* of their dioceses), Margaret Tapang, Josefina Manabat (she succeeded me as dean of the Graduate School of Liturgy in Manila), Moises Andrade, Ricardo Serrano, Timoteo Ofrasio, Florencio Salvador, Fortunato Garces, Raul Pura, and Melchor Camiña. To them I imparted loyalty to the Church, as the Dominicans had taught me, and the passion for liturgical worship that I acquired at the Pontifical Liturgical Institute.

Chapter Five

Per Ritus et Preces

The title of this chapter refers to the outward shape of liturgical worship. The phrase is found in the Constitution on Liturgy: "Through a good understanding of the rites and prayers the faithful should take part in the sacred service conscious of what they are doing, with devotion and full involvement" (48). The 1967 Instruction *Eucharisticum mysterium* reechoes the Constitution: Pastors are enjoined to explain "the meaning of the rites and prayers, especially those of the great Eucharistic Prayer, and lead the people to grasp the mystery that the rites and prayers signify and accomplish" (14). The words "rites" and "prayers" encompass the many external elements that constitute the liturgy, such as symbols, language and texts, vessels and vestments, furnishings, images, and audio-visual gadgets. Liturgical worship does not happen without these external appurtenances. They are all needed, according to a certain hierarchy of value, in order to make worship a celebration or, more precisely, a feast. While celebration denotes liturgical activity, feast describes the convivial character of liturgical worship. If we regard the liturgy as a feast, we recover its original Latin concept of *festum*, or holiday, as well as the conventional meaning of the English "feast" as a banquet and religious festival. In truth, the word "feast" embodies some of the outstanding traits of the liturgy.

LITURGY AS RITUAL FEAST

The phenomenology of feast can be verified in the celebration of liturgical worship. In his classic work *The Feast of Fools* Harvey Cox names three elements of festivity, which he defines as a special time set aside for observing an event or the memory of a person. The first element is conscious excess that involves revelry, vacation from convention, and ability to delight in the present. The second is celebrative affirmation that entails saying yes to life even in moments of tragedy. The third is juxtaposition, which means that the feast is noticeably different from the course of everyday life.

Following upon the heels of Cox, I would identify in our liturgical celebrations the elements that constitute them as feasts. The liturgy is a memorial: it always recalls the death and resurrection of Jesus Christ. It is conscious excess: its language is ceremonial and its rites solemn. It is a celebrative affirmation: even Good Friday liturgy and the funeral rite are called celebration. Lastly, it is juxtaposition: even if the liturgy is celebrated every day, it is not an element of daily routine. The manner of holding the liturgical feast is subject to the circumstances of culture, history, and the theological climate in the Church. One generation may carry out the celebration in the simplicity of a household or *domus ecclesiae*. Another may celebrate it in the splendor of a Constantinian basilica with rites that are evocative of the imperial court. In the playful fantasy of the baroque period the liturgy and its adornments may have been marked by exuberance and gaiety. The liturgical reform of Vatican II, as I noted earlier, opts for a form of celebration that focuses on active and intelligent participation. Culture, history, and theology affect the form or style of the liturgical rite; but ultimately, as long as the liturgy is memorial, conscious excess, celebrative affirmation, and juxtaposition it is in the category of feast.

What does the liturgical feast represent? For people conscious of their redemption in Christ, the celebration of the liturgy means gratitude, remembrance, and anticipation. It is an occasion to enter into that other horizon of life, which has been unveiled by Christ. It is an affirmation that there is more to life than our experience of it. The present gloom of pain will persist, but Christians will continue to be fools who celebrate with abandon and shout the yes of faith in Christ.

Saying yes to life is particularly evident in the liturgy of Sunday. Patristic literature, which the Constitution on Liturgy (106) repeats, calls Sunday the eighth day. Although there are only seven days in a week—Sunday being the first day—Christian tradition from the fourth century has called Sunday also the eighth day. This means that in the weekly cycle, Sunday is both the beginning of the week (the first day) and the day next to Saturday, which is the seventh day. The eighth day can also signify the extension of the weekly cycle outside the realm of time. In the light of Christ's resurrection we may understand the first and eighth day to mean that the weekly cycle opens and closes with the Sunday feast. We may also say symbolically that the week, which symbolizes our life on earth, begins and ends with the feast of Christ's paschal mystery.

The underlying theology behind Sunday as the first day is that we begin every week with our profession of faith in the mystery of

Christ's resurrection. On the other hand, Sunday as the eighth day signifies a break away from the cycle of normal life and activity, in order to enter, as it were, into the sphere of the eternal feast. On Sunday, the risen Lord appears to us and raises us up from the routine of daily life to the joyful feast of his resurrection. Sunday gives us an inkling of what awaits us in eternity. Hence, the Sunday liturgy is a foretaste of eternal bliss and a comforting assurance that we are no longer enslaved by the forces of evil. On Sunday we celebrate our freedom as children of God. The Liturgy Constitution sums this up: "The Lord's Day is the first holyday of all and should be proposed to the devotion of the faithful and taught to them in such a way that it may become in fact a day of joy and of freedom from work."

Speaking about Easter week as the feast day typifying the feast of an entire life, Gregory of Nyssa wrote these exquisite words: "The Easter week is meant to be a symbol for those who celebrate spiritually throughout their lives, so that all the days of their lives they may celebrate one bright and shadowless Easter" (*Homily on Holy Passover* I). To a world that has immersed itself in production, professional competition, and technological efficiency, the liturgical feast, with its qualities of excess, affirmation, and juxtaposition—to use Harvey Cox's language—is God's summons to rise above the present and to delight in his presence. The liturgical feast invites us to celebrate the "feast of fools," to cease being a machine, and to start living the life of human beings. Liturgical worship is a liberating feast of Christ's fools.

LITURGICAL SYMBOLS

"No one can live without symbols. The symbol is the true appearance of reality; it is the form in which, in each case, reality discloses itself to our consciousness, or rather, it is that particular consciousness of reality. It is in the symbol that the real appears to us." When I came across this quotation from Raimundo Panikkar, I knew I had in my hand a definition I had always wanted to formulate. Panikkar's definition is dense, but it is not impenetrable. It is linguistically compact, but it is theologically limpid. It has all the items that liturgists need in order to untangle the intricate world of liturgical symbols: the necessity of symbols, the appearance of reality, the form of reality, and the consciousness of reality. The final statement is profound: "It is in the symbol that the real appears to us."

It is obvious that symbols are the life and soul of liturgical worship. What is not often obvious is that its symbols come to life when the rites are performed. Liturgical symbols are in the category of action. This is an insight into the world of liturgical symbols that I inherited from Vagaggini. Actions breathe life into symbols. Gestures must be performed, songs must be sung, water must be poured, bread must be broken and shared, the word must be read, hands must be laid, oil must be applied, and the assembly must be convened in the name of the Holy Trinity. When this is done, symbols breathe with life and disclose to our consciousness the mystery of Christ and the Church. Paraphrasing the words of Panikkar, we can say that it is in liturgical symbols that the reality of the paschal mystery appears to us. To appreciate the full impact of liturgical symbolism, it is useful to keep before us the ideal picture of a liturgical action. The Constitution on Liturgy describes it as such: "All should hold in great esteem the liturgical life of the diocese centered around the bishop, especially in his cathedral church; they must be convinced that the preeminent manifestation of the Church is present in the full, active participation of all God's holy people in these liturgical celebrations, especially in the same Eucharist, in a single prayer, at one altar at which the bishop presides, surrounded by his college of priests and by his ministers" (41). It is the image of the liturgical assembly in full action. The assembly participates fully and actively, the rite of prayer is performed, the bishop presides, the priests concelebrate, and the ministers serve.

After several years of discussion on the meaning of liturgical symbol, there is still much fluidity in the way it is defined. I follow the school that distinguishes sign, symbol, and sacrament from one another. Sign points to another person, thing, or event. I adhere to St. Augustine's classic definition: *Aliud videtur, aliud intelligitur* (One thing is seen, but another thing is understood). Smoke is a sign of fire; the revolving red, white, and blue neon lights are the sign of a barber shop. Symbol, on the other hand, is a complicated concept to explain. A friend of mine, cultural anthropologist Crispino Valenziano, acquainted me with modern thinking on symbols. I should add that it was he who introduced me to the concept of cultural patterns, which I use extensively in my work on inculturation. I owe him much as mentor, friend, and colleague at the Liturgical Institute in Rome.

One school of cultural anthropology describes the qualities of symbol. It "contains" and reveals the presence of a person or thing. It is a type of sign that also conveys a concept. It is a device that allows us to make abstraction and form a thought or entertain an emotion. The flag is a symbol denoting national sovereignty; red roses offered to a woman convey a man's love. The idea of presence was probably the reason Hippolytus of Rome called the Eucharist "symbol of Christ's body," a phrase that some theologians could be wary about. For them it is troublesome enough to say "sacrament of Christ's body," but to refer to the consecrated host as symbol would be to take leave of one's senses.

Another quality of symbol is that it is polyvalent. This means that it can carry several meanings and, hence, is open to different interpretations. The polyvalent attribute of symbols applies to human relationship as much as to liturgical worship. Words, which fall in the category of symbols, are amply polyvalent. People play upon words and put words into someone's mouth. The effect can be disastrous to harmonious relationship. Several liturgical symbols too are polyvalent and should not be confined to one interpretation. The use of incense is one such symbol. It is normally intended as a symbol of honor and respect and is often associated with solemn liturgy. But there is no reason it cannot have a more practical use. I have heard it said, but I have not been able to verify the claim, that in St. Augustine's church, where the heat could be oppressive in summer, the deacon incensed the church and assembly every so often to perfume the environment. When I concelebrated with a bishop in a remote parish in Zaire, I was alarmed by the drove of tiny white mosquitoes that mercilessly attacked every human being inside the small church. I placed incense in the thurible and incensed the church to drive the mosquitoes away. The assembly complimented me for having added solemnity to the celebration.

A third quality of symbol is that it kindles relationship. Hebrews 4:12 tells us, "The word of God is living and active, sharper than any two-edged sword, piercing until it divides soul from spirit, joints from marrow; it is able to judge the thoughts and intentions of the heart." It can happen though that some symbols, especially words, can have the contrasting quality that unites or separates. We find an example of this in John 6:52-66, which relates that when Jesus declared himself bread of life many of his disciples withdrew from his company. The Constitution on Liturgy teaches that Christ "is present in his word, since it is he himself who speaks when the holy Scriptures are read in the Church" (7) and that "in the liturgy God speaks to his people and Christ still proclaims his gospel" (33). We listen with faith. A relationship is formed between Christ and us. Sometimes we are unable to grasp the meaning of the word we hear, but we listen just the same because we believe that Christ is addressing his word to us. Sometimes a word unexpectedly jumps out of the pages of Scriptures, and we are bathed in light. No one who listens with faith to the word of God will remain unmoved or indifferent. Similarly, baptism creates relationship between Christ and the baptized person. Such relationship is meant to be permanent. It is meant to grip the entire being of the baptized. That is why St. Ambrose exhorted the baptized with these moving words: "When you immersed yourself in the water, you took on the image of his death and burial, you accepted the sacrament of that cross to which Christ's body was nailed. You are therefore crucified with Christ, you cling to Christ, and you cling to the nails of our Lord Jesus Christ, so that the devil may not snatch you away from him. Let the nail of Christ detain you and let not human infirmity wrench you from him" (*De sacramentis II*, 23).

At the outset I plainly admitted that I belong to the old school, which distinguishes sacraments from signs and symbols. In keeping with the traditional language used by the Church, I use the word "sacrament" when I refer to specific items and actions that are essential to the performance of the sacraments. The truth, however, is that if we understand symbols as cultural anthropologists explain them, we can interchange symbols and sacraments. But, frankly, I see no reason to upset people because of semantics. For the sake of clarity, allow me to define sacraments as signs or symbols that embody, reveal, and communicate the real presence of Christ and his mystery. The three words "embody," "reveal," and "communicate" are the hinges around which sacramental theology revolves. Scholastic theology used the word "contain," which I freely render with "embody": "Sacraments contain what they signify." In this theological postulate the element of real presence is what ultimately distinguishes sacraments from signs and symbols. The *Catechism of the Catholic Church*, contrary to newer thinking that the Church is the root sacrament, continues to predicate the word primarily to the seven sacraments, which it describes as "signs and instruments by which the Holy Spirit spreads the grace of Christ the head throughout the Church" (774). The *Catechism* calls the Church a "sacrament" only in an analogical sense.

Some sacraments consist of material things that the liturgy employs. Examples are bread and wine for the Eucharist, water for baptism, and oil for anointing. These elements, as we had occasion to discuss in the third chapter of this work, embody the presence of Christ and the Holy Spirit. Through bodily contact with the sacramental bread, water, and oil recipients enter or deepen their relationship with the Divine Persons. Other sacraments are actions that may or may not involve material things. Examples are the recitation of the Eucharistic Prayer, immersion of the candidate in baptismal water, hand-laying in the rite of ordination, and anointing the sick person with oil. Other symbols are ritual actions that are not essential to the performance of the sacrament but are needed for the integrity or greater comprehension of the sacrament. Examples of these are the breaking of bread and the hand-laying at confirmation, penance, and anointing of the sick. In passing, I should make mention of the so-called explanatory rites that are found in some sacraments. After baptism certain rites are performed—anointing with chrism, vesting in white garment, and the giving of the baptismal candle. Through these rites we get a fuller appreciation of what happens at baptism. Immersion in the name of the Trinity carries with it effects that are not explicitly stated by the baptismal formula. The newly baptized is inscribed as a member of the priestly people, is vested with Christian dignity, and sent forth to live in the light of faith.

Liturgical symbols are often aligned with some human circumstances. Through symbols the liturgy grafts the heavenly reality on the earthly, the divine is encountered through the human, and the world is bathed in God's grace. Because of this, every time we break bread, that is, share food with our family, friends, and strangers, we are invited to remember the broken bread on the altar. On the other hand, the food on our table points to the food on the altar and acquires from it a fuller meaning. Liturgical symbols elevate the reality of our day-to-day lives to the higher plane of human existence.

The liturgy uses a number of material things and gestures that have transcultural acceptance. Eating and drinking together in a cultic celebration to signify vertical communion with God and horizontal fellowship is practiced in many religions. So are the gestures of bowing and prostrating to express the worshiper's attitude of reverence. However, symbols can mean different things in different cultures. The Christian cup of salvation could be resented in cultural settings where alcoholic drink is banned. Hand-laying at ordination would necessitate an extraordinary amount of convincing in some countries that regard the gesture discourteous, not to say rude. Inculturation offers solutions to the difficulties local assemblies have with regard to some traditional symbols used in the liturgy. Dynamic equivalents do exist and they express pretty much the same concept: bowing in place of genuflection, for example.

Other symbols, especially those that are used in sacramental celebrations, require closer theological attention, pastoral discernment, and serious cultural research. Pope Paul VI paved the way when he permitted the use of vegetable or plant oil as a substitute for olive oil in the anointing of the sick. But, alas, the craze to dust museum pieces and use them in the liturgy has spread and is now fashionable in some local churches. I can hear them argue, "What use do we have of modern and contemporary symbols, when the Church has a rich collection of them in museums and old sacristies? You claim that the people cannot identify with these hallowed symbols. Have you never heard of catechesis?" I confess that sometimes the frustration can be so overpowering that I muse whether this is not the time to throw up one's hands and close shop. But liturgy is the experience of the paschal mystery. Hope lies behind the dark clouds; a new day breaks after the night; and most important of all, the Holy Spirit will surely not allow to go to waste what he and the council fathers of Vatican II together had garnered.

Liturgical symbols are most eloquent when they are authentic, that is to say, when they are not mere tokens. The importance of this is obvious in a world that seeks to be genuine and real. The use of liturgical symbols that have been despoiled of their original meaning and reduced to a rubrical formality obscures the sense of the celebration, makes it less understandable, and even alienates the symbol from its true meaning. We know for a fact that lame symbols impoverish the understanding of worship.

How effectively does a trickle of water on the forehead of a child symbolize entry into the tomb with Christ? The author of *Didache* (chap. 7) prefers running water for baptism because it symbolizes the "living water." The rite of immersion is a graphic enactment of baptismal participation in the death and burial of Christ. What message is sent when the priest slightly anoints the newly baptized with chrism that in the time of Tertullian was poured on the crown of the head and "flowed down our entire body": *in nobis carnaliter currit unctio* (*On Baptism*, 7)? The early Christians knew the importance of authentic symbols. In the oriental versions of *Apostolic Tradition* attributed to Hippolytus of Rome, a picturesque detail is appended to the baptismal rite for lively effect. The person to be baptized faces the West to renounce Satan (some manuscripts direct the candidate to spit toward the West). Afterward the person faces the East to pronounce the baptismal profession of faith.

In the Eucharist, how does a thin white wafer called a host signify bread, let alone the body of Christ? As someone jested, "it is easier to believe that the host is the body of Christ than that it is bread." There was a time when Coptic seminarians boarded in our college on the Aventine Hill. I was thoroughly taken aback when at communion they returned the host back to the priest, explaining they did not think it was bread.

Finally, how expressive of married love and dedication are the legal words "I do," which neglect the romance and courtship that precede the liturgy of marriage?

Interpreting liturgical symbols can be a tricky business. A great majority of them hail from biblical times and the patristic and medieval periods. Consequently, as the Liturgy Constitution reminds us, "a careful investigation is always to be made into each part of the liturgy. . . . This investigation should be theological, historical and pastoral" (23). Failure to do so could spell liturgical and theological disaster. When infant confirmation became the normal practice after the sixth century, the kiss of peace which the bishop gave to the newly confirmed adult was, for some reason, revised to a slight fatherly pat on the cheek of the child. By the thirteenth century in France and the Germanic region the gesture had turned into a slap similar to what a man received when he was knighted. The thirteenth-century Pontifical of Durand carries the rubric: *Deinde episcopus dat ei leviter alapam super genam dicens: Pax tecum* (The bishop lightly slaps the cheek [of the child] saying, "Peace be with you"). Consequently, confirmation wound up as the sacrament that made children soldiers of Christ. The passage from kiss to slap is one of the mishaps of inculturation, and the shift from the Pentecostal outpouring of the Holy Spirit to a military sacrament is one of the misfortunes of sacramental theology. This proves that careless interpretation of liturgical symbols can negatively affect the doctrine of the sacrament.

The thirteenth-century writer Amalarius of Metz occupied himself with the allegorical interpretation of the rite of the Mass. Since the Mass is the representation of Christ's suffering and death, he construed it as the unfolding of the different phases of Christ's passion. His dubious method gained acceptance in succeeding centuries, subjecting the Mass to uncontrolled fantasy. The washing of the hand, for example, recalls Pilate's washing of hands as he condemned Jesus to death.

As rule of thumb I suggest basing the interpretation of liturgical symbols on the accompanying text, although I do not promise that this will always produce an acceptable result. The text for the rite of commingling completely ignores its history and ecclesial dimension: "May this mingling of the body and blood of our Lord Jesus Christ bring eternal life to us who receive it." At the end of the day we need to open our history books to find out what a liturgical symbol really means. Advice I have always given my students is not to add to the confusion by ingenuous guesswork.

After several decades of liturgical reform we need to ask whether the road it has chosen on the question of liturgical symbols does not permit alternatives. Simplification of rites, return to a more sober and austere form of celebration, avoidance of what appears excessive, dramatic, and colorful, and the unveiling of the Christian mystery for the intellect alone to contemplate: do not all these subtract something from the charm and conviviality of the liturgy as a feast? It is said that modern living is practical, fast, and clichéd, but must the liturgy rub it in? There is often a feeling of "ordinariness" in our liturgical rites, not in the sense of being at home with it, but of not finding an exceptional quality in it. Since the ordinary is so akin to what is routine, might we not wake up one day and discover that we have made a grand expedition in search of a new form of routine celebration? Our liturgy seems to be on the verge of turning anemic, color-blind, and utterly cold. We insist that the liturgy is celebration, but we labor to remove the "false" impression that it is a feast. Do we not perhaps overstress the spirituality of worship at the expense of the totality of human experience? We recognize the importance of lively symbols expressing exuberance, dance, and clapping the hands for pure joy, but to use them in our liturgy can strike us as something odd, if not banal. Have we not perhaps forgotten how to celebrate with symbols? Have we perhaps forgotten too that the *sobrietas romana* was meant to be the object of cultural adaptation or inculturation?

RUBRICS IN THE LITURGY

From the Council of Trent to the liturgical reform of Vatican II, or for roughly four hundred years, rubrics gained an unprecedented position in the celebration of liturgical rites. Why did it happen? Protestant reformers, led by Martin Luther, had earlier instituted changes in the liturgy. The changes were intended to de-clericalize the liturgy and make it respond to Protestant tenets, particularly the priesthood of all the faithful and the supremacy of God's word over Church teaching and discipline. As one can see in retrospect, not everything Protestant was harmful to the Catholic faith. On the contrary, several documents of Vatican II accorded the priesthood of the laity and the power of God's word their rightful place in the liturgy. Surely the Church of Vatican II can own up to the sixteenth-century watchword among the Reformed Churches: *Ecclesia reformata, sed semper reformanda* (The reformed Church is always in need of further reform).

But not everything Protestant signaled a welcome change. In the process of reform, Protestants did away with some basic Catholic doctrines, such as the sacrificial aspect of the Mass and the sacramental authority of ordained ministers. In order to eliminate from the Mass any trace of sacrifice, Luther revised its texts and rites. He took liberty with them, especially the offertory rite and the Eucharistic Prayer, purged them of any reference to the sacrifice of the cross, and practically reduced the Mass to a community meal that centered on the commemoration of the Last Supper. For Luther such matters as liturgical rubrics, formularies, vestments, and vessels were "neither prescribed nor forbidden." To prescribe them would mean to restrict the freedom of Christians. The use of Latin in the Mass was not necessary for salvation, but neither was the use of German. As humanist and teacher, he wanted the Latin language to be preserved because of its cultural value. He had great attachment to the traditional *ordo* of the liturgy and hence believed that the correct shape of liturgical worship should grow organically from its roots. His pastoral sense dictated that the prevailing rubrics of the Mass should be observed, although priests could omit references to sacrifice in the prayers and Canon of the Mass so that they could celebrate "according to the Gospel," while the common people "would not notice anything that causes scandal." He allowed time for the simple folks with "weak consciences" to gain purity of faith and did not want "to burden their consciences through precipitate changes not adequately prepared by preaching."

From the standpoint of Rome, Luther's liturgical reform was exaggerated and imperiled the faith, but do not prophets exaggerate in order to bring home the message? Luther roused the Church from its self-complacency and indirectly caused the Council of Trent to be convened. But even in his lifetime some of his partisans misunderstood the intention of his reform. While he was in Wittenberg in December 1521, to his dismay he saw armed students and townspeople invade the parish church, jeer at the friars, prevent them from offering private Masses, break sacred images, and carry away the Latin missals. In March of the following year, dressed in his religious habit, he was in the pulpit of Wittenberg daily, directing his anger not at the pope but at the hotheads who used physical force to fight abuses.

At this juncture I pause to recall two Lutheran colleagues and friends who contributed solidly to my understanding of the liturgical *ordo*. The first is Gordon Lathrop, a brother in the Lord, for his scholarly output and zeal for unity. We complemented each other, especially in our exposition of the liturgical *ordo*, so that organizers of ecumenical meetings often paired us. I consider it an honor to have teamed up with him. When colleagues offered a Festschrift in my honor, he introduced his contribution as a homage of thanksgiving for my work "with both the World Council of Churches and the Lutheran World Federation." I am particularly touched by his testimonial that I "provided a remarkable example of ecumenical affirmation and admonition, graciously, courteously but profoundly applied to liturgical celebration." In turn, on the occasion of Lathrop's retirement as professor I offered an article in his honor entitled "Liturgy: Many Becoming One" and wrote these dedicatory words: "The adage attributed to Saint Augustine, for whom Luther had the greatest respect, sums up and concludes these pages of reflection in honor of the ecumenical liturgist and theologian Gordon Lathrop: *In necesariis, unitas; in opinabilibus, libertas; in omnibus caritas* [In essentials, unity; in opinions, freedom; in all things, love]."

The other person, so dear to me, is S. Anita Stauffer. A person of broad ecclesial vision and extraordinary managerial skills, Anita organized the yearly Worship Consultation of the Lutheran World Federation that produced several volumes on liturgical contextualization (I failed to convince her to shift to the more recent term "inculturation"). She pressured me to write one or two papers for the yearly consultation, thus kindling in me the desire to serve as a liturgist in the world of ecumenism. She has preceded Gordon and me to sing the divine praises in the company of the heavenly throng.

Returning to the sixteenth century, how did Rome react to Luther? By decreeing that henceforth no one, not even priests, should dare to change or modify anything in the liturgy. In the introduction to the Tridentine Missal of 1570 Pope Pius V warned that those who changed anything in the Missal would incur his apostolic wrath. This was Rome's measure of safeguarding the essential elements of the Roman liturgy. By securing the liturgical texts and the accompanying rubrics, Rome effectively removed the danger of another liturgical reform similar to that of Luther. I believe that it was the first time that Rome stonewalled the liturgy, but under the circumstances it was to all intents and purposes an inspired act of survival. The problem occurs when centuries later, stone walls are still up as if the enemies were breaching the wall.

This brief historical review explains why rubrics gained such importance in the celebration of the liturgy and why much attention was focused on their correct observance. To undermine rubrics was considered tantamount to disregarding the Church's authority, the unity of the Roman liturgy, and, in a way, some of the doctrines the rubrics safeguarded.

The observance of rubrics is needed for a correct and dignified celebration of the liturgy. However, obsession with rubrics can be damaging. It is called rubricism, which means that the celebrant's attention is fully engaged by the servile performance of every rubrical detail. Rubricism means that rubrics and liturgy are synonymous. When seminarians studied liturgy, they memorized the rubrics. The liturgy course was distinct from systematic theology, which dealt with the meaning and purpose of the sacraments. When priests and bishops celebrated the liturgy, they executed the prescribed rubrics and were happy to have gone through the rites with as few rubrical infractions as possible. Canon law and moral theology allied themselves with rubricism. Canon law enshrined and codified rubrics. Instead of being considered guides for the proper celebration of the liturgy, rubrics were regarded as norms. Willful disregard for rubrics could result in illicit or even invalid celebration of sacraments. Cases of honest mistakes, however, were conveniently covered by the theological axiom, *Ecclesia supplet*, for example, when the faithful by mistake receive Communion from unconsecrated hosts.

In recent times the Vatican instruction *Redemptionis sacramentum* came out with a list of infractions and delicts in the liturgy that merited penalties. Moral theology, in its turn, tagged rubrics with moralistic censure. Certain infractions are classified as serious sins, like the deliberate omission of the rite of commingling. It was a standing joke that few priests celebrated Mass without committing at least ten venial sins, which were of course remitted by Holy Communion.

The overall effect of rubricism was appalling. Attention was paid to the rigid compliance with the rubrics, to the detriment of the prayer aspect of the liturgy. Prayer texts were pronounced carefully, but their message was neglected. Rites were meticulously performed, but their rich spiritual symbolism was overlooked. Instead of focusing attention on the mystery being celebrated, priests were burdened by the discipline of rubrics. Instead of weighing the doctrinal import of such a simple greeting as "The Lord be with you," priests were caught up in their concern for the correct gesture of the hands. Not surprisingly, some priests were afflicted with unhealthy scrupulosity, while others simply did not care, as long as they judged their celebration to be valid. Rubricism did not spare parishes, seminaries, and religious communities. Heated arguments that sometimes had the semblance of civil war erupted over hair-splitting interpretation of rubrics.

But all that dramatically changed, at least officially, with the advent of the liturgical movement in 1909 and the postconciliar reform of Vatican II. Theology and spirituality drawn from liturgical texts and rites are beginning to attract the interest of both clergy and laity, even if rubrical debates still arise sporadically. The Constitution on Liturgy reminds pastors that "when the liturgy is celebrated something more is required than the mere observance of the laws governing valid and lawful celebration" (11). Now, what is that "something more"? That something more, according to article 7, is the regard for the liturgy as the highest form of Christian worship. It stems from the belief that the liturgy "is considered as an exercise of the priestly office of Jesus Christ," who "associates the Church with himself." There are two persons involved in liturgical worship: Christ and the Church. Regarding Christ, Vatican II teaches that he is present in the gathered community, in the word that is proclaimed, in the consecrated bread and wine, and in the person of the celebrant. Regarding the Church, it teaches that "the liturgy is the summit toward which the activity of the Church is directed; at the same time it is the fount from which all the Church's power flows."

If Christ and his paschal mystery are really present in liturgical actions and if the liturgy is the summit and source of the Church's activity, is it not odd that we spend our energies quarrelling over rubrics and in the process miss the reality of Christ's presence? Far be it from me that I should discredit the important role of rubrics in the liturgy, but I wish to stress that rubrics are mere instruments and aids to experience more profoundly the mystery of Christ. After the Council of Trent rubrics became the liturgy's apple of the eye. After Vatican II rubrics no longer claim such importance. Perhaps this is the moment to have a more balanced outlook on what liturgical rubrics are all about.

What are rubrics? The word is derived from the Latin *ruber*, red, and from *rubricare*, to write in red. Etymologically, it says nothing except that it is printed in red color. Rubrics denote instructions or directions on how each section of the liturgy is to be performed. In the tradition of printed liturgical books these instructions are in red in order to draw attention to them and distinguish them from the texts like prayers, admonitions, and readings. Perhaps red, rather than another color like blue or green, was chosen because of the importance attached to rubrics. Students are familiar with the red ink used by their teachers when they correct papers. Corrections in red strike the eyes. People give special significance to letters or communications written in red. At any rate, rubrics are in red (the expression is redundant), because they give important notices and instructions to the celebrant, ministers, and masters of ceremonies on how to celebrate the liturgy correctly, with ease, and with grace.

It is useful to note that the medieval forerunners of our present-day Sacramentary did not have rubrics. They contained only the prayer texts to be read by the celebrant. It was expected that the celebrant who was assisted by deacons and masters of ceremonies knew what he was doing. However, the ninth-century books called *Ordines* contained the rubrics but not the liturgical texts for the papal Masses. Given the nature of such rubrical books it stands to reason that the pope himself emceed the celebration. In fact, in the first *ordo* it was the pope himself who gave the rubrical directions to the ministers. For example, he gave the sign to the choir when to stop singing the entrance, offertory, and communion songs. Rubrics were useful, but they did not rank first in the concern of the celebrant. At a later time the liturgical books developed. The books for the Mass, the rituals for sacraments and sacramentals, and the divine office were printed with accompanying rubrics (some editions do not print the rubrics in red). However, even then not all the pertinent rubrics were printed, lest the books became unwieldy or unfriendly to users. Other books had to be invented so that the rubrics could be explained in full and greater detail to the great satisfaction of the rubrical-minded liturgists. An example of such books is the Ceremonial for Bishops.

The postconciliar rubrics exhibit the reaction of the drafters of the Liturgy Constitution toward liturgical rigidity and rubricism. The rubrics are less prescriptive in tenor: they do not ring like laws and norms that accept no possible variation and the violation of which calls down apostolic wrath. Postconciliar rubrics are more indicative in tone: they set guidelines for the correct, smooth flow and graceful performance of the liturgical rite. Instead of the Tridentine rubrics that tell the celebrant to greet the people with palms that open to each other, fingers close to each other, and hands not exceeding the length and height of the shoulders, the Vatican II rubrics simply state: "The priest, facing the people, extends his hands and greets all present." How wide the hands should extend is a matter of the celebrant's stage management, his understanding of the words he pronounces, and his generosity with gestures. Stage management can include such variables as the size of the church and the number of the faithful.

Emblematic of Vatican II's reform are notices that allow the celebrant rubrical leeway. For example, he is given a set of formularies from which he may freely select what in his judgment is more appropriate for the occasion. There are three alternative forms of greetings at the entrance rite. On several occasions (only once during the Mass when the people are sprinkled with holy water) the celebrant is even offered the possibility of composing his own texts. The rubrics note that he may address the people "using these or similar words." These are rubrical innovations that sharply contrast Vatican II's rubrics with the Tridentine. What are the reasons underneath the change in rubrical policy? One reason might be the council's principle of "unity in diversity." The Constitution on Liturgy (38) directs the Church to embrace the variety of cultural traditions in the spirit of Pope Pius XII, who advocated the acceptance of cultural differences against rigid uniformity in things that are not essential to the life of the Catholic Church. Unity is not equivalent to uniformity and is not hurt or threatened by rubrical flexibility.

Another reason might be the Liturgy Constitution's decree that "the rites should be marked by a noble simplicity; they should be short, clear, and unencumbered by useless repetitions; they should be within the people's powers of comprehension and as a rule not require much explanation" (34). This boils down to the council's chief agenda, namely, full, active, and conscious participation of the faithful in liturgical celebrations. To foster it, greater attention is to be given to the theology and spirituality of liturgical actions, and certain adjustments should be made to mitigate the stringent observance of rubrical norms. I recommend that we do not read the rubrics of any liturgical book without having first studied the introduction and meditated on the texts and the scriptural readings. In short, we need to balance the observance of the rubrics with the basic agenda of Vatican II's liturgical reform, which is active participation. We should beware of ranking the rubrics ahead of good theology, historical consciousness, and pastoral care. Rubrics are meant to lead the faithful to an ever-deepening experience of the paschal mystery. If our obsessive preoccupation with them soft-pedals this primary goal of the council, there is something terribly wrong with our attitude toward liturgical worship.

We can approach liturgical rubrics from three different angles, namely, theology, culture, and pastoral consideration.

Rubrics occupy an ancillary position in the liturgy. To put some people's minds at rest, I should affirm that rubrics are not purely ceremonial in nature and purpose. The truth is they can be part of a theological discourse. Rubrics can have a theological bearing. The rubrics that direct the celebrant to lay his hands on persons and things are the ritual expression of what theology calls *epiclesis*, or the invocation of the Holy Spirit on those who receive the sacraments of confirmation, anointing of the sick, and holy orders, or on the material elements that constitute the sacrament, such as bread, wine, baptismal water, and oil. Hand-laying is not merely for dramatic effect; it is the symbol of consecration by the Holy Spirit.

There are other examples that belong to this category. One example is the anointing with chrism at baptism. This ancient practice, dating from the second century, was done by pouring the oil on the crown of the head so that it would flow down as if to envelop the entire body. By the way, candidates for baptism were baptized naked. Clothing them with baptismal garb when they came out of the baptismal pool thus made sense. In the course of time the rite of anointing was reduced to smearing the crown of the head with oil. The rubrics direct the celebrant to recite the assigned formulary, which explains in a few words the meaning of the rite: it symbolizes the participation of the newly baptized in the priesthood of Christ. Here rubrics are in close alliance with the theology of common priesthood. A third example is the *dexterarum iunctio*, or the joining of the right hands by the couple as they pronounce their marriage vows. The rite dates from Roman times and was adopted by the Roman Church as symbol of the married couple's unity in Christ. For those who appreciate the meaning of *dexterarum iunctio*, other symbols like the rings, the bridal veil, and the unity candle are repetitious, if not superfluous. The rubrics direct the celebrant to ask the couple to join their right hands. It is a simple and hardly noticed rubrical detail, but its theology is conspicuous. These examples are rubrical directives that enhance the theology of the sacraments. Surely the sacraments will be valid without them, but they will be deprived of symbols that enrich their meaning. Validity is not the only criterion of good liturgy.

We should not forget commonplace rubrics like kneeling and genuflecting, in short, the rubrics on liturgical posture. In a sense every liturgical posture is a theological declaration. Kneeling and genuflection are postures that express adoration and reverence, sitting denotes openness to teaching, and standing symbolizes priestly prayer. The commentator's rubrical instructions in this regard may sometimes sound idle, but in reality they remind the assembly of the basic components of Christian worship.

For a fuller appreciation of rubrics I suggest we see them in their historical-cultural context. The Constitution on Liturgy decrees that "the rites should be marked by a noble simplicity; they should be short, clear, and unencumbered by useless repetitions; they should be within the people's powers of comprehension and as a rule not require much explanation" (34). Noble simplicity, brevity, clarity, and functionality are, among others, the qualifying traits of the Roman culture and consequently of the Roman liturgy. Not only texts and symbols, but also rubrical instructions reflect the culture of the people. It is well known that the rubrics of the Roman rite represent various strata of Western culture from the Greco-Roman to the medieval world. Some rubrics have remained practically unchanged over the centuries. An example is the rubrical instruction of the first-century *Didaché* that the water should be poured three times on the head of the candidate, if there is scarcity of water. Other rubrics have been subjected to change: some were revised and others replaced as cultural or pastoral needs arose. What this is telling us is that we should not be overly distressed when rubrics are modified or even eliminated in favor of new ones. History teaches us to free ourselves of our inordinate attachments to the past, if this is not of the essence of life, and to welcome legitimate change and progress.

Culture plays a significant role in understanding the meaning of liturgical rubrics and how they could be adjusted (or inculturated) today. Beginning in the fourth century the newly baptized were dressed in white robes that symbolized their dignity as Christians. Roman citizens paraded themselves in white tunics that heralded their dignity. In accord with a peculiar color-code system, Filipino Catholics use blue and pink, respectively, for boys and girls. This type of rubrical adjustment answers the problem of white, which does not have the cultural meaning for Filipinos that blue and pink have. But the shift from white to blue and pink does not answer the underlying theology of the white garment, namely, the symbol of Christian dignity. Blue and pink do not signify dignity. Perhaps the real issue is not the color of the baptismal garment. Perhaps the real issue is whether Filipinos possess a symbol that typifies dignity and can, like the white robe of old, express Christian dignity.

Pastoral consideration should feature in any discussion about rubrics. In the past, rigidity led to rubricism, and rubricism turned the liturgy into a code of laws that were strictly enforced in order to ensure that the liturgy is both licit and valid. In all this the assembly had little role. The size of the assembly, the kind of church, the season of the year or the time of day, and the community environment mattered little, if they mattered at all. The liturgical reform has rectified this. Rubrics cannot be divorced from the reality of the assembly. Rubrics should be carefully read in the context of the faithful assembled together in a particular place, at a particular time, and with the concrete reality of their lives. Rubrics should be viewed in the light of pastoral care. A helpful aid to this manner of understanding the rubrics is semiotic analysis. The following example will illustrate how it works.

The entrance rite of the Mass carries the following rubrics: "After the people have assembled, the priest and ministers go to the altar while the entrance song is being sung." This brief rubrical direction raises the basic questions of who, why, where, how, when, and what. If we are able to answer these questions, the rubrics will have a concrete context and a particular meaning. "After the people have assembled . . . " Let us take note of the words: "When the people have assembled." The rubrics do not say, when the celebrant has arrived and wants to start the Mass regardless of whether or not the people have assembled. This segment of the rubrics rightly gives due regard for the role the people have in the celebration of the Mass. They are, after all, major actors (not mere onlookers) in the liturgy. We need to ask the question, who are these people? Are we speaking of urban or rural community? What is their socioeconomic status? Are we dealing with a community of farmers or a mixture of employees and professionals? Are there a large number of children and senior citizens in the assembly?

Our knowledge of the type of people in the pews will help us to make the necessary adjustments in the celebration. Certain texts might have to be slightly modified, alternative scriptural readings chosen, and suitable songs for this particular assembly selected. We should also ask where they are gathered: in a cathedral, parish church, village chapel, or perhaps a shopping mall. Does the venue have the required liturgical space, furnishings, books, vestments, and vessels? How are the people assembled in the church? Are there reserved pews? Are there enough seats for all, so that they do not have to stand throughout the Mass? Where are the ministers stationed? Finally, we consider the time or the occasion for the gathering. Is it in the heat of the day, or during a storm? Is it Sunday, or a weekday? Is there a particular occasion for which they gather, such as a marriage or funeral Mass?

What this short exercise in semiotics intends to impress is that rubrics should be read and performed in the context of the worshiping community. Rubrics do not have a life of their own. They exist for the sake of the assembly.

THE USE OF THE VERNACULAR LANGUAGE

Active participation convinced the council fathers to finally approve the hotly debated article 36 of the Liturgy Constitution, which still elicits good cheer or annoyance, depending on who reads it: "Since the use of the mother tongue, whether in the Mass, the administration of the sacraments, or other parts of the liturgy, frequently may be of great advantage to the people, the limits of its use may be extended." The cause for the vernacular liturgy made giant strides in articles 37–40, where the basic principles and criteria of inculturation are laid out. To promote active participation texts need to be translated into the vernacular so that their message can be communicated in the cultural setting of the audience. Inculturation begins with the use of the vernacular. The revival of Latin in the liturgy is to all intents and purposes a deplorable attempt to seal the fate of liturgical inculturation that merited four conciliar paragraphs. In sharp contrast to the revival of Latin in the liturgy is the reminder of the ill-fated 1969 Instruction *Comme le prévoit* issued by the Consilium: "Texts translated from another language are clearly not sufficient for the celebration of a fully renewed liturgy. The creation of new texts will be necessary." Not only should we translate the texts into the vernacular, we should also compose new ones. Now it becomes clear why the 2001 *Liturgiam authenticam* unceremoniously expunged the 1969 Instruction from the official list of liturgical instructions. According to *Comme le prévoit*, translation, inculturation, and creativity are the three progressive movements toward the full realization of the liturgical reform.

We presume that the first Christian community at Jerusalem worshiped in Aramaic, though it is to be assumed that the scriptural readings were in Hebrew. As the Church spread to the other centers of the Roman Empire, a popular type of Greek became the language for worship. It was a language distinct from the *koinè* and was widely spoken in the major cities of the empire, including Rome itself. In fourth-century Jerusalem the situation was somewhat different. The bishop addressed the assembly in Greek, while an interpreter translated what he said into Syriac. What a messy way of celebrating the liturgy! Eventually the biblical readings were translated into Syriac and Latin for those who did not speak Greek.

As Christianity made its presence in other parts of the world where the people were less familiar with Greek, local languages began to be used in the liturgy. In the peripheries of Antioch people continued to speak Syriac, and this became their established liturgical language. Alexandria spoke Greek, but by the sixth and seventh centuries Coptic was introduced into the liturgy for nationalistic and sectarian, that is Monophysite, reasons. Today it uses Greek, Coptic, and Arabic. Ethiopia still celebrates the liturgy in ancient Ge'ez, which is a Semitic language, although the local Church was influenced by Coptic, Greek, and Syrian missionaries. Seleucia, on the lower Tigris and the center of the Assyrian Church (Nestorian Church) that brought Christianity to India, Java, and China, used Syriac, the language in which Mesopotamia and Persia had been evangelized. The Nestorian Church is credited for translating the biblical readings and its liturgical books into local languages. Armenia, which was evangelized in the third century and received influences from Antioch and Constantinople, keeps its ancient Armenian language in the liturgy. Georgia celebrates the Byzantine liturgy in the Georgian language. Lastly, most of the other Churches in Eastern Europe from Bulgaria to Russia, which inherited the liturgy of Constantinople, use Slavonic for their liturgical language.

All this demonstrates that the use of the vernacular language in the liturgy was a living tradition of the early Church. It is obvious that the vernacular was the only available means of effectively communicating the message and eliciting the active response of the liturgical assembly. The problem arose in the second half of the ninth century when the Thessalonian missionaries of Moravia, Cyril and Methodius, translated the Latin and Greek liturgies into Slavonic. Their exceptional work was met with hostility by the Frankish clergy who had been the original missionaries of Moravia. The clergy argued that God could be worshiped only in Hebrew, Greek, and Latin. These were the three languages in which Pilate wrote the cause for which he condemned

Christ to death. This fanciful argument is called "tri-linguism." It sacrificed tradition and pastoral care at the altar of the jealous clergy.

When the Christian community was established in Rome before the year 60, Greek was the dominant language among the inhabitants of the city. This is explained by the cosmopolitan and international character of the city, which attracted the Orientals in great numbers. In fact, during the first two centuries the Church of Rome raised ten Greek-speaking bishops to the throne of Peter. The Romans themselves preferred to speak Greek because it was the language of culture and civilization. Interestingly, the introduction of Latin in the liturgy began, not in Rome, but in the Churches of North Africa. Did it forebode the storm during the council caused by the Roman Church's attachment to its existing conventions? The writers that contributed to the use of Latin were Tertullian, Cyprian of Carthage, Arnobius, Lactantius, and Augustine of Hippo. From them the Church in the West inherited such liturgical words as *sacramentum*, *ordo*, *plebs*, *disciplina*, and *institutio*. The first official Latin version of the Bible for use in the liturgy appeared in North Africa around the year 250. In his writings Cyprian constantly quoted from this translation.

The first attempt to introduce Latin in the Roman liturgy was made not by a Roman pontiff but by Victor I (+203), who was an African by birth. It was toward the year 250 when the Latin Bible made its appearance in the Roman Church. By the second half of the third century, when the number of migrations from Eastern Europe dropped, the use of Latin in the liturgy became more frequent. It was then that the Roman Church adopted the celebrated *via media* or Roman compromise: a bilingual liturgy in which Greek was used for the Eucharistic Prayer (until the Roman Canon appeared in the fourth century) and Latin for the biblical readings. This transitional stage lasted until the end of the fourth century, when Pope Damasus I (+384) initiated a definitive transition from Greek to Latin. It is commonly held that the transition involved the composition of new liturgical texts in Latin, not the translation of Greek prayers. Latin liturgical language developed on its own, thanks to the Roman bishops, especially Pope Leo I (+461), who authored Latin prayers that are still used today. The Roman Church is branded as traditional and conservative, and there is truth in this, but we have to admire its amazing flexibility in responding to changing circumstances. Thus in the seventh century it returned to some form of bilingual liturgy to accommodate the Eastern migrants who poured back into the city. In fact, from 638 to 772 nine popes were from the East. Rome's bilingual liturgy covered the readings and some rites of the catechumenate. Readings were in Latin and Greek on such occasions as Easter and Christmas, at the Vigils of Easter and Pentecost, on Ember Saturdays, and the ordination of a pope.

In the third century the liturgy of Rome was still in Greek, although the great majority of the population spoke Latin. It took the Roman Church one century to submit to the inevitable, but when it finally did, it did so with a shepherd's care, aware that it was abandoning the language of the apostolic times and the language of its martyrs. The liturgy had to speak the language of the people so that the gospel message it contains could be communicated to them. This same pastoral spirit came alive in the seventh century when the Roman Church shifted back to a bilingual liturgy in favor of the migrants from the East. It took the Roman Church several hundred years to adjust to the reality that the liturgical assemblies no longer understood Latin. This time it had to be a decision enacted by an ecumenical council.

When the Second Vatican Council approved the use of the vernacular in the Roman liturgy, it implied that the Latin liturgical books would have to be translated into the local languages. How to state this fact without intimidating a fairly large number of the fathers was a feat of intelligence and prudential judgment on the part of the conciliar commission. Article 36 of the Liturgy Constitution caused a tempest in the council hall that did not abate until a formula that pleased the majority was proposed. The final text is a classic example of the *via media*, which reaffirmed as a matter of principle that "particular law remaining in force the use of the Latin language is to be preserved in the Latin rites." After doing homage to the traditional language of the Roman liturgy, the Constitution penned a most innovative declaration that still reverberates in the hall of history. The text reads: "Since the use of the mother tongue, whether in the Mass, the administration of the sacraments, or other parts of the liturgy, frequently may be of great advantage to the people, the limits of its use may be extended." The article originally considered the readings, instructions, and some prayers and chants. But the provision empowering bishops "to decide whether and to what extent the vernacular is to be used" became a blanket approval to translate the entire corpus of liturgical texts into the vernacular.

However, the implications of a translated liturgy were not lost on those who supported the use of the vernacular. Norms were needed to safeguard the liturgy's doctrinal purity and message. The permission to use the vernacular did not mean opening the door to the creation of new liturgical texts. A petition was submitted to the conciliar commission to add a clause requiring that "translations from the Latin text into the mother tongue intended for use in the liturgy must be approved by the competent, territorial authority." The reason was "to avoid dangerous freedom and variety of translations which can threaten the true meaning and beauty of the texts." It is evident that in the thinking of the council fathers the translated texts enjoy the same worth and dignity as the Latin from which they have been translated. It is still claimed in some sectors that Latin is the official language of the Roman rite. The Constitution does not say this. It merely reminds us that the Latin language is to be preserved in the Latin rites, which is what the Latin *editio typica* does. Vernacular languages, if approved by the Holy See and used in liturgical worship, share with Latin the status of official liturgical language.

The first area where the vernacular was introduced was the Liturgy of the Hours. In his1964 *Motu proprio, Sacram Liturgiam*, Pope Paul VI started the ball rolling. Priests could pray the Liturgy of the Hours in the vernacular. I suspect that the Holy Father was not oblivious to the fact that even among the clergy Latin was as unintelligible as Greek. When a council father begged for the retention of certain Latin prayers like the *Kyrie eleison*, it must have dawned on Paul VI that the time had come for the Church to march with the times. I could not hide my amusement when a bishop asked what I thought about *Summorum Pontificorum*. Paul VI laid down the norm that the translated version should be drawn up and approved by the conferences of bishops and submitted to the Holy See for approval or confirmation. "This is the course to be taken whenever any Latin liturgical text is translated into the vernacular by the authority" of the conferences of bishops.

In the same year the Consilium issued the farsighted Instruction *Inter oecumenici* in which the criteria for vernacular translations are set forth. Among other things, the Consilium made it clear that the basis of the translations is the Latin liturgical text, because translation is not the creation of new liturgical texts. Furthermore, the work of translations should be interdisciplinary, involving institutes of liturgy and experts in Scripture, liturgy, the biblical languages, Latin, the vernacular, and music; where applicable, there should be consultation with bishops of neighboring regions using the same language; in nations of several languages there should be a translation for each language; and the liturgy may be celebrated anywhere in the language of migrants, members of a personal parish, or other like groups.

RITUAL LANGUAGE

To develop this elusive topic I present a synthesis of the principal points raised in the works of Christine Mohrmann, Gail Ramshaw, and Gianfranco Venturi. To their expert treatises I add some personal insights, which I developed from an earlier article that I wrote for Kathleen Hughes's *Finding Voice to Give God Praise*. I met Mohrmann when I was a student in Rome. She made history as the first woman to enter the classroom of the Pontifical Liturgical Institute, but Nocent brushed away our wariness by noting that she was holding a cigar in her hand. I met Ramshaw and Venturi on several occasions.

Mohrmann presents the philological aspect of liturgical Latin in her two classic works *Liturgical Lati: Its Origin and Character* and *Latin chrétien et liturgique*. Ramshaw's *Christ in Sacred Speech: The Meaning of Liturgical Language* treats the subject in a metaphorical perspective, while Venturi's article *"Lenguaje liturgico"* (*Nuevo Diccionario de Liturgia*) makes a semiotic study of ritual language. I purposely use the word "ritual" instead of "liturgical" to stress the fact that it is performative and that it comes alive as a symbol when it is said, sung, or proclaimed in the liturgical assembly. The word "ritual" reinforces the connotation of language as something that is performed or carried out through words, gestures, and use of material things. Ritual language indicates that the liturgy, being a conjunction of interrelated words, formularies, gestures, and symbols, is by definition a ritual action.

Experts on the science of linguistics understand language in its broadest sense as a system of communication through the use of conventional signs, symbols, gestures, and sounds. These represent meanings that are commonly understood by the people to whom they are addressed. When applied to the liturgy, language denotes the entire system of signs and symbols, words and speech or song, moments of silence, gestures and postures, sacred images or icons, and some material elements of biblical origin, such as water, bread, wine, and oil, with which the Church celebrates the saving mystery of Christ. In a broad sense the totality of this type of "language" is called ritual because it refers to rites or to the prescribed system governing the words, actions, and material things needed for a ceremony. The ceremony itself is an action, more or less solemn, which people set apart from the normal routine of the day. Though people tend to use the word "ritual" rather loosely, as in the expression "daily ritual," a rite in itself is always something special, even when it is performed daily or several times a day.

At the outset it is useful to note that the ritual language of the Roman liturgy is anchored in the medieval culture of Europe from the time of the classical patristic period (represented by Popes Vigilius, Gelasius, Leo the Great, and Gregory the Great) down to the late Middle Ages. This consideration is reason enough why the texts of the Roman liturgy, even in their most recent translation, sometimes sound to modern ears as rather quaint and distant.

What is ritual language or, better yet, what is it not? Ritual language is not a bearer of dogmatic statements of the faith. Although *lex credendi* sometimes weighs heavily on *lex orandi*, as in such feasts as the Holy Trinity, Corpus Christi, Immaculate Conception, and the Assumption of the Blessed Virgin Mary, it is not normal to construct ritual language with elements derived from dogmatic statements. The only dogmatic formulary in the liturgy is the Nicene Creed, but we know that it was not composed originally for liturgical proclamation. I am not saying that liturgical texts do not contain doctrine. They do speak about God, about Jesus Christ and his saving work, about the Church, and about the rule of Christian life. The Constitution on Liturgy confirms this: "Although the liturgy is above all things the worship of the divine majesty, it likewise contains rich instruction for the faithful" (33). The liturgy communicates to the assembly the faith of the Church. However, it does so not in the language of systematic theology and speculative philosophy but in the language used for acclamations and narrations. The liturgy is not exposition but persuasion: in the prayers we, as it were, remind God about his divine deeds (anamnesis) in order to persuade God to renew them in our day (epiclesis). Even the homily is not meant to be a doctrinal treatise, but a persuasive speech addressed to the assembly to regard people, events, and things in the light of God's proclaimed word.

It can be an exercise in futility to formulate doctrinal statements using liturgical texts. While it is true that Pope Pius XII invoked the ancient feast of the Assumption as a living witness to the dogma, the liturgical texts available then did not offer sufficient material to articulate a dogmatic statement. Those who expect liturgical texts to provide them with a corpus of Christian doctrine will be disappointed or, what is worse, might naively detect dogma where there is in reality a polyvalent symbol. Dogma-hunting in every liturgical text can be a frustrating exercise. Likewise, those who are excessively fastidious about the use of abstract and technical terms in liturgical texts can miss the basic premise that ritual language is more persuasive than systematic.

Finally, those who demand that every doctrine should be laid out fully in liturgical texts forget that the liturgy is not a dogmatic compendium but a memorial of persons and events. To mention at every possible occasion that Mary is the Mother of God or that she is ever-virgin is not always a catechetical advantage. Liturgical formularies need not say everything that is contained in the *Catechism of the Catholic Church*. Obviously, literary language is not an excuse to ignore the requirements of orthodoxy, but it does not follow that ritual language is in the category of systematic theology.

Ritual language is not colloquial speech. When we speak to God in public or address a community assembled in worship, we do not engage in familiar and informal conversation. The occasion is always solemn, even if it involves only two or three worshipers in the austerity of a village chapel. It is always solemn, because the object of the memorial is the sublimity of Christ's saving act and the people celebrating represent the one, holy, catholic, and apostolic Church. Ritual language should be in the vernacular and it should be accessible to the majority in the assembly, but it should not be colloquial. Even if colloquial language is not banal or trite, it is nonetheless not ritual. The cheery greeting "Good morning, how is everyone today?" that sometimes replaces the liturgical "The Lord be with you" is at best a failure to distinguish one occasion from another. Someone has noted that it might even offend those who have suffered recent loss or misfortune. The following prayer is familiar and intimate, but it does not pass as a ritual text for liturgical worship: "We pray to you, dear Lord, please do something quickly about this painful situation." Similarly, the ritual context is ignored by extemporized exchange of marriage vows like this one: "Annie, for so long I have searched for a partner but never found the right girl. Now at last God led me to you. I promise to be a loving and faithful husband for as long as I live."

The language of popular religiosity, like that of the liturgy, is ritual, but it belongs to a different ritual genre. There is much that the former can learn from the latter, especially in its content and the use of language suited for public prayer. But in situations where people are more at ease with the language of popular worship it might not be altogether uncalled for to allow liturgical language to integrate some characteristic traits of popular religious language. It is useful to note that colloquial language is distinguished from the popular religious language that we use for novena prayers. The language of popular religiosity can be solemn, though often florid, discursive to the point of rambling, and vividly picturesque. The following novena prayer is surely not colloquial, but it is neither liturgical: "To whom can I turn if not to you, whose heart is the source of all graces and merits? Where should I seek if not in the treasure which contains all the riches of your kindness and mercy? Where should I knock if not at the door through which God gives himself to us and through which we go to God?"

Finally, ritual language is often poetic, though it is not subjective. It is not subjective because its beauty does not arise merely from the heart of the composer but above all from the poetry of the divine mystery. Ritual language that is poetic is the product of contemplation, of pondering the beauty of God, the paschal mystery, the Church, the human family, and the world. The poetic character of ritual language does not well up from the writer's stream of consciousness but from the silent experience of God that breaks into song of thanks and praise and pleads for salvation. The liturgy often makes use of poetic language when it records the history of God's dealings with humankind. Good poetry has the power to move and touch the heart of worshipers. The ancient Church used biblical psalms in the liturgy, but at the same time it encouraged people, as Tertullian in the third century informs us, to stand in the assembly to sing or recite poems, called "idiotic psalms" that narrated their personal encounters with Christ. A good number of hymns composed specifically for liturgical celebrations are masterpieces of poetry. We recall the hymns that writers like Ephrem of Edessa, Ambrose of Milan, Fulgentius, and Rhabanus Maurus composed for the liturgy. Poetic context alone can explain or even justify such liturgical compositions as the *improperia*, or reproaches, on Good Friday. It is extremely difficult to imagine that Jesus who was led to the cross like a lamb and forgave those who crucified him would now reproach the people that he loved and for whom he suffered so much. Likewise, how do we explain, except in poetic context, such outbursts in the *Exsultet* as: *O certe necessarium Adae peccatum! O felix culpa! Ut servum redimeres, Filium tradidisti*. I venture to translate these poetic outbursts as follows: "O truly necessary sin of Adam! O fault that was a blessing in disguise! To redeem a servant, you handed your Son to death." I should note that *tradidisti* often connotes betrayal.

In common usage ritual language is the type of speech used in the performance of a rite. Speech in this context refers to the system of communication that employs spoken words to express a desired message. Speech is composed of words and phrases, but these are not independent units. Rather, they combine to create a denotation, a connotation, a context or, in short, a message. It is useful to note that every word, being in the category of symbols, is polyvalent: it can carry several meanings and nuances. Dictionaries normally enumerate them, carefully indicating the different contexts in which they are used. The word "foot" can mean a part of a body; a system of measurement; a metaphor, as in "foot of a mountain"; a synecdoche, as in "the feet of one who brings good tidings"; or an idiomatic expression, as in "foot in the door." But in combination with other words a word assumes a particular or definite meaning that is needed in order to articulate, in conjunction with those other words, the message of a text.

Thus, no word should be read singly as an independent unit but in context, that is, in conjunction with the other components of language, including the signs and gestures that accompany the spoken word. To understand fully the meaning of a word in a linguistic unit, it is necessary to do the process of what authors call "decomposition," "decoding," or "dehistorization" of the entire unit in order to determine the "kernel." This process aims to discover the relationship between the kernel and the other segments of the text or, in other words, its global historical, cultural, doctrinal, and literary context. Someone was mortified by the sentence "the couple pronounced their solemn vows before God's altar," because the expression "solemn vows" brought to mind the profession in religious orders! Context and the conjunction of surrounding circumstances define the meaning of a word. This explains why translations should not be done word for word. I will not mince my words: it is a crude method and I hazard a guess that those who advance it have a rudimentary understanding of language.

Ritual language takes on various forms. The list comprises formularies, acclamations, poetic compositions or hymns, songs, and addresses in the form of homilies or instructions. In a word, ritual language is anything spoken, read aloud, proclaimed, or sung in the liturgy. It is primarily intended to be performed orally in celebrations with an assembly. Since the early Middle Ages liturgical formularies and hymns have been put down in writing. This should not, however, lead us to regard them as literary pieces for private reading. Liturgical texts come alive as symbols when they are read aloud or sung in public. Ritual language is the type of language appropriate for this because it is able to convey the meaning and purpose of the liturgical. Thus the vocabulary, lexicon, and the grammatical construction of ritual language are shaped and developed by the liturgy itself. Hence, the vocabulary and lexicon of ritual language, though not necessarily reserved for the liturgy, are best understood in the context of the liturgical action.

In the liturgy words like "blessed" and "rejoice" have a more felicitous effect than "happy" and "be happy," which can sound trite and commonplace. "Behold," as in "Behold the lamb of God," is more fitting than the conversational "This is the lamb of God." Rituality suffers when presiders extemporize, as in this fashionable but obtrusive formulary: "This is Jesus, our brother and friend, the Son of Mary, the lamb of God who takes away the sins of the world." The ability to recite extemporaneous prayers with dignity, style, and depth is a rare gift. From the third century on liturgical texts began to be written down not only to ward off heresy but also to maintain a literary style suited for solemn worship. In the heyday of Latin liturgical creativity authors paid detailed attention to the literary properties of the medieval Latin language. The number of syllables was counted, accents were positioned for cadence and rhythm, and the appropriate imagery was chosen to make the text memorable.

It is true that we use ritual words sparingly in normal life, but because the liturgy is not normal life but one of its solemn ritual moments, we expect to hear ritual words when we gather for worship. The following sentence, which is exclamatory, is constructed to suit the nature of ritual language: "Lord, you are holy indeed; you are the fountain of all holiness." Outside the context of the liturgical rite this linguistic construction sounds contrived. At times ritual language also dispenses with normal syntactic arrangement. The formula of blessing, "May almighty God bless you, the Father, and the Son, and the Holy Spirit," is an unusual form of speech in English, though not in medieval Latin. However, the normal construction, "May almighty God, the Father, the Son, and the Holy Spirit, bless you," is prosaic. The declarations "The body of Christ," "The word of the Lord," and "The gospel of the Lord" are striking in both English and Latin, but they have neither verb nor predicate. Such irregular sentence construction is justifiable within the ritual parameter. The long and short of it is that the liturgy produces its ritual language with specific and suitable lexicon and grammar.

THE RITUAL LANGUAGE OF ICEL

How did the International Commission on English in the Liturgy (ICEL) deal with the question of ritual language before its Advisory Committee, which first met in 1965, was replaced in 2000 by a

Consultants' Committee? In some ways this discussion can be judged moot and academic, but in many ways the method of translation it used, especially in the aborted revised Sacramentary on which it worked for ten years, is a shining example of how ritual language is designed. It is regrettable that the Congregation for Divine Worship is patronizing a less-suitable method, but I want to hope that the inner dynamism of living language will eventually prevail.

My many years of association with the Advisory Committee of ICEL are as memorable as they were liturgically enriching and ecclesially challenging. It was a closely knit group of bishops and advisors from every part of the English-speaking world that we fondly called the ICEL family. We argued, debated, critiqued, and laughed as we went over every word and phrase to pass judgment on their doctrinal content and suitability for public proclamation. Some persons are unforgettable: Executive Secretary John Page, whose person, loyalty to the Church, and managerial skills I highly esteem; Gilbert Ostdiek, who was chair of the committee when I was named advisor; Kenneth Larsen, a delightful scholar of Elizabethan English; Frederick McManus and Godfrey Diekmann; Mary Collins; Christopher Walsh; Kathleen Hughes; Ronald Krisman; Margaret Mary Kelleher; Geoffrey Steel; Margaret Daly-Denton; Edward Matthews; and James Schellman. I was greatly encouraged by the full support given to ICEL's work by the members of the Episcopal Board: Maurice Taylor, Peter Cullinane, and Denis Hurley.

A subtle form of attack hurled by organized groups (such as Credo) at ICEL's translations took cover under the wing of "doctrinal concern" that smeared the credibility of ICEL, its fidelity to the original texts because of its use of dynamic translation, and its alarming use of inclusive language. The question of inclusive language in the liturgy is not an insignificant matter. It seems to me that the evolution of language is a cultural, linguistic reality that the liturgy is obliged to accept. When we insist on calling women "men" or "brethren" and refer to our ancestors in faith as "fathers," we do not even pay lip service to the rightful place of women in salvation history and the life of the Church. In all honesty, I can assure ICEL's critics that it had no other agenda than to communicate faithfully, nobly, and memorably to the English-speaking faithful the message of the liturgy.

To ensure the dignity and solemnity of the new ICEL Sacramentary the Advisory Committee went to great lengths to revise or modify the translations and original compositions in the 1975 Sacramentary. The group took seriously the process for shaping a ritual language for worship that involved several conferences of bishops and experts in every field significantly related to the liturgy. The following translation of the opening prayer for the Seventeenth Sunday in Ordinary Time, which the Advisory Committee drafted, is remarkable for its attention to English cadence and rhythm and to the qualities of ritual language.

O Gód, protéctor of thóse who hópe in yóu,
withóut whom nóthing is stróng, nóthing is hóly,
enfóld us in your grácious cáre and mércy,
that with yóu as our rúler and gúide,
we may úse wísely the gífts of this pássing wórld
and fíx our heárts even nów on thóse which lást for ever.

Nothing is colloquial here, nothing is improvised: every word and every accent have been thoroughly considered.

The Latin liturgy gives us instructive examples of how to design ritual vocabulary. The following example from the Roman Canon is admirable for the use of Latin rhetoric: *Unde et memores, Domine, nos servi tui sed et plebs tua sancta . . .* It is a hieratic speech about the solemn (*unde*) memorial (*et memores*) addressed by the Church to God, the ministers that serve at God's table (*nos servi tui*), and the assembly gathered as a holy people (*sed et plebs tua sancta*). This hieratic property of ritual prayer is present in the translation prepared by the Advisory Committee:

All-merciful Father,
we come before you with praise and thanksgiving
through Jesus Christ your Son.

The sentence "we come before you" expands the Latin *igitur*, which cannot be translated with one word without sounding flat and unconnected, except for expert ears. The conjunction of these words gives the phrase the unmistakable mark of ritual language and matches the solemnity of *igitur*. On the other hand, the words "with praise and thanksgiving" serve as a strong link between the preface and the rest of the Eucharistic Prayer.

There is a set of ritual words that details the meaning of epiclesis as petition for God's grace, salvation, consecration, holiness, offering and sacrifice, and intercession for the needs of the Church and humankind. The Roman Canon expresses such elements of epiclesis in these words:

Per Iesum Christum Filium tuum, Dominum nostrum, supplices rogamus ac petimus, uti accepta habeas et benedicas haec munera, haec sancta sacrificia illibata. The Advisory Committee's version captures this in typically crisp English without injury to the qualities of ritual language.

> Through him [Christ] we ask you
> to accept and bless these gifts
> we offer you in sacrifice.

Because the spoken language of the liturgy is by nature ritual, it is consequently also a literary language. It is contemporary and hence accessible to the majority of people in the assembly, but it uses a literary genre or style suited for proclamation. This ritual quality of liturgical language is confirmed by the experience of the medieval Latin Church. Historians tell us that when Latin became the liturgical language of Rome after the fourth century, several prayer formularies were authored by persons who had been formed in the school of Roman rhetoric and the classics. They were bishops of Rome: Vigilius, Gelasius, Leo the Great, and Gregory the Great. Through them the literary style of medieval Latin permeated the language of Latin liturgy. Rhetoric, which unfortunately acquired a pejorative meaning in our day because of grandiloquent political discourses, was actually a literary style that the solemnity of the occasion required. Conversational style would have been frowned upon as trite and impertinent. Theodore Klauser gives the name *Kulturlatein* (as opposed to *Volkslatein*) to the type of literary Latin that the popes crafted for liturgical use.

Yet I believe it is a mistake to think that the rhetorical style of these medieval Latin prayers belonged to a wholly other kind of language that is reserved exclusively for religious purposes. Latin liturgical language is surely literary, elevated, and noble, in short, rhetorical, but it is not sacred like the Sanskrit or the cryptic language used by the mystery religions. At the time of these four great popes of the liturgy, the Roman people gathered in liturgical assembly would have noted that the same style of language was being used by State leaders in public discourses. That is why it is not correct to regard the Latin liturgical language as sacred language. Ritual language is not synonymous with sacred language, at least in the experience of the Latin Church. Perhaps a comparison can be made with the Christian places of worship. The early Christians did not gather in temples but in houses, which acquired the title *liturgical* because of the presence of Christ in the assembly. Sacred language is a form of ritual language, but not every ritual language is sacred language.

To press this point it might help to cite a few examples of the more commonly used forms of classical Roman rhetoric. An understanding of the Latin original can contribute to a greater appreciation of what the Advisory Committee tried to achieve.

A familiar literary form is the *cursus*, which consists of a rhythmic arrangement of the final words of a sense line. The aim is to highlight word cadences, express sentiments of joy and wonder, and produce a sound pleasing to the ears of listeners. Scholars detect three types. The first is *cursus planus*, as in *órbis exúltat*. The second type is *cursus tardus*, as in *ástra caeléstia*. The third type is *cursus velox*, as in *consília respondémus*. A classic example of the use of *cursus* is found in one of the Christmas formularies in the Veronese Sacramentary (1239):

> *Deus, qui humanae substantiae dignitatem*
> *et mirabiliter condidisti*
> *et mirabilius reformasti . . .*

The lines ending with *mirabiliter condidisti* and *mirabilius reformasti* are in the *cursus velox* and are meant to evoke by their swift rhythm the sense of admiration, joy, and gratitude for God's work of creation and redemption. The Advisory Committee's revision of the Sacramentary has in more ways than one remarkably seized the sense being conveyed by the *cursus*. In the alternative opening prayer for the Mass on Christmas day we detect an English equivalent of *cursus*. The text is concise and moves quickly but with grace, as it elicits a response of wonder and thanksgiving. Its aural effect has a quality that is comparable to the Latin *cursus*.

> We praise you, gracious God,
> for the glad tidings of peace,
> the good news of salvation:
> your Word became flesh,
> and we have seen his glory.

Another rhetorical device is binary succession, a type of embolism, which develops in pairs the principal theme of the prayer. Pope Vigilius often used this in the prefaces he penned. The following preface in the Veronese Sacramentary (501), which scholars attribute to him, is a remarkable example of the use of binary succession:

Nullis quippe forinsecus miseriis adfligemur,
si vitia frenemus animorum;
nec visibili dedecori subiacebit,
qui foedis cupiditatibus obviaverit;
nulla inquietudo praevalebit extrinsecus,
si agamus corde sincere . . .

ICEL's Advisory Committee employed binary succession in its translation of the second preface of the Passion. After the solemn proem "This is the hour" the text develops the theme of Christ's victory through his passion in a binary succession of "when" clauses to define the "hour":

This is the hour
when we celebrate his triumph over Satan's pride,
when we solemnly recall the mystery of our redemption.

A third type of Latin rhetorical device is antithesis or juxtaposition of contrasting concepts like *ascensio* and *discessio*, *invisibilis* and *visibilis*. The Latin sacramentaries have a fondness for antithesis, especially in the prefaces. The preface for the Ascension in the Veronese Sacramentary (176) uses it copiously. It reads in part:

Quia in caelos ascensio mediatoris . . .
a nostra non est humilitate discessio.

The Advisory Committee's revision of the second preface of Christmas takes into consideration the antithetical device used by the Latin original:

The God we cannot see
has now appeared in human form.
The one begotten before all ages
begins to live in time.

A fourth type of Latin rhetorical device is *concinnitas*. This consists of a balanced arrangement of the parts of an oration, which is obtained through symmetry of words and concepts. The postcommunion prayer in the Veronese Sacramentary (1068) is a masterly example:

Quod sumit, intelligat;
quod gustu delibat, moribus apprehendat;
quod iustis orationibus expetit, tua misericordia percipiat.

ICEL's original texts, which the Congregation for Divine Worship declared to be outside the bounds of ICEL's mandate, are often characterized by symmetrical sentences. Below are typical examples, one for the first Sunday of Lent, the other for the fourth.

> When we walk through the desert of temptation,
> strengthen us to renounce the power of evil.
> When our faith is tested by doubt,
> illumine our hearts with Easter's bright promise.

> Lifted up from the earth,
> he is light and life;
> exalted upon the cross,
> he is truth and salvation.

The foregoing discussion leads us to believe that some traits of ritual language are cross-cultural. Ritual language is oral and aural; it is a component of ritual action; and it uses rhetorical devices to draw out the meaning and enhance the beauty of the message. There is, to be sure, a world of difference between Latin and English syntax construction and between Latin and English literary devices. Yet both own in common such cross-cultural qualities as cadences, accents, and rhythm. Likewise, our discussion shows that the translations and original texts crafted by ICEL's Advisory Committee are singularly attentive to the properties of formal spoken English. These are: accent on key words, avoidance of internal rhyme and too many unaccented syllables in a row, and effort to end each line strongly on an accented syllable. The inclusion of these and other properties of modern English language in the aborted revised Sacramentary of ICEL resulted in more ways than one in liturgical texts that match the beauty and nobility of the original Latin.

PRINCIPLES OF LITURGICAL TRANSLATION

In his address to the translators of liturgical texts in 1965 Pope Paul VI summed up the conciliar and postconciliar thinking on the matter. The address is brief, but it covers the basic principles governing liturgical translations. In many ways the 1969 Instruction *Comme le prévoit* is an elaboration of several points raised by the Holy Father. First, he reminded the translators that their aim is principally to promote active participation in the liturgy, as the council desired. He recalled that for the sake of active participation the Church willingly let go of its centuries-old Latin liturgy and permitted "the translation of texts venerable for their antiquity, devotion, beauty, and long-standing use." The sacrifice of so noble a heritage should thus be compensated by vernacular texts that are "within the grasp of all, even children and the uneducated." Translations should bridge the cultural gap between the Latin liturgy and the local assemblies everywhere.

Second, while the preconciliar translations assisted the faithful to understand the Latin rite, the official translations after the council "have become part of the rites themselves; they have become the voice of the Church." In a word, vernacular translations enjoy the same value and respect as the original texts: they too are the Church's official languages for liturgical worship. That is why translated texts, approved by the local authority and the Holy See for liturgical use, "are as such to be held in all reverence." To take liberties with them is to be unmindful of their status as prayer of the Church. After the council, new languages across the globe were introduced for liturgical use. The Roman liturgy ceased being monolingual. It does not follow, however, that the Church has instituted new liturgical families because it welcomed other languages for worship. "The voice of the Church remains one and the same in celebrating the divine mysteries and administering the sacraments, although that voice speaks in a variety of tongues."

Third, the type of language to be used in the liturgy should, according to the pope, "always be worthy of the noble realities it signifies, set apart from the everyday speech of the street and the marketplace." This requires that translators "know both Christian Latin and their own modern language." This is the crux of the problem in many places today where Latin is a language that is foreign even to the clergy. Consequently, some translations are based on other existing translations such as ICEL's. A translation from a translation is sometimes as good as a new composition. ICEL, from what I know, is saddled with responsibility to serve as a basis for other languages. No wonder the Congregation for Divine Worship importunes it with the demand for literal translation. In view of a truly musical liturgy the pope prompted translators to take the rules of music into account and choose words that could be set to local music. As he concluded his discourse the pope appeared to convey mixed feelings about the sacrifice the Church had made: "For pastoral reasons, the beauty and richness of Latin, which the Latin Church used for centuries for prayers, petitions, and thanksgiving to God, have been partially lost."

He thus challenged translators to "make a similar clarity of language and dignity of expression shine forth in the vernacular translations of liturgical texts." The message or content should always be the chief consideration of translators, but it is not the only consideration. Translators should develop the kind of ritual language that reflects the best in local culture.

The problem of translating from one language to another is not new. We have much to learn from the experience of the great biblical translator St. Jerome. In his *Eusebii Interpretata Praefatio* he writes: "If I translate word by word, it sounds absurd; if I am forced to change something in the word order or style, I seem to have stopped being a translator." With these words he voiced the sentiment of anxiety or insecurity of every conscientious translator. The Italian warning *traduttore, traditore* (a translator is a traitor) should not fall on deaf ears. Word-by-word translation often does not make sense, but a change in the meaning of the word will betray the message. The translation of liturgical texts is perhaps the most delicate and complicated matter arising from the council's decision to shift from Latin to the vernacular languages.

To define "translation" it is useful to review several of its components. I have availed myself of the scholarly work of Eugene Nida and Charles Taber entitled *The Theory and Practice of Translation*, Charles Kraft's *Christianity in Culture*, and Noam Chomsky's *Syntactic Structure* and applied their findings to the liturgy. What happens when we do a translation? Basically we reexpress in the receptor language the message of the source language. In our case the vernacular is the receptor language, while Latin is the source language. The message is the doctrinal, spiritual content of the Latin text, that is, the message that the Church originally intended to communicate to a particular assembly for which the Latin text was prepared. The aim of translation work is to share the original message with another assembly, one of a different culture and speaking a different language. In order that this assembly will grasp the full meaning of what is communicated, it is necessary that the message be reexpressed using the values, traditions, and linguistic patterns proper to the assembly.

It is senseless to try to separate physically the doctrinal content from the cultural form, but it will be necessary to make a mental distinction between them in order to allow the content to take on another cultural form. Sometimes the translator has to subject the original text to the process that I mentioned earlier on. It consists of "decomposition," "decoding," or "de-historization," which should result in identifying the "kernel" or basic doctrinal content. The process also aims to discover the relationship between the "kernel" and the other segments of the text or, in other words, its global historical, cultural, doctrinal, and literary context. The process concludes with the "re-composition" of the text in the new form of the receptor language. We can describe the process of translation as the passage of the content from one cultural form to another, which represents equivalently the original form. In short, it is the transferal of the message whole and entire from the source to the receptor language. A good translation produces in the audience of the receptor language the same effect the source language had on its original audience. It achieves the same purpose as did the original text.

This theory of translation requires the method of dynamic equivalence in order to operate. The method won the approval of the Consilium that issued the 1969 Instruction *Comme le prévoit* on the translation of liturgical texts. Sad to say, the Instruction was shelved in 2001 by *Liturgiam authenticam*, which is rather hostile to dynamic equivalence. Nevertheless, because the principles on which the 1969 Instruction rests stand on scholarly research and solid scientific ground, I believe that it remains as a valuable guide for liturgical translators. The Instruction appeals to the method of dynamic equivalence when it affirms that "a faithful translation cannot be judged on the basis of individual words: the total context of this specific act of communication must be kept in mind, as well as the literary form proper to the respective language" (6). The context, according to the Instruction, includes the message itself, the audience for which the text is intended, and the mode of expression. This is what the method of dynamic equivalence is all about.

The foregoing definition of translation discredits the method of translation that does not take into account the culture represented by both the source and the receptor languages. Such method merely renders the original text word by word or phrase by phrase, unmindful of the cultural underpinnings in them. The method is descriptively called "formal correspondence." There is no doubt as to the sincerity of those who embrace this scientifically dubious method. They profess to be faithful to the original text but, alas, the method they have adopted treats fidelity on the surface level of the source language and hence occupies itself with the literal transferal of the message to the receptor language. Apropos Marsili ("Liturgical Texts for Modern Man,"

*Concilium*1959) calls to the attention of translators the unsuitability of formal correspondence: "We would not regard as scientific a translation based on the belief that the sense of a Latin text could be captured by a simple recourse to a dictionary and the study of the grammatical and logical form in question." He points out that the text possesses a "genius" of its own, "which is in turn the genius of the people, the age, and the culture giving rise to the text." A Latinist colleague at the Pontifical Liturgical Institute, Ildebrando Scicolone, gave a humorous example of what happens if we translate liturgical texts with the use of the Latin dictionary alone. The *vere dignum* preamble of the preface can be rendered thus: In spring (*vere*) it is right and just to greet (*salutare*) also (*et*) the horse (*equum*).

The work of liturgical translation rests on certain premises. It is a scientific endeavor that observes the systems particular to linguistics and liturgy. Translators are required to possess an adequate knowledge of the principles and structure of language. Ferdinand de Saussure's *Course in General Linguistics* has made a solid contribution to the scientific understanding of language. Modern linguistics has moved away from the traditional notion of language as nomenclature, which means that the words used by different languages are regarded merely as sound labels for the same reality. Hence, translation is only a matter of transferring names. The truth, however, is that every language has its distinctive cultural patterns and unique genius that translators are expected to know, respect, and work with. The syntax, literary genres, and idioms manifest the receptor language's cultural patterns and linguistic uniqueness. At the same time they provide the users of the language a prism with which to view reality.

It is obvious that since we deal with the liturgy, translators should work according to liturgical requirements. I realize that I am repeating this ad nauseam: translators do not create new liturgical texts. That is why they work on existing liturgical texts provided by the Latin typical edition of liturgical books. We know that texts originated in different epochs of Church history and were authored by various people for the use of a particular assembly in a particular time and situation. Their authentic and original message will be understood better if translators keep this in mind. *Comme le prévoit* gives a piece of advice that in this regard is probably the only kind of practical advice one can offer: "To discover the true meaning of a text, the translator must follow the scientific methods of textual study as used by experts" (8). Liturgical exegesis and hermeneutics are now regarded as integral components of the study of liturgy. They consist of philological analysis of the text, textual identification (authorship, theological and cultural ambient, and literary properties of the text), and the identification of the redactional sources of the text. The Instruction requires that "if need be, a critical text of the passage must first be established so that the translation can be done from the original or at least from the best available text" (10a). Such is the seriousness that should mark liturgical translations. The mind boggles at the verdict that critics pass on *Comme le prévoit*. They brush it off as a "dated" document because dynamic equivalence, which it champions, is now a moot issue.

Liturgical translation is a work of art. It requires creative skill for producing translations that display form, beauty, and perception. Aesthetics in the best sense of the word is an integral element of Christian worship. Liturgical tradition has always put stock in the beauty and nobility of texts, ceremonies, vestments, music, sacred images, books, architecture, and environment. A translation may be doctrinally faithful and linguistically correct, but if it lacks beauty or aesthetic form and is not memorable, it is an amateur piece of liturgical art. Prayers proclaimed in assembly should be pleasing to the ears, evoke beautiful images of God and the universe, and raise the hearts to what is sublime and noble. The Latin prayers, especially during the heyday of liturgical creativity, were products of literary skill that knew how to employ the finest rhetorical figures in the Latin language, such as redundancy, repetition, sound, vivacity, parallelism, argumentation, and imagery. I assume that when listening to the orations of Pope Leo the Great, the Roman assembly took special delight in his expert use of such rhetorical devices as binary succession, antithesis, *cursus*, and *concinnitas* or symmetry. There is no reason to think that modern congregations are indifferent to the beauty and nobility of liturgical prayers that are proclaimed in their own language. In some parts of the Philippines discourses that are marked by the use of idioms, rhymes, and rhythmic cadence are highly valued as artistic language worthy of a formal gathering. Why should translated texts sound trite, when their source is a polished product of art?

Liturgical translation is the interpretation of a text in the context of a particular assembly. We are dealing here with the need to contextualize translation. Even after the authentic, original text is established through exegesis and hermeneutics, translators should still pose the question whether the translated text communicates to a given assembly and in their own particular circumstances the message intended by the original text for its original audience. This seems to be the concern being addressed by the Instruction *Comme le prévoit* when it remarks that "in the case of liturgical communication, it is necessary to take into account not only the message to be conveyed, but also the speaker, the audience, and the style" (7). Liturgical texts communicate the message in a performative manner. In the liturgical celebration the texts are performed as actions that express the relationship between God and the assembly. In the words of *Comme le prévoit*, "a liturgical text is a linguistic fact designed for celebration" (27). It is not enough to transmit the original message. It is necessary that the message be contextualized or made relevant to the circumstances of the assembly. After all, the liturgy is not a historical celebration, nor is it merely a remembrance of what God did in ages past. It is also the experience of what God does for the people gathered for liturgical worship. The Instruction points out that "the prayer of the Church is always the prayer of some actual community, assembled here and now. It is not sufficient that a formula handed down from some other time or region be translated verbatim, even if accurately, for liturgical use. The formula translated must become the genuine prayer of the congregation and in it each of its members should be able to find and express himself or herself" (20).

Related to contextualized translation is inculturation. The fact that good translations are generated by dynamic equivalence argues for the application of the principles of inculturation. With the openly hostile attitude toward dynamic equivalence, I sometimes entertain a nagging doubt that inculturated translations will ever see the light of day. Nonetheless, I console myself with the thought that historical developments are relative: people and events come and go. The present should not put a damper on tomorrow's hope.

The subject of inculturation is broad, and I have discussed it separately in a number of my works, but the following points have immediate relevance to translation. First, inculturation is achieved when the receptor language is able to comfortably use idiomatic expressions and elements of local proverbs, maxims, and aphorisms to communicate the message of the source language. They are integral components of linguistic patterns and reveal the people's understanding of God, history, and the reality of life. I have heard the remark that the use of idioms is proof that the person knows the language. Theologians and liturgists regularly use idioms in daily conversation, but they have this lurking suspicion that idioms do not have a place and a role in liturgical prayers. Understandably, when we are preoccupied with stating the correct doctrine, the safest thing to do is to use the theological vocabulary we learned in the classroom.

The second point is that inculturation in certain receptor languages will unavoidably touch on the question of inclusive language. This is a delicate matter that translators need to address, and some conferences of bishops have already issued guidelines regarding the vertical language (when addressing God) and the horizontal (when referring to humans). Mary Collins's article "Naming God in Public Prayer" (*Worship* 59) clarifies many points of this unsettled issue. What really escapes comprehension is that some "official" English translations cold-shoulder the progress of the debate and simply use masculine nouns and pronouns on the horizontal level. The question of inclusive language stems from the evolution of verbal and lexical usage brought about by cultural and social changes. Inclusive language is the modern protagonist of the centuries-old movement working for the recognition of the equality of human persons, male or female, and the promotion of the rightful place of women in the Church and society. To ignore it is to disregard the historical process. The problem is not universal. Some receptor languages, especially outside the Western hemisphere, do not encounter this problem. My native tongue Tagalog, for example, names God in the third person form *siya*, which is inclusive. People are *tao*, brothers and sisters are *mga kapatid*, and sons and daughters are *mga anak*. These words are all inclusive. To refer specifically to a brother one needs to say *kapatid na lalaki*, and to a sister, *kapatid na babae*.

Translators are of course aware that the Latin liturgical language has its peculiarities in grammar and lexicon. The Instruction "The Roman Liturgy and Inculturation" (53) makes the timely reminder that "liturgical language has its own special characteristics." Examples are words and phrases that are biblical in origin or inspiration and "certain Christian expressions that can be transmitted [by transliteration] from one language to another, as has happened in the past, for example in the case of: *ecclesia, evangelium, baptisma, eucharistia.*" The Instruction *Comme le prévoit* (11–29) is an authoritative exposition of the criteria governing the translation of Latin texts that cause special difficulties in modern receptor languages. With vision and pastoral insight it crosses the borders of liturgical translation as it urges local Churches to be creative: "In many modern languages a biblical or liturgical language must be created by use. This will be achieved rather by infusing a Christian meaning into common words than by importing uncommon or technical terms."

To flesh out the above discussion I will go over some Latin words that frequently occur in the liturgy and how they can be translated. A more proximate purpose is to acquaint my readers with those Latin words that regularly appear in liturgical publications and in liturgical circles where it is often presumed that everyone knows what the words mean. From the sixth to the eleventh centuries the usage of several of them acquired specific and definitive meanings. Like other branches of specialization, the Latin liturgy possesses a corpus of traditional words and phrases that liturgists should be familiar with. Mary Ellebracht's extraordinary research produced an equally extraordinary work entitled *Remarks on the Vocabulary of the Ancient Orations in the Missale Romanum* (Utrecht, 1966).

1. *Altare*: Pagan writers used this noun in the plural (*altaria*), while Christians used it in the singular to denote the altar of sacrifice. In exceptional cases the plural is used, but the meaning is the single altar (classical Latin often used plural nouns for a single object). Regarding the case of the seven silver altars donated by Constantine to Pope Sylvester, the word *altaria* seems to refer to the seven side tables upon which the offerings of the faithful were placed: *Tua muneribus altaria cumulamus*.

2. *Apostolus*: from the Greek *apostolos* (sent). In the Roman liturgy this word always referred to one of the Twelve, not to an apostle in the broad sense of the word, i.e., one who preached the gospel. The Latin texts use the word *praedicator* for this second type.

3. *Baptisma* or *baptismus*: from the Greek *baptisma* (washing in water). These words exist side by side with the Latin *lavacrum* (washing), as in the phrase *lavacrum regenerationis* (washing of rebirth).

4. *Benedictio*: "blessing." While it means "we praise or bless God" in the hymn Gloria, the Latin prayers use this word to mean the sanctification effected by God. It is a synonym of *sanctificare*. The petition *benedictio tua descendat* refers to God's act of sanctification. *Benedictio* refers also to the effect produced by the sacraments, which is sanctification. In the Veronese Sacramentary *benedictio* is interchangeable with *consecratio* and is the title of the ordination of a bishop (*benedictio*

episcopi). The word is no longer used for ordination, but it is retained for the blessing of abbots and abbesses.

5. *Catechumenus*: from the Greek *katechumenos* (one who receives instruction or catechesis). The word later replaced the original Latin *audiens* or *auditor* (one who "listens" to pre-baptismal catechesis), whose instruction centered on the preaching of the word of God by a catechist.

6. *Celebrare*: Classical Latin used this verb to signify public festivities like the imperial games that were attended by a great number of people. In liturgical Latin this verb refers frequently to the yearly celebration of the feasts (*solemnia celebramus*). Since the Mass was the principal rite to celebrate the Christian feast and to start the Lenten observance, the verb came to be associated with it (*huius hostiae commemoratio celebratur*). Today we commonly use the expression "to celebrate Holy Mass" and call the authorization to celebrate Mass *Celebret*. The word *celebrare* does not lend support to the current use of the word "celebrant," referring to the presider of a liturgical rite. The original meaning embraced the entire Christian community gathered together in worship without specific reference to the role of the minister. Later, the verb *celebrare* was applied to other liturgical functions, such as baptism, marriage, funerals, and Liturgy of the Hours.

7. *Confessio*: This is a native Latin word that acquired three different meanings in liturgical usage. It is the profession of faith and is a technical term for "being a Christian" (*confessio nominis*). It is the act of martyrdom, a meaning that is derived from the legal term *confessio*, or admission of guilt in court (the martyr's admission of being a Christian meant martyrdom). Lastly, it refers to the confession of sins and is the equivalent of the Greek *exomologesis*, or confession of personal sins to a priest.

8. *Credere*: This verb normally takes the dative case in classical Latin and means "to trust someone." Christians introduced a new grammatical syntax by affixing the preposition *in* with the accusative case. *Credere in* designates the act of professing the Christian Faith (*Credo in unum Deum . . . in Iesum Christum . . . in Spiritum Sanctum . . . in Ecclesiam*). It is also used with the accusative to express acceptance of a revealed truth: we believe Mary to be the Mother of God (*eam Genetricem Dei credimus*). Lastly, when used as participle, it means true believer or the faithful (*credentes* is another word for *fideles*, or those who practice the Faith).

9. *Ecclesia*: from the Greek *Ekklesía* (a gathering of people). The Christian usage refers to an individual Christian community or to the Church as a whole. In the Latin texts *ecclesia* has the same meaning as the Hebrew *qahal Yahweh*, i.e., the people of God assembled especially for worship. Hence, in liturgical books *ecclesia* frequently refers to the congregation assembled for liturgical worship. I note, however, that the adjective *tota* or *universa* is attached to *ecclesia* to signify the universal Church, not in the cultic, but in an administrative sense. Ellebracht makes an interesting observation about *ecclesia*: it is never used in Latin liturgical prayers to mean church building.

10. *Eucharistia*: from the Greek *eucharistein* (to give thanks). Medieval Latin liturgical books did not use this word to signify the celebration of Mass. In its place they used such phrases as *sacrificium, sacrificii immolatio, sacramentum, mysterium* (particularly for the consecrated bread and wine), *hostia, hostiae commemoratio, oblatio* (hence, *oratio super oblata*), and *munera oblata*. These Latin words and phrases underline the sacrificial character of the Mass. The word *Eucharistia* to mean Mass was introduced in modern times, perhaps to stress that it is the Lord's Supper. The phrase *Prex Eucharistica* (Eucharistic Prayer) normally signifies the new Eucharistic Prayers that were introduced in the Roman Missal after the council. The technical name of the first Eucharistic Prayer is *Canon Missae, Canon actionis,* or *Actio sacrificii*.

11. *Familia*: This word evokes the legal system of Roman society, e.g,, the assembly of all the members of the household (wife, children, and slaves) under the leadership of the *paterfamilias*. Used in the liturgy, it has practically the same meaning as *Ecclesia* or the Church gathered for liturgical worship. However, unlike *Ecclesia*, it connotes a certain intimacy among the members of the assembly, which is described as God's own family (*respice familiam tuam, tuere familiam tuam*). Although there is a kind of hierarchical ranking among the members (as in the Roman *familia*) because of roles and ministerial functions, all belong to the household of God.

12. *Fides*: "Faith." This word is used in Latin prayers in a variety of ways. It means gift of God (*auge fidem catechumenis nostris*), personal decision of a Christian (before baptism or martyrdom), an interior act that is outwardly expressed by authentic Christian life (*ut sacramentum vivendo teneant, quod fide perceperunt*), and the body of revealed Christian truths (often with the adjective *vera*).

13. *Hostia*: In the sense of "victim" this word was commonly used by Latin authors in connection with sacrifice. In the Vulgate it translates the Greek *thysia*. The Latin liturgy uses it frequently, especially in the prayers over the gifts. The gifts of bread and wine offered by the faithful are called *hostiae*, or offerings, with a sacrificial nuance. There are several instances when this word is used with sacrificial overtones: *hostias deferimus, hostia immolatur, hostias offerimus*. It is possible to explain this in the light of their subsequently becoming sacraments of Christ's sacrifice. The Latin medieval texts refrained from calling the consecrated bread *hostia*. Other words are used for it in the prayers after communion, mostly in reference to spiritual food and nourishment, not in the context of sacrifice. The practice of calling the bread for Mass *hostia* was popularized by hymns like *O salutaris hostia*.

14. *Mysterium*: This many-sided word is a transliteration of the Greek *mysterion*, which was the technical name of the rite for initiating candidates to a religious sect. It acquired the New Testament meaning of "God's plan of salvation that had been hidden and is now revealed in Christ." From this developed the meaning of mystery as a revealed truth of faith that surpasses human understanding. In liturgical usage *mysterium* generally refers to the Eucharistic celebration. The word can mean either the outward liturgical rite or the grace of the sacrament. There are instances when the word *mysteria* refers specifically to the sacred species (*sumpsimus divina mysteria*). *Mysteria paschalia* (paschal mysteries) means the sacrifice of Christ made present in the Eucharistic celebration, especially during the feast of Easter. The diaconal proclamation *"Mysterium fidei"* was mistakenly inserted in the words of Christ over the cup. It was probably to call the assembly's attention to the act of consecration that was being performed by the priest in silence. Sometimes *mysterium* is applied to the sacraments of baptism and marriage and is used synonymously with *sacramentum*.

15. *Offerre*: This is one of the earliest verbs to describe the Eucharistic celebration. Tertullian was one of the first to use it with this meaning. There are several instances when this verb refers to the material gifts people bring to Mass. For this reason, this part of the Mass came to be known as "Offertory Rite." The postconciliar Order of Mass reverted to an earlier name, "Preparation of the Altar and the Gifts," although it continues to call the prayer over the gifts *Oratio super oblate*. *Oblata* is the past participle of *offerre* and stands for the gifts of the faithful, like the word *hostia*.

16. *Paenitentia*: This word translates the Greek *metanoia*, meaning conversion, total change of heart and attitudes. It was used for the first conversion that took place at baptism and for the subsequent acts of repentance after baptism. It carries primarily the meaning of inner attitude of conversion or radical change of heart. Oftentimes it is equated with the performance of the penitential act imposed by the confessor. *Paenitentia* and its verb form *paenitere* are used to express conversion from grave sins some of which merited excommunication. The postconciliar sacramental rite has preserved the original title of the sacrament (*Ordo Paenitentiae*).

17. *Plebs*: This was one of the first words that translated the Bible's "people of God." As a technical term drawn from the profane Latin *plebs*, meaning the Roman society, this word makes no distinction between clergy and laity. Used always in the singular, it stresses the unity of all the members of the Christian community. In the Latin prayers it often connotes the assembly gathered for worship.

18. *Populus*: This original Latin word designated the Roman people (*Senatus populusque Romanus*). It became the Christian technical word for the people of God assembled in worship, although sometimes it was used also for the Jewish people and the catechumens. *Populus* and *plebs* are almost identical in meaning and usage, except that *plebs* generally embraces both clergy and laity. At any rate, one should be careful not to confine these two words to the laity. Used in prayer, they normally signify all the Christian people regardless of their status in the Church.

19. *Redemptio*: Literally "the act of buying back," it translates the Greek *apolytrosis* and means liberation from sin and union with God. In the Latin prayers *redemptio* does not refer to the historical act of Christ on the cross by which he bought back humanity at the price of his blood. Rather, it means the redeeming effect that the liturgical rite produces on each member of the assembly. The Eucharist is thus *pignus redemptionis* and *munus redemptionis*.

20. *Sacramentum*: This word was borrowed by early Christian writers from the profane Latin word that described the rite of allegiance made by soldiers to the emperor (*sacramenti testatio*). For Christians it was the same as their sacred rites. St. Jerome sometimes translated the Greek *mysterion* as *sacramentum*. As a synonym of *mysterium*, it refers primarily to the Eucharist (*paschale sacramentum*), which is the ritual

actualization of Christ's paschal sacrifice. It is frequently used in the prayers after communion and for the consecrated species (*perceptio sacramenti*). It is also applied to the other liturgical rites and to the liturgy as a whole. It is preferred to its counterpart *mysterium*, when it is a question of the efficacy of the sacramental rites.

21. *Sacrificium*: This word was used in a broad sense by pagan and Christian writers. In the liturgy, in accord with St. Cyprian's expression *celebrare sacrificia divina*, it acquired different meanings. First, the Mass as a whole was called *sacrificium* insofar as it is the anamnesis of the sacrifice of the cross. Second, the gifts offered by the faithful for the Eucharistic celebration were likewise called *sacrificium*, as we see in the prayers over the gifts (*accipe sacrificium a devotis tuis famulis*). Used in this particular occasion, it has the same meaning as *hostia*. Third, *sacrificium* pertains to the discipline of fasting that people observed for the benefit of the poor (what was saved through fasting was given as alms). *Sacrificium* stands for the gifts of the faithful, which they offer to the Church as their personal sacrifice and their union with the sacrifice of Christ.

Several of the above words can be rendered perfectly by their equivalents in the receptor language. However, some simply defy translation. Such, for example, are *mysterium* and *sacramentum*, which are often best transliterated and explained through catechesis. But I would encourage translators to give dynamic equivalence a chance to prove its worth as a method of translation. While formal correspondence can give the impression of propinquity to the source language, in reality it can obscure the message and raise more questions than it can answer. Servility is not the same as fidelity. For example, the frequent use of superlatives, a linguistic trait that Latin acquired in the Middle Ages, can have the opposite effect in some receptor languages. The English "exceedingly" for the Latin *nimis* in the medieval *Confiteor* is a clear case of hyperbole. In the second century before the Christian era Terentius Afer had already warned about excess: *ne quid nimis*, which is the equivalent of the classic *sobrietas romana*. Too many superlatives can nauseate. In the English language understatement is sometimes a more effective means of emphasis.

In conformity with *Liturgiam authenticam* and *Ratio translationis* issued by the Congregation for Divine Worship, translators of the *Ordo Missae* are inclined to render *et cum spiritu tuo* and *pro multis* literally, using formal correspondence rather than dynamic equivalence. Earlier the Congregation issued a statement to the effect that any problem the assembly might experience regarding a literal translation could be resolved by the explanation of the text in question. One can only pray that we all have the tools to give the correct explanation. The greeting "The Lord be (is) with you" is biblical and is found in both Old and New Testaments. The answer in both Greek and Latin liturgies mentions the spirit (*pneuma* or *spiritus*). In Hellenistic philosophy humans have three ascending levels of existence: the body (*soma*), the soul (*psyché*), and the spirit (*pneuma*). *Pneuma* represents the highest and noblest level of the human being. Thus the meaning of *et cum spiritu tuo* is a sophisticated and courteous manner of returning the greeting by referring to what is noblest in the greeter. The origin and liturgical usage do not consent to the explanation of spirit as sacerdotal or priestly spirit. It is true that the original meaning of spirit is not carried by the English "And also with you." But will the translation "and with your spirit" be understood today as referring to what is noblest in the priest? The problem of literal translation will be felt in some vernacular languages, like Tagalog, where the word *espiritu* (without the modifier "holy") can mean evil spirit.

A confounding issue is the literal translation of the consecratory words *pro multis* (Matt 26:28 has *perì pollōn*, while Mark 14:24 has *hyper pollōn*; Luke 22:20 and 1 Cor 11:25 do not insert the phrase). The third-century Eucharistic Prayer in *Apostolic Tradition* omits it. According to Daniel Harrington (*The New Jerome Biblical Commentary*, 626), the phrase *hyper pollōn* in Mark "means for all, not just for a few." He cites as the basis for Mark and Matthew the words of Second Isaiah 53:12: the Servant by his suffering "bore the sin of many." "Many" is a collective, not restrictive, word; it means "all." Several current versions render *pro multis* in the collective sense of "for all" in conformity with the doctrine of the universality of Christ's work of redemption. He died for all of humankind, from the time of the first parents to the time of the parousia. He did not die just for many but for all. I am certain that those who claim that the literal translation is more faithful to the original Latin do not deny the universality of salvation, but the literal translation can engender elitist exclusivity. Catechesis is supposed to explain away the problem by saying that "many" is the same as "all." As someone rightly exclaimed in frustration, "If that's what it means, why not say it?"

Another case of an infelicitous literal translation of a biblical passage is "under my roof" for the Latin *sub tectum meum*. The Latin text lifted this phrase from the Centurion's declaration (Matt 8:8) but changed *servus* to *anima*. Even liturgical Latin does not reproduce *in toto* the biblical text. It is well known that in order to conform to the rhetorical properties of Latin, the composers of Latin orations rarely quoted the Scriptures word for word. It would be a Herculean task to put the biblical quotation in Latin *cursus*. The literary quality of Latin was a major consideration for the great popes who authored the majority of the liturgical prayers we use today. The point is, why translate the phrase *sub tectum meum* literally when the phrase "to receive Jesus under one's roof" is a far-fetched literary figure for Holy Communion?

It is understood that translators read Latin. The perennial value and importance of the Latin language was vindicated by Pope Paul VI in an address to Latinists in 1968. He stated that he himself "had taken every step to have all the modern languages introduced into the liturgy." However, "without the knowledge of Latin something is altogether missing from a higher, fully rounded education—and in particular with regard to theology and liturgy." I believe that the scarcity of those who read Latin is sufficient reason to reaffirm the most innovative and courageous statement of *Comme le prévoit*: "Texts translated from another language are clearly not sufficient for the celebration of a fully renewed liturgy. The creation of new texts will be necessary." The Instruction notes, however, that "translation of texts transmitted through the tradition of the Church is the best school and discipline for the creation of new texts" (43). The question is whether local Churches are privileged to have translators who are Latin experts and liturgists at the same time.

A Note on Liturgiam authenticam

Wilton Gregory wrote in my Festschrift that I had been "a staunch defender and promoter" of *Comme le prévoit* and that when its successor was published I would "review whatever is established as a new set of principles and . . . examine scrupulously how they can advance the work of allowing the Church's worship to inspire and speak to the heart of people in a contemporary world."

The Fifth Instruction, *Liturgiam authenticam*, published by the Congregation for Divine Worship and the Discipline of the Sacraments on March 28, 2001, is one of those rare Vatican documents that entirely ignore their predecessors. It is de rigueur for Vatican documents to do homage to preceding ones. Such a practice provides a sense of organic unity in the Acts of the Holy See. However, nowhere does the Fifth

Instruction mention, much less give credit, to the Instruction *Comme le prévoit*, which the Consilium issued in 1969 as a guide to the translation of liturgical texts. When the new Instruction was being planned, a minor official of the Congregation "indiscreetly," that is, unofficially, informed me that the Holy See had actually never considered the 1969 Instruction an official document. That explains why it did not merit being a player in the new Instruction. But how do we explain away the embarrassment of having translations made into major languages for over thirty years on the basis of an unofficial document? Why did it take the Holy See such a lengthy span of time to address an issue of such magnitude as liturgical translation?

In fairness we take cognizance of what the Fifth Instruction states: "Ever since the promulgation of the Constitution on the Sacred Liturgy, the work of the translation of the liturgical texts into vernacular languages, as promoted by the Apostolic See, has involved the publication of norms and the communication to the Bishops of advice on the matter" (6). The 1969 Instruction was, of course, the most significant of those norms. What follows appears like a subtle censure of preceding norms: "Nevertheless, it has been noted that translations of liturgical texts in various localities stand in need of improvement through correction or through a new draft." The Instruction reveals that there are "omissions or errors, which affect certain existing vernacular translations." It baffles me to think that the Holy See approved such defective translations, allowing them for a good number of years as an integral part of the local Church's *lex credendi, lex orandi.*

The Holy See has finally issued a translation document whose ownership it officially claims. Only time will tell what the future holds in store for this document. Even if translators adopt its principles and criteria, how long will they stick to it, especially when the product of their work is not consistent with the aim of translation, which is to transmit the original message in the living culture and language of the people? Will it command the kind of respect, not to say eager welcome, its predecessor had? Or will it suffer ultimately the fate of other reactionary documents, such as *Veterum sapientia* (on the study of Latin in seminaries), which became obsolete soon after it hit the front pages of Catholic dailies and was read by those who were meant to implement it?

In a sense the Fifth Instruction can be considered a sequel to the Fourth Instruction "The Roman Liturgy and Inculturation," which dealt with the question of inculturation. Translation is in reality a form, perhaps the highest form, of inculturation. What is liturgical inculturation but the dynamic translation of the cultural components of the Roman Rite into the equivalent cultural components of the receptor local Church? Strictly speaking, inculturation should not be identified with the creation of new liturgical rites and texts. Although the Fifth Instruction is rather shaky on several issues, as we shall have occasion to see later, it hits a bull's-eye when it affirms that "the work of inculturation, of which the translation into the vernacular languages is a part, is not therefore to be considered an avenue for the creation of new varieties of families of rites" (5). The basic question underlying the Fifth Instruction is: what type of translation is it talking about?

Not every type of translation falls under the category of inculturation. It appears to me that the Fifth Instruction leans heavily on formal correspondence as it subtly warns against the dangers of dynamic equivalence. Formal correspondence, which consists basically of word-for-word translation, cannot advance the cause of liturgical inculturation. In its obsession for lexical accuracy and verbal fidelity to the original text, it ignores the culture of the recipient or the people for whom translation is made. Because formal correspondence does not bother about the cultural situation of the recipient, it cannot be considered a form of inculturation. The Instruction supports inculturation at the same time as it promotes formal correspondence. It sees danger in dynamic equivalence that it fears could eventually distance the translated text from the original to the point that it would no longer be recognizable. It seems to me that what the Fifth Instruction would want to happen is that if the translated text is rendered back to the original language, which is Latin, every Latin word can be retrieved and accounted for.

Liturgiam authenticam rightly affirms that "the Roman Rite is itself a precious example and an instrument of true inculturation. For the Roman Rite is marked by a signal capacity for assimilating into itself spoken and sung texts, gestures and rites derived from the customs and the genius of diverse nations and particular Churches both Eastern and Western into a harmonious unity that transcends the boundaries of any single nation" (5). But there remains in my mind the nagging question regarding the Instruction's understanding of inculturation and the type of translation that is at work in inculturation. In short, what does it mean by liturgical inculturation? The answer can be gathered from various statements it makes. In number 20 it states that "the translation of the liturgical texts of the Roman liturgy is not so much a work of creative innovation as it is of rendering the original texts faithfully and accurately into the vernacular language." I agree with the statement, but I have difficulty with how the Instruction envisages its implementation. Although it permits the reordering of words for the sake of flow and rhythm, it lays down the rule that "the original text, insofar as possible, must be translated integrally and in the most exact manner, without omissions or additions in terms of their content, and without paraphrases or glosses. Any adaptation to the characteristics or the nature of various vernacular languages is to be sober and discreet." We are bombarded by such words and phrases as "faithfully," "accurately," "integrally," "in the most exact manner," "without omissions or additions," and "without paraphrases or glosses." In short, what the Instruction requires is formal correspondence.

The Instruction wants translators to keep in mind that "the adaptations of the texts" should not be an excuse for "supplementing or changing the theological content" of the Latin typical edition (22). Obviously, when translators supplement or change the theological content, they no longer translate: they create. But through dynamic equivalence the doctrinal content can be enriched by situating it in the context of the local assembly. *Comme le prévoit* observed that the Latin orations are succinct and abstract. "In translation they may need to be rendered somewhat more freely while conserving the original ideas. This can be done by moderately amplifying them, or, if necessary, paraphrasing expressions in order to concretize them for the celebration and the needs of today" (34). If we follow the thinking of *Liturgiam authenticam* there would be no opportunity for the liturgy of local Churches to grow in doctrine and spirituality. The orations the popes wrote for their people in the fifth and sixth centuries are what we must pray today without supplement or change. This is all very stifling. To ensure that no translation would trespass the bounds of formal correspondence the Instruction prohibits translations from other translations: "New translations must be made directly from the original texts, namely the Latin, as regards the texts of ecclesiastical composition" (24). Realistically, I can foresee that several local Churches will have no translated liturgical texts for lack of medieval Latinists.

I find even more disenchanting the suggestion to retain "a certain manner of speech which has come to be considered somewhat obsolete in daily usage" (27). This suggestion is prefaced by a caution to avoid "excessively unusual or awkward" expressions that hinder comprehension. On the other hand, the Instruction directs that the work of translation "should be free of an overly servile adherence to prevailing modes of expression." Besides, the Instruction continues, words or expressions, "which differ somewhat from usual and everyday speech" become truly memorable and capable of expressing heavenly realities. The obsolete expresses better the heavenly realities than do contemporary modes of expression! Why recommend the use of the unusual and somewhat obsolete words? The answer comes as a bombshell: the use of obsolete words will "free the liturgy from the necessity of frequent revisions when modes of expression may have passed out of popular usage." The truth is that the liturgy is not a monolith that cultural and linguistic changes can affect. That was the thinking after the Council of Trent, which Vatican II set out to correct. The liturgy is not a museum piece; it is as alive as the Church that celebrates it. We all remember what happened to the Latin liturgy when Europeans no longer knew Latin and spoke only modern languages. I detect a theological concern. It is obvious that the less we touch the liturgy, the more secure will its deposit of faith be.

The norm of using the obsolete is developed in numbers 47 and 50, which introduce the public to the new term "sacral vernacular." What does it mean? It is the language of worship that "differs somewhat from ordinary speech"; it is "characterized by a vocabulary, syntax and grammar that are proper to divine worship." Why say "sacral" when there is a more suitable word, namely, "liturgical"? I suspect that the use of the word "sacral" belies the agenda to save the liturgy from the false perception that it has become secular. Or perhaps it is an outright reaction to the existing English translation of the Roman liturgy that minimized or dropped the use of "sacred" before such words as ministers, vessels, furnishings, and vesture, and substituted cup for chalice, plate for paten, and so on. Number 50 instructs the translator to maintain the distinction of sacred persons and things "from similar persons and things pertaining to everyday life and usage." The dichotomy between the sacred and profane is nowhere as firmly established as here.

But what if the assembly understands little or nothing of what is proclaimed in liturgical prayer because of its obsolete expressions? The Instruction has a simple answer: "It is the task of the homily and of catechesis to set forth the meaning of the liturgical texts" (29). Vatican II's program of active participation means that the assembly, including children, understands the liturgical texts while they are being proclaimed. As a rule of thumb, a good test for the suitability of a liturgical text is that it needs little or no explanation. The homily and catechesis should deepen the assembly's comprehension, but not set forth the meaning of the translated text that is obscure. At any rate, what assurance do we have that the homilist and catechist can correctly interpret the true sense of the liturgical text?

Liturgiam authenticam set out on a momentous journey, completely ignoring its 1969 predecessor. It evidently lacks the pastoral insight of a document that is suffused with the enthusiasm and vitality of the council. It does not build on the past. It ignores the wisdom and the positive contributions of its predecessor to the shaping of contemporary ritual language. It is a reactionary document that practically confines its concern to the avoidance of errors. It lacks a clear, broad, and far-sighted vision of what liturgical worship should be in the third millennium.

MUSICAL LITURGY

The Constitution on Liturgy declares: "The musical tradition of the universal Church is a treasure of inestimable value, greater even than that of any other art. The main reason for this preeminence is that, as sacred song closely bound to the text, it forms a necessary or integral part of the solemn liturgy" (112).

One of the great achievements of the liturgical movement and the conciliar reform is making the assembly sing the liturgy. After the Council of Trent there were remarkable efforts to involve the assembly through songs, even if most of the time these had nothing to do with the Order of Mass. There was singing during Mass, but the liturgy of the Mass was not sung. Strictly speaking, the liturgical notion of music is that music that is joined to the liturgical text. Liturgical music means singing the assigned text at the appointed time: an antiphon or song, a formulary, a greeting and a response. One of the aims of liturgical music is to develop a musical liturgy wherein the liturgical action is carried out in song, not merely accompanied by music. In this sense purely instrumental music, like a sonata for organ, would not pass today for liturgical music, although it may be used in liturgical celebrations to add solemnity or sometimes to fill a vacant "acoustic space." *Musicam sacram* assented to it: "Musical instruments either accompanying the singing or played alone can add a great deal to liturgical celebrations" (62).

Over the centuries the types of music for the liturgy were given different names: ecclesiastical or church music, religious music, sacred music, and liturgical music. While each of these names has a particular history and usage, it is not possible at this point in time to give a hard-and-fast definition of each. The truth is that today there is still fluidity in the use of these terms. Ecclesiastical or church music, a name which comes from ancient times, distinguished itself from the music used at secular gatherings. Today it denotes virtually any type of music used at congregational worship, whether liturgical or devotional. Thus Gregorian chant, the Lutheran hymns for worship (like "A Mighty Fortress Is Our God"), and Catholic novena songs (like "Immaculate Mother") all fall under the general category of church music. Religious music, on the other hand, refers to any type of music whose text is considered to have a religious theme, even if its rhythm is not traditionally used in church services, for example, jazz and rock. Religious music has a rather wide range of denotation: from the rock music "Jesus Christ Superstar" and African-American spirituals like "Were You There" to baroque music like J. S. Bach's *St. Matthew Passion*.

Sacred music is the official term used by Roman Church documents for the type of music composed for the celebration of the liturgy. The Instruction of 1958 is called *De Musica Sacra*. Chapter 6 of Vatican II's Constitution on Liturgy carries the title "Sacred Music." In line with this, the 1967 Instruction on music is entitled *Musicam Sacram*. This particular Instruction explains that "music is 'sacred' insofar as it is composed for the celebration of divine worship and possesses integrity of form" (4). The definition is rather broad. It embraces "Gregorian chant, the several styles of polyphony, both ancient and modern, sacred music for organ and for other permitted instruments, and the sacred, i.e., liturgical or religious, music of the people." Thus, before the council the concept of sacred music was not necessarily tied to the liturgical text. It could be purely instrumental, provided it was considered suited for worship.

Liturgical music is a more recent term and has enlisted a growing number of liturgists who prefer it to other words. In his book *Voices and Instruments in Christian Worship* Joseph Gelineau makes a useful and necessary distinction between music in the liturgy and music of the liturgy. This distinction clarifies the nature and role that music plays in liturgical worship. It is not any kind of music that is sung during a liturgical celebration, regardless of whether it corresponds to the meaning of the rite that it accompanies. One can think of such examples, which are not unheard of even today, as a novena song to Our Lady at the communion rite or an offertory song at the entrance procession. Liturgical music is the music whose lyric or text comes directly from the liturgical *ordo* or has been approved for liturgical use.

In his article "Liturgical Music" (*The New Dictionary of Sacramental Worship*) Edward Foley defines liturgical music as "that music which weds itself to the liturgical action, serves to reveal the full significance of the rite and, in turn, derives its full meaning from the liturgy." Foley's definition gives the three components of liturgical music. First, it is woven into the liturgical rite and becomes an element of the celebration. The singing of the *Gloria* or the *Sanctus* at the prescribed time is the performance of a liturgical rite. The offertory song while the gifts are brought to the presider is not merely for the sake of musical accompaniment. When performed, it becomes an element of the offertory rite; it becomes a liturgical action. Second, liturgical music has a symbolic nature and role: it reveals the meaning of the liturgical action. This means that its lyric corresponds to the rite that is being performed and explains its meaning. The text is basic to the notion of liturgical music. And third, liturgical music derives its full meaning from the liturgy. The purpose of liturgical music cannot be isolated from the purpose of the liturgy itself: it is composed and performed for the service of the liturgy. Liturgical music has a ministerial role outside of which it has no meaning.

It is not my intention to record the development of liturgical music. Gelineau's work extensively does that. I wish to call attention to the recent fact that the council's open-minded attitude toward the musical traditions of other people (art. 119) has prompted a new practice in the Roman liturgy of substituting the psalms with original compositions. The tradition of Rome is to accompany the entrance procession, the offertory, and the communion rite with the chanting of psalms.

Because of the Church's strong synagogue tradition, which is probably the basis of St. Paul's admonition "to sing psalms, hymns, and spiritual canticles to God" (Col 3:16), we may suppose that from the start psalms already formed part of Christian worship. Since the "great Hallel" (Psalms 112–117) was an element of the Passover meal, we can assume that Christians would have revived this Jewish tradition during the Easter season. The practice of the early Christians to chant psalms is recorded in the apocryphal *Acts of Paul*, which was written toward the year 190: "Each shared in the bread, and they feasted . . . to the sound of David's psalms and hymns" (7). Tertullian, in his work *On the Soul*, informs us that in liturgical gathering "the scriptures are read and psalms are sung, allocutions are delivered, and prayers are offered" (9). The liturgy he speaks about was held *in ecclesia inter domi-nica sollemnia*, that is, Sunday Eucharist. Its *ordo* consisted of scriptural reading, followed by the chanting of psalms, the homily, and prayers, or the equivalent of what is known today as the liturgy of the word. The position of the psalms between the readings and the homily can be taken as witness to the early tradition of responsorial psalm at Mass.

Nonbiblical psalms, known to scholars as *psalmi idiotici*, began to appear at this time. These were compositions by Christians in the style of the psalms, and thus they could be sung like psalms. According to Gelineau, the earliest are the *Odes of Solomon* written in the second century. Part of Ode 27 reads: "I extended my hands and hallowed my Lord, for the extension of my hands is his sign. And my extension is the upright cross. Hallelujah." Nonbiblical psalms answered the Christian need to sing "psalms" that are directly and explicitly Christian. Although we read in Luke 24:44 that everything written in the psalms about Christ had to be fulfilled, it requires some mental, even laborious, process to recognize Christ in them. The later tradition of concluding the psalms with the Trinitarian doxology supports the Christian interpretation of the Jewish psalms. The singing of nonbiblical psalms in liturgical assembly was in all probability a normal practice. The more gifted members must have grabbed it as an opportunity to sing about their faith and experience of Christ, comparable to the modern personal witnessing of faith in charismatic gatherings. In *Apologeticum* Tertullian mentions the practice of singing privately composed psalms: "After the ritual hand-washing and the bringing in of the lights, each one is invited to stand and sing to God as one is able: either something from the Holy Scriptures or of one's own making" (39). Tertullian was in character when with typical irony he answered the pagan accusation that Christians got drunk in their assemblies: "Hereby we are able to prove how much one has drunk!" It was indeed an era of spontaneity and improvisation, and we may surmise that the manner of singing these songs depended to a large extent on the talent of the individual. It is important to remember that the liturgy then was celebrated in a domestic setting where one would expect a good measure of spontaneity.

I would consider Marty Haugen's composition "We Remember" a modern example of nonbiblical composition that admirably sums up in musical prose what liturgical worship is all about: "We remember how you loved us to your death, and still we celebrate, for you are with us here; and we believe that we will see you when you come in your glory, Lord. We remember, we celebrate, we believe." The first time we met many years ago I was flabbergasted when Haugen knelt beside me "to learn at the feet of the master." In reality, it was I who learned from his humility, mastery of music, and zeal for the liturgy.

Hymns were also part of the early Church's worship. In the words of Joseph Gelineau, they have always been "on the threshold of liturgy." Unlike psalms, hymns are metrical poems divided into stanzas of at least two lines. Each stanza has the same meter, number of syllables, scheme of word accent, and number of verse lines. This trait allows for the singing of each stanza in the same way as the first. When such a trait is not observed by the composer, as in the case of *Gloria* and *Te Deum*, singing suffers because of the adjustments that need to be made on notation. The singing of the psalms, on the other hand, which are not metered like the hymns, requires modification of the music, however slightly, in order to accommodate the varying meter, number of syllables, and word accents.

Some examples of early hymns are worth mentioning. The letter of Pliny the Younger to Emperor Trajan in the year 112 reports that the assembled Christians sang hymns alternately among themselves, which suggests that the assembly was divided into two groups. Pliny writes: "They were accustomed to meet on a fixed day before dawn and sing alternately among themselves a hymn to Christ as to a god." A famous hymn to Christ, in Greek, dating from the early third century was composed by Clement of Alexandria, whom authors suspect to have been influenced by second-century Gnostic hymns. In translation that appears in Foley's work *From Age to Age* it reads: "King of saints, almighty Word of the Father, highest Lord, Wisdom's head and chief, assuagement of all grief; Lord of all time and space: Jesus, Savior of our race." The only example of a musically annotated hymn dating from the third century was discovered in a papyrus from Oxyrhyncos in Egypt. Musicologists have been able to transcribe its melody. Composed in Greek, the fragment in translation reads: "Neither the stars, sources of light, nor the springs whence flow the raging torrents are silent! While we sing the praises of Father, Son, and Holy Spirit, let all the powers cry out: Amen, Amen! Power and glory to the sole giver of all good things: Amen, Amen!"

St. Ambrose of Milan is regarded as the father of Western hymnody, and it is possible that his hymns were sung to well-known secular tunes of the time, as Martin Luther's hymns centuries later. Since hymns were not sung in the Roman Mass, they remained in the periphery of the liturgical action. The variable songs for the entrance, offertory, and communion rites were always drawn from psalms, though the antiphons that were introduced later were sometimes non-biblical compositions. After the Council of Trent there were efforts to encourage the faithful to sing at Mass. In 1605 the *Cantuale of Mainz* was produced so that the congregation could sing popular hymns at the time of the gradual or responsorial psalm, after the narration of the institution, in place of *Agnus Dei*, and at communion. At a time when the liturgy of the Roman Mass had already acquired its definitive texts and chants, such an attempt, though pastorally praiseworthy, did not make the people sing the liturgy; all it did was to make them sing during the liturgy. Perhaps influenced by Lutheran tradition, Roman Catholics unquestioningly substitute the psalms for the entrance, offertory, and communion songs for the sake of active participation.

The English language is blessed with a sizeable collection of Christian hymns, many of which enrich today's liturgical worship. Two of my favorite hymns are nineteenth-century compositions marked by profound theological insight and uplifting melody. They are: "The Church's One Foundation," composed by Samuel Stone (+1866) and set to music by Samuel Sebastian Wesley (+1864), and "For All the Saints," by William Howe (1897) and Vaughn Williams.

Liturgical hymns did not always and everywhere receive the sympathy of Church authorities. The Roman divine office, in fact, did not have hymns. It was St. Benedict who introduced Ambrosian hymns in the monastic Liturgy of the Hours, whence they passed over to the Roman office. Hymns were popular because the assembly found their melody simple and engaging. No official prohibition could put a stop to the practice of singing hymns during public worship. In 563 the first Council of Braga (canon 12) decreed that except for the psalms or other biblical passages from the Old and New Testaments, no poetic compositions, that is, hymns, may be sung in liturgical gatherings. If I read the motive correctly, the prohibition was meant to hold at bay heretical doctrines that could easily creep into such poetic compositions. But harsh measures did not stifle the production of liturgical hymns. According to the stunning estimate of Adolf Adam (*Foundations in Liturgy*), "about 35,000 hymns in all were composed" after the fourth century.

Although I enjoy singing hymns and find most of them spiritually uplifting, I have to admit that the flowering of hymnody was symptomatic of the gradual decline of active participation. When hymns were first introduced in the Roman Mass, singing hymns meant singing during Mass, rather than singing the Mass. Earlier, the rise of professional singers confined the role of the assembly to the recitative parts of the liturgy. But even the recitative parts were abandoned in later centuries in favor of the more ornate and talent-demanding genre called melismatic music. Thus the assembly had to content itself with hymns, which were not integral elements of the Roman Mass. Today, however, hymns are no longer extraneous to the Roman Mass. This is surely a welcome development, even if it requires a great effort on the part of local churches to be creative and at the same time attentive to the requirements of the liturgy and the musical tradition and lyrical genius of the people. Apropos the local churches with native musical tradition distinct from the Western, Gelineau writes: "It is particularly desirable that in mission countries native compositions should be encouraged rather than the imported tunes of European hymns, for they can suit the musical idiom of the country and the poetry which belongs to the language concerned."

In Jewish and other ancient cultures proclamation and public speaking, because of their solemn character, were not merely read or spoken. They were cantillated. This was observed in the synagogues from which Christians inherited it. It consisted of reciting a text with simple musical tones or a set of melodic formula like the music for chanting the psalms in the divine office. For the early Christians, whose liturgy centered on the word of God and prayer formularies, cantillation was the best available form of music, because it transmitted more effectively the message of the text. As a musical genre it reinforced the words and enhanced their meaning. The piling up of musical notes on the words of the lyric tends to obscure the meaning of text as it calls attention to the melody. In the early centuries the Church underlined the primacy of the text over music, which it subjected to serving the purpose of the *ritus et preces* of Christian worship.

Hymns express poetically deep theological thoughts and spiritual insights. If the melody has outstanding musical quality the mind plays the hymn for extended periods of time. Thus good hymns can be our good companions in the course of the day and the night. But liturgical hymns also play a significant part in evangelization. When the missionaries first evangelized the Congo, they immediately saw to it that the children memorized and sang the hymns of the Mass. As the children walked back to their homes they sang these hymns, arousing the interest of their elders. It is said that a contributing factor to the success of Arius in spreading his heretical doctrine about Christ was the popularity of the hymns he composed about the Logos. Hymns, as much as the orations or prayer texts, are a powerful vehicle of doctrine. Should it come as a surprise that the General Instruction on the Roman Missal (48; cf. 87) requires that the Conference of Bishops approve songs that it judges to be suited to the sacred action, the day, or the season? The Instruction (393) goes a step further when it includes for the approval of the Conference the melodies, especially for the texts of the Ordinary of Mass, for the congregation's responses and acclamations, and for special rites that occur in the course of the liturgical year.

Recovering the "recitative" genre of the past in order to foster a better understanding of the lyric does not seem to be the solution to the problem of shaping a musical liturgy in which the words are prayed and communicated in songs. Music has an ancillary role in the performance of the liturgical rite. Nevertheless, music is an integral part of solemn liturgy, as the Constitution on Liturgy affirmed. The classical liturgical movement successfully called our attention to the fact that texts should be first in our ranking the components of liturgy. I believe that the time has come to treat music in the liturgy not only as a servant but "as worship," as Jan Michael Joncas rightly maintains (*The New Westminster Dictionary of Liturgy and Worship*). Some churchgoers complain that music distracts them during the liturgy. But by and large musical culture has evolved, and it is not rare to find people who can concentrate on the lyric of an aria in an opera, cantata, or oratorio amid their prolix musical notes.

Today what reason have we to declare that polyphony is not suited for the liturgy because it sidetracks our attention from the mystery? Why should an assembly not sing in voices? Why should we be content with mediocre congregational singing and equally mediocre, if not absolutely trite, musical compositions because people sing them with greater ease? I do not find valid reason why a trained choir should not occasionally render greater solemnity to the liturgy by singing certain parts of the Mass, such as the entrance, offertory, and communion songs. I am not convinced that liturgy should always and everywhere be performed through the congregational singing of all the parts of the Mass normally assigned to the assembly. I regard musical liturgy as the performance of the rite through the singing of the parts appointed to be sung. Who actually sings each part is very much a matter of musical discernment. The quality of musical performance is highly prized in our cultural world. Surely there are occasions when the assembly should not be deprived of an uplifting experience of worship through exceptional musical performance. I believe in progressive solemnity, which distinguishes times and seasons and promises something we can look forward to. Surely we need to enhance the word and foster active participation through congregational singing, but we should not forget that music is a ritual language that progresses according to the solemnity of the occasion.

LITURGICAL VESSELS AND VESTMENTS

The Mass as celebration of the Lord's Supper requires vessels to hold the bread, wine, and water. This to me is the simple explanation for why we use table vessels. To this explanation I should add that by origin and tradition the Mass is a domestic liturgy in the form of community meal. From the beginning the Church has used the dining table and vessels, rather than the altar and temple vessels for sacrifice, for the celebration of Mass. It was due largely to the theology of the Mass as the memorial of Christ's sacrifice on the cross that the Church adopted the sacrificial language of the Old Testament, such as altar, temple, sanctuary, and priest. Fortunately ritual language in this case did not affect the ritual symbols and outward components of the Mass. Jewish or pagan altars, which were normally square structures of stone or marble upon which victims were slain or burned, never had a foot in the door of a Christian church. The bread began to be called host, but it remained bread that was broken and shared at table. The plate and cup were renamed *paten* and *chalice* in deference to the sacrificial theology of the Mass, but they contained the sacraments of Christ's body and blood rather than the realities themselves.

The types of vessels the Church has used since the early centuries confirm the meal aspect of the Mass. In the first century the Eucharistic bread was kept in baskets, since these were the normal bread containers used at home. Mattthew 14:20 and John 6:13, which are Eucharistic passages, speak of twelve wicker baskets in which the leftover from the five loaves shared by the crowd were gathered together. One of the frescoes in the catacomb of Callixtus depicts seven baskets containing the Eucharistic bread. Wine, on the other hand, was stored in pitchers or jars. These were often earthenware, though some were made of metal. It is likely that communal cups, rather than individual ones, were normally used during family meals. They were made from a variety of materials, including glass. The wealthy might own drinking goblets made of precious metals. We gather from 1 Corinthians

10:16-17 that a communal cup was used for the Eucharist in order to accent the unity of the assembly.

The tradition continued unbroken through succeeding centuries. In the third century wicker baskets were discarded in favor of glass and metal plates. They were dish-shaped vessels large enough to hold loaves of bread. Pope Zephyrinus made the rule that glass plates should be used for the Eucharist. In his turn Pope Urban I donated twenty-five silver plates for the Eucharist. There is a story about church vessels that is very informative. It is told that in 303 the church in Cirta in North Africa was searched by pagan authorities. Bishop Felix surrendered the possessions of the church, which were for liturgical use. The inventory included two golden cups, six silver cups, six silver jars, a silver dish, seven silver lamps, two torches, seven short bronze candlesticks, eleven bronze lamps, and several items like tunics and slippers for men and women, presumably for baptism. The Church in Cirta could not have been poor by any standard, as is demonstrated by these expensive vessels. In the fourth century Emperor Constantine donated to the Lateran Basilica seven golden plates, each weighing thirty pounds, and sixteen silver plates, each also weighing thirty pounds. Around the sixth century the plate for the fraction at papal Mass was carried by two subdeacons. This suggests that the plate was large and heavy. I am intrigued by the information that in papal Masses toward the sixth century the loaves of bread offered by the faithful were deposited in linen sacks, rather than plates, and that at communion the Eucharistic bread was put again in linen sacks for distribution to the assembly. It seems that Eucharistic plates made from such materials as glass, pottery, and wood continued to be used as late as the eighth century.

The table and vessels used for the Eucharist attest to the Church's theology of the Eucharist as the memorial of the Lord's Supper. It is the meal that the household of God shares together in the setting of a home. The shift from wicker baskets and glass cups to adorned plates and silver and gold cups does not detract from the original domestic setting of the Eucharist. It merely suggests that some communities counted among their members wealthy patrons who donated generously to the Church. The important consideration here is that the trend to sacralize ritual words in order to restore to the Mass an aura of mystery is consequential. It is true that ritual symbols and language are polyvalent and there is no clear-cut nomenclature for many things we use in the liturgy. The Eucharistic table is also altar and the presider is a priest. But when people systematically discard "secular" words like cup and replace them with words that carry the sense of sacrifice, I sniff danger in the air. There is a canny obsession to "free the Mass" from what is claimed as "Protestant influence." In other words, let us switch back to sacrifice and downgrade the meal. For the people in question it is obvious that the Tridentine Mass perfectly typifies sacrifice, while the Vatican II Mass sleeps with the enemy. Naming or renaming the liturgical vessels is not a semantic issue. It is a continuing theological debate on the nature of the Mass.

Regarding the baptismal vessels, it is useful to review some historical data. The celebration of baptism uses water, but water must be found or kept somewhere. In the beginning baptism was done in rivers, but eventually the water for baptism was kept in pools, fonts, or vessels. In the New Testament and the first century baptism was administered "where there is water." The flowing water of rivers and streams was preferred because of the symbolism of life. However, any pool of natural water did serve the purpose. Since baptism was performed normally by semi-immersion, the candidate and the minister went down into the river, stream, or pool. The water would normally reach up to the waist or even knee, and with the help of a cup or seashell the water scooped from the river was poured three times on the head of the candidate. In the third century there were cases of total immersion. This implies that there was a pool, and that the water reached up to the breast, so that the head could be lowered to the water. Gradually, after the sixth century, as more children were baptized, elevated baptismal fonts rather than pools came to be used. This had a significant effect on the mode of baptism, which shifted from immersion or semi-immersion to infusion.

At this time I will include in my book of liturgical lamentations a heartbreaking reality. In a number of parishes I visited the baptismal font that the sacrament had hallowed for many generations of Christians had disappeared. I was shocked to see some of them reduced to a kind of utility receptacle. In its place were an all-purpose plastic receptacle and a bottle containing the baptismal water. I can go on with my liturgical lamentations. The baptistery was abandoned and used as a stockroom. I was told that the more liturgically meaningful place for baptism is the sanctuary.

The dignity, beauty, and cleanliness of the baptismal font express our awe at God's work of adoption. The baptismal font is next in importance only to the altar. Patristic and liturgical tradition honors the baptismal font as the womb of Mother Church from which God's children are born in water and the Holy Spirit. It is also, according to some early Christian writers, the tomb of Christ, for "we have been buried with him by baptism into death, so that, as Christ was raised from the dead by the glory of the Father, so we too might walk in newness of life" (Rom 6:4). The baptismal font contains the sacrament of water. I have insisted time and again that the baptismal water should not be equated with "holy water" that reminds us of our baptism. Baptismal water is sacramental water. In that water the Holy Spirit, according to the teaching of tradition, is present so that those who are washed in it are also washed in the Holy Spirit. They are "born in water and the Holy Spirit." The consideration of what the baptismal font contains and signifies argues strongly for the dignity of its shape and material and the appropriateness of its location.

Under this heading I deal briefly with liturgical vestments. People can be fussy about dress. Convention requires that we wear the proper attire for the occasion. Filipino Catholics expect their priest to wear the appropriate vestments for worship. A great number of worshipers still come to church in their Sunday best. When I visited Western Samoa several years ago I was impressed by the festive white lava-lava the Samoans wore to Mass. It was a spectacular sight to watch hundreds of them dressed in white walking to church. The question arose in my mind whether the clothes people wear for Mass should not be regarded as liturgical vestments. Filipino Catholics dress the images of saints during holy week, in black on Good Friday and gold or white on Easter Sunday. Unfortunately many urban residents no longer observe the tradition of Sunday best. Many come in sportswear.

What meaning do we give to the different garbs we use for liturgical worship? Scripture has interesting data. Psalm 93 describes God as "king, robed in majesty," and Psalm 104 exclaims: "O Lord my God, you are very great. You are clothed with honor and majesty, wrapped in light as with a garment." These words proclaim the "otherness" and supreme status of God: God is beyond all. Luke 2:7 relates that Mary wrapped the infant Jesus in swaddling clothes. Mark 9:3 reports that at his transfiguration the clothes of Jesus became dazzling white, such as no fuller on earth could bleach them. John 19:2 narrates that in order to deride Jesus the soldiers arrayed him in a purple robe as befitted a king. Finally, John 19:23 likewise narrates that when Jesus was crucified he was despoiled of his tunic that was without seam, woven from top to bottom. There is an interesting Filipino apocrypha that his mother wove it for him. After his death, as John 19:40 notes, his body was bound in linen cloths. These biblical passages present Jesus in his human condition clothed in the poor peasant's swaddling clothes, although as Son of God his garment shone like the sun.

In the liturgy garbs or vestments are worn to signify a person's state of life and role in the Church. Although these clothes often originate in the culture of local Churches, they acquire a new meaning: they become signs of participation in the life and mission of the Church. Liturgical vesture is not just a convention. It also signifies the relationship between Christ and the person who wears it. In the first three centuries those who were baptized stripped before they entered the baptismal pool. Stripping symbolized the action of "putting off the old man." As they stepped out of the baptismal pool, they were clothed in white robes to signify that they had clothed themselves in Christ" (cf. Gal 3:27) and that they had acquired the dignity of the adopted sons and daughters of God. For eight days, which symbolized their entire lives, they wore the white robe to signify that throughout their lives they would be faithful to their baptismal commitment. The Conferences of Bishops are authorized to adopt another color of the baptismal garment that better suits the people's color patterns. A timely consideration is that the baptismal robe is really worn by the newly baptized. The practice that still persists in some places of imposing a white cloth on the newly baptized child is a parody of the rite of vesting the newly baptized with the robes of Christian dignity.

But Christians can sully and even cast aside their baptismal robes. To recapture baptismal innocence they pass through the tears of repentance that replace the water of baptism. In the early Church a new garb was given to public penitents: the sackcloth. It was a coarse cloth of goat's or camel's hair. It underlines the state of the Christian who had taken off the white and smooth robes of baptism. In the Middle Ages, when the rite of anointing the sick came to be connected with the rite of penance, the sick had to wear the sackcloth during the celebration of anointing. Sickness was often regarded as the result of a sinful life that engaged the bodily senses. Thus the senses were anointed to signify forgiveness of sins and bodily healing.

Another sacrament where certain vesture has a weighty importance is marriage. In Roman antiquity, as in other parts of the world, the woman was subject to her husband. The veil she wore symbolized obedience to him. The saying in Ephesians 5:24 that "just as the church is subject to Christ, so also wives ought to be, in everything, to their husbands" comes from a dated cultural tradition. Today we would rather speak of mutual respect and obedience. Unfortunately, Christ's revolutionary code of conduct toward women and children did not have an immediate impact on the Jewish and Roman cultures and in the other parts of the world. Thus when Ephesians 5 was written the prevailing situation of women was one of subjection to men. Wives are compared to the Church and their husbands to Christ. The comparison is unfortunate, because it is mono-directional and exalts husbands as images of Christ at the expense of wives, who in good theology should be regarded also as images of Christ. To my mind Ephesians 5 should be reread in the light of Christ's message of equality between woman and man. Both husband and wife represent Christ and the Church. When the husband respects, cares, and dedicates himself to the welfare of his wife, he plays the role of Christ who loves the Church. When the wife does the same for her husband, she plays the role of Christ who loves the Church. When the husband accepts the love showered on him by his wife, he is the image of the Church. When the wife receives the love of her husband, she is the symbol of the Church. In light of this, I interpret the bridal veil as a reminder of the Church's total adherence to Christ rather than the subjection of the bride to her husband.

Through the rites of ordination a person enters into the clerical state as deacon, presbyter, or bishop. The chief duty of the ordained minister is to preach the word of God, celebrate the sacraments, and exercise spiritual leadership in the community. These threefold functions describe the clerical state and its responsibilities. To express them the ordained person receives the principal vesture that symbolizes his life and ministry: the stole. This they use every time they exercise the office of preaching and celebrating the sacraments. The other vestments, like the alb or tunic, chasuble, cope, and dalmatic, though distinctive and traditional, should be ranked after the stole in value and symbolism. Historians of liturgical vesture inform us that the alb and chasuble (now also the maniple that priests who say the Tridentine Mass have pulled out from sacristy drawers) are modern versions of early medieval garments, religious or otherwise. On the other hand, we are told that the stole is the modern interpretation of the shawl (square or oblong fabric garment used as a covering for the head or shoulders) used by the Jewish rabbi during the Sabbath services in the synagogue. It seems that the "woman at prayer" painted in Roman catacombs is wearing the earliest version of the stole. The combined alb and chasuble with the stole over it is an attempt to simplify the vesture for Mass. It has the advantage of focusing on the stole, unlike the traditional chasubles that hide it.

I quote some pertinent directives of the General Instruction on the Roman Missal. It makes the following reminder: "In the Church, the Body of Christ, not all members have the same function. This variety of offices in the celebration of the Eucharist is shown outwardly by the diversity of sacred vestments, which should therefore symbolize the office proper to each minister. But at the same time the sacred vestments should also contribute to the beauty of the sacred action" (335). It also ordains that "unless otherwise indicated, the chasuble, worn over the alb and stole, is the vestment proper to the priest celebrant at Mass and other sacred actions directly connected with Mass" (337). It leaves the matter of the design of vestments to the decision of the Conferences of Bishops (342). Finally, it states that "the beauty and nobility of a vestment should derive from the material used and the design rather than from extraneous and lavish ornamentation" (344).

SACRED IMAGES IN THE LITURGY

In several parts of the Catholic world the question of sacred images in the liturgy cannot be isolated from the doctrinal issues being raised by fundamentalist groups. There is no doubt that gross exaggerations regarding the veneration of sacred images exist among some of the Catholic faithful. But the fundamentalist response, which often involves outright destruction of sacred images, is impiously irreverent and offensive. The Catholic faithful as well as their fundamentalist sisters and brothers need to exercise moderation, which is the mother of all virtues. The words addressed by Pope Gregory the Great to Bishop Serenus of Marseille are relevant and timely: "We commend you for forbidding the adoration of sacred images, but we reprimand you for destroying them."

The Constitution on Liturgy rules that "the practice of placing sacred images in churches so that they may be venerated by the faithful is to be maintained" (125). With this Vatican II reaffirmed the doctrine of the Second Council of Nicea (787) and the Council of Trent (1545–1563) concerning the use and veneration of sacred images. But in the spirit of the *romana sobrietas* the Constitution adds that "there is to be restraint regarding the number and prominence of images so that they do not create confusion among the Christian people or foster religious practices of doubtful orthodoxy." The General Instruction on the Roman Missal elaborates this conciliar decree: "In keeping with the Church's very ancient tradition, images of the Lord, the Blessed Virgin Mary, and the Saints may be displayed in sacred buildings for veneration by the faithful, and may be so arranged there that they guide the faithful to the mysteries of faith celebrated there. . . . As a rule, there is to be only one image of any given Saint" (318).

Since the church is primarily for liturgical celebrations and not as a kind of "pantheon" that houses every imaginable sacred image, it is obvious that there should be restraint regarding the number and prominence of sacred images in the church. It is not easy to define the limit. Much depends on the devotion of the faithful, which should be, in the final analysis, the criterion for deciding how many and which images are to be kept in the church. The Consilium, in the document *Le renouveau liturgique*, observed that "in the adaptation of churches to the demands of liturgical renewal there has sometimes been exaggeration regarding sacred images. At times, it is true, some churches have been cluttered with images and statues, but to strip bare and do away with absolutely everything is to risk the opposite extreme" (8). Regarding works of art, the Congregation for the Clergy, in its circular letter *Opera artis*, in 1971 made this appeal: "Works of art from the past are always and everywhere to be preserved so that they may lend their noble service to divine worship and their help to the people's active participation in the liturgy." The Congregation bewailed that "more than ever before there is so much unlawful transferal of ownership of the historical and artistic heritage of the church, as well as theft, confiscation, and destruction." However, we note the instruction of the Constitution on Liturgy to the bishops: "Let the bishops carefully remove from the house of God and from places of worship those works of artists that are repugnant to faith and morals and to Christian devotion and that offend the true religious sense either by their grotesqueness or by the deficiency, mediocrity, or sham in their artistic quality" (124).

In his 1969 address to the Pontifical Commission for Sacred Art in Italy, Pope Paul VI explained that "the place of images and everything connected with their veneration in worship is purely relative and symbolic." Sacred images direct the attention of the assembly to the Eucharist on the table, the sacrament of rebirth at the baptismal font, and the mystery of the Church assembled in worship. The cross in the sanctuary expresses the relationship between Calvary and the Mass, and the picture of Christ being baptized by John reminds us that we belong to the priestly people of God. Sacred images of Christ and the saints on the occasion of their feasts are visual aids for devout participation in the liturgical celebration. Sacred images are not pieces of decorative art nor are they purely catechetical. Nevertheless, sacred images have a subordinate role in the liturgy and hence should not be so prominently displayed that they command total attention to themselves. Nor should they be of such gigantic proportion that they dwarf the Eucharistic table. In the sanctuary the principal furnishings that should be given prominence are the table, the ambo, and the chair of the presider. The Rite of Dedication of a Church and Altar directs that "in new churches statues and pictures of saints may not be placed above the altar" (10). The rite speaks of new churches, not of the older ones where sometimes the niches or *retablo* for sacred images behind the table are part of the architectural design. Normally, if there is to be an image above the altar, it should be the image of the cross.

The discipline of one image of any one saint is a good measure to dispel superstitious and erroneous beliefs, sometimes nurtured by devotees, that the image of Our Lady of Fatima, for example, is more powerful than the image of Our Lady of Lourdes! Some of the devotees play it safe by moving from one image to another. However, I do not have a one-track mind on this matter. It may very well happen that several images of the Blessed Virgin under different titles will be a source of catechesis and foster devotion when carried together in a procession or placed in church on the occasion of a Marian celebration.

Fundamentalist groups, based on a literal interpretation of Exodus 20:4-5, unjustly assail the Catholic practice of venerating sacred images. There was a time in the Philippines when their proselytes were required to break sacred images, burn them, or dump them in garbage bins. History has given the ugly word "iconoclasm" to the destruction of sacred images. There is a need to correct misconceptions and to instruct Catholics on the meaning of sacred images.

According to the Second Council of Nicea II, sacred images are material representations of the cross, Christ, the Blessed Virgin, the angels, and the saints. They may be painted or sculpted from any material. The council allowed them to be placed on vessels, clothing, walls, at home, and in public places for the veneration of the faithful. It noted that "the more we look at these images, the more we are reminded of the persons they represent and are inspired to exert effort to imitate them." The council makes a clear distinction between veneration (*proskynesis*) and adoration (*latreia*). Adoration is a total and absolute submission of one's entire being. This is offered to God alone. Sacred images are not adored, even if they are images of Christ; they are merely venerated. *Proskynesis* refers to prostration, a gesture commonly practiced in the Byzantine court as a sign of respect for the emperor. It did not imply adoration or worship. It will be remembered that from the time of Pope Gregory VII until the late Middle Ages the popes were honored with the gesture of prostration and the kissing of their feet. Nicea encouraged the burning of incense and the lighting of candles before sacred images as sign of veneration. In the liturgy of Vatican II the only image before which the faithful genuflect—and this is done only once a year on Good Friday—is the cross.

Many practices of devotion to sacred images are the object of cynicism and contempt by fundamentalists who label them idolatrous. The truth is that images are in the category of signs and hence ultimately refer to the persons they signify. Nicea teaches that "the honor given to an image is given to the one it represents. Whoever venerates an image venerates the person it represents." Thus when we perform gestures of respect before an image and make our prayers, we do not address them directly to the image, as if it could see and hear us, but to the person it signifies. The image stands for the person of Christ or the Blessed Mother or a saint, but it is not the person of Christ or the Blessed Mother or the saint. The honor and veneration we direct to the image are not received by the image but by the person represented by it.

The Council of Trent reiterated Nicea, but made a significant point of clarification: we are not to believe that in the images "the divinity or a power is present, for which they are venerated, or that there is anything we can ask from them, or that we can put our trust in them as did the pagans who put their hope in idols." Sacred images do not contain the power of God or the saints, but we venerate them because of the persons they represent. We do not trample on the pictures of persons we revere or love. There is always some connection between a lifeless picture and the person it represents. Iconoclasm failed to understand the yearnings of the human heart. In stark contrast to Trent was the claim of St. John Damascene (+749), which regarded sacred images as "channels" of divine grace, in the manner of sacraments. In consideration of the persons they represent a sanctifying power is attached to them. Sacred images possess a quasi-sacramental power. Neither the Council of Nicea nor the Council of Trent appropriated this doctrine. However, it is a doctrine that characterizes the Oriental veneration of sacred images: They are not only in the category of signs. They are also in the category of sacraments—they contain in the manner of sacraments what they signify. I confess that I am of two minds over this matter, especially when I deal with popular religiosity. How does one explain (away) "miraculous" images in which devotees perceive the presence of Christ, his mother, or the saint? Is real presence an attribute exclusive to sacraments? The most I can say is that when a sacred image is called "miraculous," it is understood that it is God that performs the miracle, using the image to transmit the grace. I realize that I am really just begging the question.

The *Book of Blessings* gives useful pointers on sacred images. I limit my discussion to the cross and the images of the Blessed Virgin Mary. Among the sacred images the cross of Christ holds the place of preeminence in churches and in the homes of the faithful. The cross of Christ is the symbol of Christ's passion, death, and glorification. It was on the cross and there alone that Christ offered his human life for our redemption and bestowed the Holy Spirit on his Church. The cross was the instrument of his passion and the throne of his glory as the *Kyrios* who bestows the Holy Spirit. Raised on Calvary between heaven and earth, the cross became the symbol of our reconciliation with God. The cross accompanies us from the time of baptism up to the moment of death. It reminds us that when we were baptized we were crucified to the world and to sin, and that our life of suffering in union with Christ does not end in death but in resurrection. It reminds us that ours is a life of discipleship, of following the example of the Master who carried his cross and was nailed to it for the sake of others.

The cross is the one sign that distinguishes Christianity from other religions. It is displayed on the roofs and towers of churches and in places where Christians assemble. It leads the people during processions. In churches the cross is placed over or near the Eucharistic table in order to convey the relationship between the Supper of Jesus and his sacrifice. The cross adorns the homes of the faithful as well as the public places used by Christians. It is also worn by the faithful as a sign of their Christian identity and devotion. In some countries or territories occupied by religious groups inimical to Christianity it is forbidden to display the cross in public. Sometimes Christians carry the blame when, out of a false sense of security that their country is Christian, they neglect the cross. The diocesan directors of liturgy in the Philippines who met in September 2008 on the island of Mindanao where Muslims are active addressed this disquieting issue: "Religious objects are powerful signs of faith. They promote Christian piety and the awareness of God's presence. Among the sacramentals that are objects, the cross of Jesus Christ or crucifix possesses preeminence. We recommend that whenever it is opportune or feasible the cross should be raised in strategic places in towns and cities in order to foster the Christian environment."

Marian images represent the Blessed Virgin under different titles, such as Mother of God, Immaculate Conception, and Assumption, or according to the event or place of apparition, such as Our Lady of Lourdes and Our Lady of Fatima. But whatever their title or appearance, Mary's images summon our attention to two principal teachings of the faith, namely, the human nature of Christ and the Church. Mary's foundational title is *Theotokos*, or Mother of God. The Church believes that because she had been chosen to bear in her womb the Incarnate Word, she was conceived without sin and was assumed body and soul into heaven. The special gifts she received personally from God were in consideration of her role in salvation history as the Mother of the Savior. We can give her a litany of titles and invoke her under every conceivable name, but she is first and foremost the Mother of God. The Oriental Churches value this title so eminently that their icons of Mary almost always show her with the Child. The person of Mary cannot be understood, pictured, or venerated apart from her title of Mother of God. There is so much the Western Church can learn from the Orient in the manner it depicts her. Images and paintings of Mary all by herself do not tell the whole story about her.

At the foot of the cross Mary stood for the Church, the bride of Christ who emanated from his pierced side like the first woman Eve. There Mary stood not only as the Mother but also as the image of the Church and the Mother of the redeemed people of God. Assumed into heaven, she is the image of the Church whose glory will be revealed at the end of time.

MASS MEDIA IN THE LITURGY

Vatican II's Decree on the Means of Social Communication (1) vouches for the Church's particular interest in modern mass media inasmuch as they directly touch the human spirit and open up new avenues of communication. Modern mass media influence not only individual persons but also the entire human society. The decree calls them "media of social communication" and enumerates their types: "These are the press, the cinema, radio, television, and others of a like nature." Today we include in the list the internet and the ubiquitous mobile phones that have reduced the size of the globe to a tiny mobile unit.

The question of how the liturgy can profitably employ modern mass media was treated earlier by the council in the Constitution on Liturgy (20). The use of mass media in the liturgy links up with the oral and aural features of Christian worship. When the Instruction *Inter*

Oecumenici launched the reform in 1964 it reminded pastors that in the design of churches the active participation of the assembly should be a preponderant consideration. According to the instruction, "care is to be taken to enable the faithful not only to see the celebrant and other ministers but also to hear them easily, even by use of modern sound equipment." The liturgy is an oral-aural experience of Christ's mystery, just as Christianity is a religion of oral proclamation and aural demeanor. Words like "preach," "read," and "sing," as well as "listen," "hear," and "respond" describe how the liturgy is performed. The written word of God has to be proclaimed to the assembly. It is normal to assume that in the celebration of the liturgy texts are read, songs are sung, and responses are said.

The oral-aural feature of Christian worship is at the heart of any discussion on the use of mass media. In its 1967 Editorial *Mécanique et Liturgie* the Consilium took up the issue concerning the introduction of sound systems in the liturgy. It gratefully noted that "microphones permit even those at the back of the largest churches to hear the voice of the celebrant, preacher, reader, or commentator." We all know that the microphone is a dangerous gadget in the hands of a forgetful minister. Modern sound devices are aids to enhance the oral character of the liturgy; they do not replace it. The document assails the use of taped music in place of active singing as "artificial and, in fact, a lie." Active participation means that the assembly is engaged in the performance of the rite by responses and songs. Unskilled but hearty singing by an assembly is to be preferred to a polished choir song played from a tape recorder. Authenticity is the formula of a good and fulfilling liturgy. To drive home its point the Consilium scoffed at the use of artificial devices: "No electrical lighting will ever have the value of the living flame of wax or oil being visibly consumed as an offering to the Lord. The illumination of the church with the candles of the congregation at the Easter Vigil is a rite simple yet full of meaning, bringing to mind both the resurrection and the faith. How ridiculous it would become if candles were exchanged for flashlights."

In the liturgy we speak of the Book of the Sacramentary, Book of the Gospels, the Lectionary, Book of Psalms, and Book of Antiphons. I do not exclude the possibility that in the course of this millennium there could be a technological breakthrough, but for now let us enjoy the tradition of using books in our liturgical celebrations. The Consilium explained its reticence: "The liturgical reform has its own distinctive way of safeguarding the nobility of objects and of actions. Any reaction it has against the danger of mechanization in worship is not based on antiquarianism. The motive rather is that the worship of God ought to lead people to a sense of the sacred and of mystery and to make the whole creation be permeated with the renewal of the New Covenant."

But the liturgy is not only oral and aural. It is also visual. The General Instruction on the Roman Missal directs that "the place for the faithful should be arranged with proper care so that they are able to participate rightfully in sacred celebrations visually and mentally." Furthermore, "care should be taken to enable the faithful to see the priest, the deacon, and the readers" (311). Seeing generally facilitates hearing. We live in the age of audiovisuals. For many of us listening to the radio or CD is not as engaging as watching DVD, cinema, television, or live performance. Although the sense of hearing is more basic than the sense of sight, we tend to value our eyes more than our ears. Listening to readings and homilies is not a gift many people enjoy. Perhaps this is the reason why in Masses with children silent dramatization or mime sometimes accompanies the scriptural reading.

The *Directory for Masses with Children*, which the Congregation for Divine Worship published in 1973, is still relevant. The Directory calls attention to the fact that "the liturgy of the Mass contains many visual elements and these should be given great prominence with children" (35). I should add, also with adults. Examples are the veneration of the cross, the Easter candle, and the lights on the feast of the Presentation of the Lord. But we do not have to wait for these yearly occasions. The daily Mass has a good number of visual elements, such as hand-laying and the raising of the Eucharistic species, not to forget the table, ambo, presider's chair, the large crucifix in the apse, and the shape and color of the vestments. In a word, we should make the most of existing visual elements of the liturgy, even before we consider power-point presentations. It is bad for the liturgy when we are indifferent to the size and appearance of the bread and the chalice, the quality of the furnishings, and the appearance of the vestments. Liturgy is a performative rite. It is heard and seen, and hence should appeal to both the ears and the eyes. Technological gadgets do not conceal the priest's and ministers' clumsiness and the poor quality of liturgical appointments. When we speak of the visual aspect of the liturgy, we mean that the assembly is able to discern the presence of the mystery through what they see happening in the sanctuary.

In the 1970s the use of audiovisual media during liturgical celebrations became popular in many parts of the world. Liturgists were engaged in producing what they termed "multi-lit." Slide shows accompanied the general intercessions at Mass. This was also the peak of the movement called "liberation theology" that spilled into the liturgy. It was not unusual to see pictures of police brutality while prayer was being recited for the victims and against the perpetrators. Sometimes certain passages from the scriptural readings were illustrated by corresponding slides. But this type of visual illustration did not outlast the decade. In the eighties people turned to dramatization, especially of the gospel reading. This caught on in rural areas where the parish could not afford a slide projector but had a good reserve of young people willing to perform in the sanctuary.

The Constitution on Liturgy dealt with the question of mass media in the liturgy only once, namely, in article 20. This article, which reaffirms the 1958 Instruction *De musica sacra*, reads: "Radio and television broadcasts of sacred rites must be marked by discretion and dignity, under the leadership and direction of a competent person appointed for the office by the bishops. This is especially important when the service to be broadcast is the Mass." In 1971 the Pontifical Commission for the Media of Social Communication (*Communio et progressio* 151) treated the question at some length. It advocated the use of mass media, especially radio and television, to enrich the devotional and religious life of the faithful and to serve the ill and elderly who are prevented from direct participation in the life of the Church. The Instruction affirms that "the most desirable and fitting religious broadcasts are those of the celebration of the Mass and other sacred rites. Everything about the liturgy itself and the technical details must be prepared with absolute care. The diversity of the audience must be taken into consideration as also, in the case of international broadcasts, regional religious opinions and customs. In number and length these broadcasts should respect the desire of the audience."

Both the Constitution on Liturgy and the Instruction speak of discretion and dignity in the use of radio and television. Discretion means discernment and good judgment, circumspection, and cautious reserve, while dignity refers to the worthy and formal manner of presenting the celebration as a sacred function. In the case of the television what is broadcast are principally the word of God and the sacramental rite. While transmission should be aesthetic, engaging, and enhanced by special effects, it is focused on the word and the sacrament. As much as possible the word of God should be broadcast in its entirety and the important moments of the sacramental rite should be faithfully recorded.

Running commentaries on the celebration should not interfere with the reading of the word of God and the prayers of the presider. Discretion requires that the liturgy not be presented on the screen as an entertainment show. The priest, the ministers, and the assembly are not stage actors. They are the Church at prayer. These people are worshiping; they are praying. *Eucharisticum mysterium* directs the local Ordinaries to see to it that "the prayers and participation of the faithful in attendance are not disturbed" (22). For this reason, close-ups of persons, showing the different facial angles of the presider or the faithful, should be done with caution and reserve, if it should be done at all.

The Pontifical Commission for the Media directs our attention to the different types of audiences watching or listening to the transmission of a liturgical celebration. The audience for the regular Sunday televised Mass is mostly the "shut-ins" due to illness or old age. On the other hand, the audience for special telecasts, like the papal Mass and diocesan or national celebrations, can range from the devout to the merely curious. In 1969 a query was put to the Congregation for Divine Worship regarding the propriety of delayed telecast of the Mass. Delayed telecast means that the liturgy is taped while it is being celebrated, but it is transmitted at a later hour that day. The answer of the Congregation is: "The purpose of broadcasts of the Mass is that those unable to participate may join in mind and heart with the actual celebration. Should grave difficulties make it impossible for the broadcasts of the celebration to be live, the listeners or viewers should be advised accordingly." The liturgical principle the Congregation invokes here is that liturgical worship is an actual celebration of a community. That is why preference is given to televised celebrations held in a parish or a cathedral church over those performed in a television studio. In a parish the people gather together to celebrate the Mass, while in the studio the group of people who are invited come for the purpose of televising the Mass. Definitely, the liturgy in the studio will be technically flawless and the ambience more ideal compared with the parish liturgy where children wail or run about, people keep looking at the camera, and the noise of the street blurs the sound of prayer and song. But the natural setting of a parish liturgy portrays more convincingly the image of the Church gathered in liturgical worship.

Conclusion:
Liturgy and Spirituality

Throughout this book I applied myself, whenever opportune, to developing some insights on the spirituality that emanates from the theology, history, and ritual performance of liturgical worship. As conclusion to this book, I sum up the principal elements of Christian spirituality in general and liturgical spirituality in particular.

Spirituality in General

The following quotation from the Constitution on the Church is a clarion call to Christian holiness: "All in the Church, whether they belong to the hierarchy or are cared for by it, are called to holiness, according to the Apostle's saying: For this is the will of God, your sanctification" (39). The Constitution assures us that the call to holiness is directed to all, regardless of their state of life, whether one is shepherd or member of the flock. It affirms that personal holiness does not depend upon the office one holds in the Church, however exalted that office might be. History informs us that the office of the papacy has not always had worthy occupants. The *Book of Popes*, or *Liber Pontificalis*, passes severe judgment on Pope John XII (955–964): *Iste denique infelicissimus, quod sibi peius est, totam vitam suam in adulterio et vanitate duxit.* A word to the wise: this is not a passage I want to translate. There were very trying moments in the history of the Church, especially in the fifteenth century, which historians call the "autumn of the Middle Ages," when the Church was in dire need of reform *in capite et in membris* (in its head and members).

It is true that the ecclesiastical office can inspire its holder to a greater holiness of life. But it is also true that the personal life of the minister can affect the faithful's perception of the office he holds. Does it not happen, sadly, that the faithful lose their respect for the office because of the office holder? On the eve of the Council of Trent some Catholic reformers began to call the Church the paradoxical yet endearing title *casta meretrix*. The title points out the paradoxical reality of the Church. Left to its own devices, the Church is no better than the people of Israel whom God accused of prostituting themselves to foreign gods. But because of the presence of Christ, the guidance of the Holy Spirit, the transforming power of God's word and the sacraments, and the conspicuous witness of saintly pastors and faithful, the Church can claim that it is the chaste bride of Christ. Throughout history the community of the faithful struggles between light and shadow, between being chaste and being unfaithful. We are consoled that by the grace of God and in spite of human weakness a great multitude of pastors and faithful keep alive the people's perception that the Church is indeed holy.

The Constitution on the Church teaches that "the forms and tasks of life are many but holiness is one" (41). Genuine spirituality is possible in every state and walk of life. This explains why the calendar of saints carries the title of each saint: pope, bishop, martyr, religious, missionary, educator, married man or woman, virgin, and so on. The intention is to show that holiness is possible in every walk of life and that God does not discriminate on the basis of the office or rank a person holds in life. Accordingly, the calendar of saints did away with the discriminatory or politically incorrect title "neither virgin nor martyr" for married women who did not enjoy the privilege of martyrdom.

The same Constitution explains that spirituality consists in the full and faithful performance of the duties demanded by one's station in life. To imagine that one will be holier in another situation or in another post or assignment can be a form of spiritual daydreaming. Holiness does not depend on the kind of work we do, provided of course that the work is upright, but on the quality and the intensity of our dedication to duty. For the pastors of the Church holiness is linked with the office of shepherding. Pastors strive to be holy in the concrete reality of their ministry. When priests preach, build and animate their flock, and celebrate the sacraments, they lead the spiritual life proper to their calling. The more profoundly they are aware of their identity as ministers of Christ and the Church, the more intensely they will live the life in the Spirit. The years immediately following Vatican II witnessed the tragedy of priests' exodus from the ministry. Many left, not because they no longer loved the Church, but because in the confusion of the time they were no longer sure what they had been ordained for.

Spirituality entails the tranquil acceptance of and joyful commitment to one's own state of life as a person and as a Christian, especially when this involves sacrifice. It leads to a sense of personal fulfillment in one's occupation, however humble this may appear in the eyes of the world. Spirituality is the endeavor to discover the face of God in the daily routine of life at home, in school, or place of employment. It is the ability to find peace of mind and contentment of the heart in one's work and enjoy it to the full. The unrestrained desire to become someone else or to be somewhere else can cause restlessness of the heart.

An important trait of spirituality is its being holistic. Spiritual people blend all aspects of life so that they form a harmonious unity. They live an integrated life that has no compartments separating one life experience from another. There is no dichotomy between their prayer and their work or the performance of one's daily tasks, as if these realities were estranged from one another. For holistic persons everything leads to God and everything becomes a factor of growth in the spiritual life.

Christian spirituality is holistic. Attending interminable committee meetings that someone called the devil's invention to test our patience, enjoying meals with members of one's household, relaxing with friends, sitting back to absorb shocking news, listening patiently to complaints and lamentations, calming the anger of others or perhaps one's own, keeping oneself well informed through books and periodicals, the internet, radio, newspaper, and television: these are occasions when we can encounter God and experience God's presence in particular circumstances of life. Christians live their spiritual lives not only when they perform acts of worship in church but also when they deal with people and events both small and great. Christian spirituality is integration, not dichotomy. In a word, everything in life, including daily routine, is a moment to experience the presence of God, who can be found not only in prayer but also in the reality of human life. Because spirituality is holistic, nothing is wasted: everything turns unto good for those who seek and love God. The Decrees of the Second Plenary Council of the Philippines (art. 36) rightly call for "the integration of prayer and action." Paragraph 167 of the document observes that "in the Philippines worship has unfortunately been often separated from the totality of life. Rather, it is seen as one department of life without an intimate connection with social, economic, and political life." In stirring words the document makes the timely reminder that "we cannot worship God in our churches and shrines, and then disregard him in the daily business of life."

Liturgical Spirituality

What is liturgical spirituality? According to the Constitution on Liturgy, the celebration of liturgical worship is the fountainhead of spirituality: the liturgy is "the summit toward which the activity of the Church is directed; at the same time it is the fount from which all her power flows" (10). The Constitution on the Church describes liturgical spirituality by enumerating its chief practices: listening to the word of God; celebrating the sacraments, especially the Eucharist; participating in other liturgical rites, and as prerequisites or consequences, carrying out God's will with deeds; applying oneself to prayer, self-denial, and active service to others; and the practice of all the virtues (42). The enumeration is rather exhaustive and can appear to make spirituality a tall order. What the two conciliar documents seem to say is that liturgical spirituality is the only spirituality for all, because it directly gushes forth from the cross of Christ. It is from this spirituality that particular types of spirituality evolve. The Benedictine, Dominican, Franciscan, Jesuit, Augustinian, Carmelite, and Salesian, to name a few, are interpretative variations of the Church's foundational spirituality. After all, no form of spirituality is possible without the liturgy of the Eucharist, sacraments, sacramentals, liturgical year, and the Liturgy of the Hours.

The liturgy is source of the Church's spirituality because Christ and his saving mystery are present and active in it. The Constitution on Liturgy teaches that "from the liturgy as from a fount grace is poured forth upon us and the sanctification of people in Christ and the glorification of God is achieved in the most efficacious way possible" (10). The liturgy quickens our spiritual life: in the liturgy we experience spiritual rebirth, communion with the Lord, reconciliation, and spiritual comfort. The liturgy transports us to the historical *kairós* of Christ's saving work that now appears to us in the form of liturgical *hodie*. We recall the lapidary words of Pope Leo the Great in *Sermon* 72: *Quod conspicuum erat in Christo transivit in Ecclesiae sacramenta* (What was visible in Christ [his person and mission] passed on the sacraments of the Church).

The liturgy is the summit to which all the other activities of the Church are directed. The Liturgy Constitution states that "the aim and object of apostolic works is that all who are made children of God by faith and baptism should come together to praise God in the midst of the Church, to take part in the sacrifice, and to eat the Lord's Supper" (10). If the Church engages in the apostolate of education, ministry of healing, political liberation, and the moral and social uplifting of the people, it is in order to lead them to the fount of spirituality, which is the liturgy.

The following are some of the chief components of liturgical spirituality. The first is a phrase that the Liturgy Constitution (90) borrowed from the Rule of St. Benedict (chap. 19): *Ut mens nostra concordet voci nostrae* (that our mind may be in harmony with our voice). It is an exhortation to monastics to attune their minds to their voices as they chant the psalms, or in short, concentrate on the prayer and avoid distractions. Liturgical spirituality requires that we pay full attention to the meaning of the words we recite and the ritual actions we perform. Someone inquired whether it was a form of distraction to gaze on the crucifix with full concentration during the Eucharistic Prayer such that the prayer serves as a kind of backdrop to meditation. Liturgical spirituality means that we are consciously engaged in the celebration and are able to relish its spiritual wealth and beauty. Obviously, the ritual action should be marked by beauty, which Pope Benedict XVI (*Sacramentum caritatis* 35) calls "a sublime expression of God's glory and, in a certain sense, a glimpse of heaven on earth. . . . Beauty, then, is not mere decoration, but rather an essential element of the liturgical action, since it is an attribute of God himself and his revelation." A disciple of the great theologian of beauty Hans Urs von Balthasar, the Holy Father understandably requires beauty in the celebration of the liturgy, a beauty that he perceives more clearly in the former liturgical rite and its appurtenances. Who can blame him when, contrary to the mind of his predecessor Pope Paul VI and the council, some liturgical celebrations neglect the noble beauty of the Roman rite because of a misguided application of *sobrietas romana* and inculturation?

Concentration is a very demanding exercise. Presiders in particular are expected to give a great deal of attention to the words they say or read and the ritual actions they perform. They are expected to understand the word of God they read in order to mean what it says. They are the first hearers of the word they proclaim to others. When ministers greet the people with "The Lord be with you," they should understand the greeting and mean every word of it. When the people answer "Amen" at the conclusion of the Eucharistic Prayer, they should know what it signifies and mean it. For the assembly, liturgical spirituality is the act of meeting God in the prayers, gestures, and symbols of the rite and above all in the assembly itself, which is the epiphany of Christ's presence. Often this may involve great faith and humility, especially when the celebration is clumsy and lacking in proper decorum, or, alas, when the ministers are inattentive to the mystery they celebrate. In such circumstances one should profess faith in the power of God who can make us holy through the liturgy in spite of ourselves. The axiom *ex opere operato* is a handy formula, but we know in the depths of our hearts that to make the sacraments truly effective and beneficial, the ministers should possess the proper disposition, and the liturgical rite itself should be worthy of the mystery it contains.

The second component of liturgical spirituality is the word of God. I have treated the subject in another chapter of this book. In the context of liturgical spirituality, allow me to add that the divine Logos, which became the Incarnate Word, descends upon us as the proclaimed Word when the words of Scripture are read in the liturgical assembly. The time allotted to the reading is the sacramental moment when we encounter the Logos. During the reading of Scripture I can truly say: Christ is now speaking to me. I may or may not understand his message, but I believe that he is present in the words I hear. Faith assures me that he is speaking to me. In a sense, it is the experience of his presence that ultimately matters, not the ability of the intellect to grasp the meaning of the words. It is always useful to keep in mind that Christ is the preacher of the word. At times we are tempted to think that because the reading is too difficult to interpret even for exegetes, it would be practical to omit it and choose another pericope that is more easily accessible to the people. The problem with such thinking is that we limit the power of God's word to what we personally perceive to be comprehensible to the people. We might forget that there is the possibility of personal encounter with Christ by the mere fact that the word is proclaimed. The lector too may be an obstacle. The personal life and reading skills of the lector can at times be so disenchanting that we focus on the voice rather than on the word. St. Augustine (*Sermo* 293) makes a useful distinction between "the voice that passes away" and "the divine Word that remains." Referring to the preaching of John, St. Augustine said, "Because it is hard to distinguish word from voice, even John himself was thought to be the Christ. The voice was thought to be the word."

The sacraments constitute the third component of liturgical spirituality. Allow me to reiterate by way of conclusion what I discussed earlier in this book. For the ministers liturgical spirituality consists in their performance of the sacramental rites and prayer. These are the Church's prayer for the faithful, but the ministers adopt them as their personal prayer for themselves and for the people they serve. Ministers become personally involved in the unfolding of Christ's mystery in the faithful who receive the sacraments. The official prayer of the Church becomes the personal prayer of the ministers. There is no more distinction between what they officially read from the book and what they utter in their hearts as personal prayer. The sacramental words they recite, like "I baptize you" and "I absolve you," are not merely sacramental formulas required for the valid administration of the sacraments; they are their personal petitions for the recipient of the sacrament. Thus the ministry of baptism is an occasion for the minister to experience the love of the Father who graciously adopts the candidate to be his son or daughter. Ministers exercise their spirituality in the act of presiding or celebrating the sacraments. For them spirituality and liturgical ministry are one and the same.

The fourth component consists of the psalms, which occupy a fairly significant place in the prayer and ministry of the Church. Psalms are used in practically all the liturgical celebrations, particularly in the Liturgy of the Hours. Based on Christ's own declaration that everything written about him in the Law of Moses, in the prophets, and in the psalms had to be fulfilled, the Church interprets the psalms in reference to Christ and the Church. Liturgical spirituality means that when we chant the psalms, we clothe ourselves with the person of Christ; we put on the vesture of the Church. When we pray the psalms in this manner, we can relate better with them. For example, if we find ourselves saying a psalm of joy, while in fact we are sad, we can appropriate the sentiments of the psalms, forgetting the personal disposition of our mind and heart. We can thus imitate the example of Christ who took unto himself the suffering of humankind. In like manner when we recite a psalm of sorrow, while in fact we are in a happy mood, we can use it as an occasion to experience vicariously in our hearts the misfortunes of other people. When we recite the psalms in the name and spirit of Christ, we fulfill the exhortation of St. Paul (Rom 12:15): "Rejoice with those who rejoice, weep with those who weep." In our communities, the Church, and the world there are millions of people who are happy or sad. The psalms allow us to unite ourselves vicariously with them. The psalms are thus like a school of the Lord's service where we can learn to share vicariously the joy and misery of the world. I came across a quotation from Martin Luther who explains what vicarious experience means: "If we cannot feel in our body the pains and sorrows of others, let us experience them at least in our hearts."

The Office of Readings for Friday of the Tenth Week in Ordinary Time reproduces a passage from St. Ambrose's treatise on the psalms that I find very relevant to liturgical spirituality: "In the Book of Psalms there is profit for all, with healing power for our salvation. There is instruction from history, teaching from the law, prediction from prophecy, chastisement from denunciation, persuasion from moral preaching. All who read it may find the cure for their own individual failings." He concludes with these marvelous words that echo the *hodie* of liturgy: "In the psalms, then, not only is Jesus born for us, he also undergoes his saving passion in his body, he lies in death, he rises again, he ascends into heaven, he sits at the right hand of the Father. What no one would have dared to say was foretold by the psalmist alone, and afterward proclaimed by the Lord himself in the Gospel" (*Explanations of the Psalms*, Ps. 1).

The awareness of being Church is another component of liturgical spirituality. It is the lively perception of the worshiping community that it represents the one, holy, catholic, and apostolic Church gathered here and now. I have treated this topic earlier in this book. Allow me to recall here that the worshiping community embodies the universal Church because it enjoys the presence of Christ and keeps unity with its bishop. Liturgical spirituality is the experience of being Church, the avowal of faith that the assembly is the gathering here and now of the one Church of Christ. Thus the liturgical assembly appears before God with the concerns of the global Church. As St. Theresa of Avila reminded her sisters, "When the world is on fire, we cannot pray for little things." Our prayers of petitions are at times quite confined to our local, personal concerns. They have an intramural character, circumscribed by the walls of our homes and communities. Sometimes our general intercessions can be so markedly individual that they lack ecclesial and universal attributes. Those that compose them seem to turn their eyes away from a world that is on fire with war, racial hatred, terrorism, poverty, natural calamities, and human violence. These are the concerns of the greater Church, and when we gather as a local community of worship we should clothe ourselves with the concerns of the one, holy, catholic, and apostolic Church.

On September 3, 1969, Pope Paul VI said these stirring words, full of gratitude and optimism: "Praise be to God that the liturgical movement, taken up and advanced by the Council, has spread throughout the Church and entered into the awareness of clergy and people. The choral prayer of the Mystical Body, which the Church is, is reaching and stirring the people of God, who are consciously becoming a community and experiencing an increase in faith and grace. Therefore, supernatural faith is reawakening, eschatological hope is guiding ecclesial spirituality, and charity is reassuming its life-giving, active primacy. And all of this in a pagan, worldly century, deaf to the cries of the soul."

That in all things God may be glorified.

Index of Ecclesiastical Documents

Index of Persons

Haugen, Marty, 212, 213
Hernandez, Virgilio, 153
Hippolytus of Rome, 52, 78, 158, 161
Hopkins, Gerard, 115
Hugh of St. Victor, 84
Hughes, Kathleen, 178, 184
Hurley, Denis, 184

Ignatius of Antioch, 74, 138, 139, 143
Isaac of Stella, 120

Jerome, 147, 191, 201
John Chrysostom, 55, 124
John Damascene, 226
John Paul II, 1, 6, 21, 24, 42, 105, 142
John XXIII, 2, 4, 5
Joncas, Jan Michael, 152, 216
Jungmann, Josef, 5, 10, 101, 113

Kelleher, Margaret Mary, 184
Kraft, Charles, 191
Krisman, Ronald, 184
Krosnicki, Thomas, 15, 80
Küng, Hans, 152

Lactantius, 175
Lanne, Emmanuel, 26, 78, 79
Larsen, Kenneth, 184
Lathrop, Gordon, 165
Lefèbvre, Marcel, 1
Leo the Great, 44, 56, 107, 136, 175,
    179, 186, 194, 236
Löhrer, Magnus, 142
Lopez, Bernardo, 66

Manabat, Josefina, xiv, 153
Manicheans, 43
Marsili, Salvatore, 23, 26, 31, 51, 67,
    78, 83, 93, 131, 137, 192
Martimort, Aimé-Georges, 5, 18, 26,
    63, 80
Martin Luther, 48, 163, 213, 239
Matthews, Edward, 184

Mayer, Augustinus, 26
McManus, Frederick, 5, 15, 184
McMillan, Sharon, 152
Metzger, Marcel, 140
Michelangelo, 44
Mohrmann, Christine, 178
Monophysite, 174

Nestorians, 174
Neunheuser, Burkhard, 5, 19, 26, 31,
    32, 72
Nida, Eugene and Taber, Charles, 191
Nocent, Adrien, 2, 11, 15, 26, 29, 33, 46,
    48, 51, 67, 73, 99, 107, 114–115, 178
Noè, Virgilio, 6, 26, 148

Ofrasio, Timoteo, 153
Origen, 73
Orwell, George, 21
Ostdiek, Gilbert, 184
Ottaviani, Alfredo, 3

Page, John, 184
Palgius I, 56
Pamelius, Jacques, 53
Pandora, 76
Panikkar, Raimundo, 156, 157
Paul V, 14
Paul VI, 1, 3, 4, 5, 9, 7, 18, 19, 41, 49,
    95, 114, 157, 161, 177, 189, 204, 224,
    237, 240
Pecklers, Keith, xi, 152
Peter Chrysologus, 70
Pinell, Jordi, 26, 78, 79
Pius V, 25, 165
Pius XII, 42, 60, 130, 132–133, 169, 179
Pliny the Younger, 213
Pomarius, Johannes, 71
Pura, Raul, 153

Quiñones, Francisco, 22

Rahner, Karl, 152
Ramshaw, Gail, 178

Index of Subjects